TRANSATLANTIC   SUBJECTS

IOANNA LALIOTOU

TRANSATLANTIC SUBJECTS

ACTS OF MIGRATION
AND CULTURES OF
TRANSNATIONALISM
BETWEEN GREECE
AND AMERICA

The University of Chicago Press

Chicago and London

IOANNA LALIOTOU is a lecturer in contemporary cultural history in the Department of History, Archaeology, and Social Anthropology at the University of Thessaly. She is also a member of the editorial committee of the journal *Historein*.

The University of Chicago Press, Chicago 60637
The University of Chicago Press, Ltd., London
© 2004 by The University of Chicago
All rights reserved. Published 2004
Printed in the United States of America
13 12 11 10 09 08 07 06 05 04   1 2 3 4 5

ISBN: 0-226-46855-0 (cloth)
ISBN: 0-226-46857-7 (paper)

Library of Congress Cataloging-in-Publication Data

Laliotou, Ioanna.
    Transatlantic subjects : acts of migration and cultures of transnationalism between Greece and America / Ioanna Laliotou.
        p. cm.
    Includes bibliographical references and index.
    ISBN 0-226-46855-0 (cloth : alk. paper)—ISBN 0-226-46857-7 (pbk. : alk. paper)
    1. Greek Americans—Social conditions—20th century. 2. Greek Americans—Ethnic identity. 3. Greek Americans—Intellectual life—20th century. 4. American literature—Greek American authors—History and criticism. 5. Greek Americans in literature. 6. Immigrants in literature. 7. Immigrants—United States—Social conditions—20th century. 8. Greece—Emigration and immigration—History—20th century. 9. United States—Emigration and immigration—History—20th century. 10. Transnationalism—History—20th century. I. Title.

    E184.G7 L26 2004
    304.8'730495—dc22

                                        2003016604

IN DEAR MEMORY OF MY FATHER

ACKNOWLEDGMENTS

Books owe their creation to many people, and their origins can be traced in many locations. This book was written between 1998 and 2003, but my research in the transatlantic world of migration and the cultural universe created by Greek migrants in the United States began in 1995, when I was a researcher at the Department of History and Civilization at the European University Institute at Florence. In the process of researching and writing about migration, I have been inspired, encouraged, and assisted by many people in different locations including Florence, New York, Princeton, Athens, and Volos.

Professors and fellow researchers at the European University Institute provided a supportive intellectual community and contributed to the formation of the original orientation of my research. I am grateful for all the friendships and lasting collaborations that grew out of this nurturing academic environment, for they continue to make academic labor a meaningful process of learning. A large debt of gratitude is due to John Brewer, whose encouraging interest, active support, and confidence in my project were indispensable to the writing and publication of this book. Luisa Passerini has generously provided me with intellectual inspiration, support, and stimulating criticism. Her guidance in the study of subjectivity, her active belief in the imperative of critical and innovative thinking, and her dedication to the practices of collegiality and the value of collective work have formed my intellectual outlook in ways that are difficult even to recognize. I cannot thank her enough. Richard Johnson took an active interest in my project at its early stages. My confidence in his integrity and critical spirit made me take seriously his view that publication of this book would not be merely an act of academic vanity.

The Idrima Kratikon Ipotrofion (State Scholarship Foundation) in Greece and the European University Institute provided the necessary funds for the initial stages of my research. The Ted and Elaine Athanassiades postdoctoral fellowship at the Program in Hellenic Studies at Princeton University gave me the opportunity to expand the thematic range of my project. Special thanks are due to Dimitri Gondicas, the program director, for his valuable support and his interest in providing and sustaining such a hospitable and inspiring climate of intellectual exchange and research. Karen Van Dyck and the community of the Modern Greek Studies program at Columbia University provided me with hospitality, support, and friendship as I revised different parts of the manuscript in New York. As a fellow at the International Center for Advanced Studies at New York University in spring 2001, I had the opportunity to participate in a truly inspiring international environment of intellectual exchange. I thank Thomas Bender, Marilyn Young, and the entire group of researchers and the staff of the center for their support during that period. I owe thanks to Vassilis Lambropoulos and Artemis Leontis for their informed readings of different parts of the manuscript and for giving me the opportunity to present and discuss parts of this book with colleagues and students at Ohio State University and the University of Michigan. I am also grateful to Alexander Kitroeff for offering guidance and support at the early stages of my research.

While exploring and researching the history of Greek migrant culture in the United States, I often felt like a participant in the process of diaspora and dispersion of material, information, historical traces, and sources. My navigation through this web of sources was assisted greatly by the staff in different archives and foundations. Many thanks to the staff at the Historical Archive of the Ministry of Foreign Affairs, Gennadeios Library, the Theater Archive. Special thanks to the staff at the Hellenic Literary and Historical Archive (ELIA) in Athens and to Manos Haritatos for kindly offering material from the photographic archive of ELIA. I am grateful for the assistance provided by the staff at the National Archives and Records Administration, the Balch Institute for Ethnic Studies, and the Tamiment Archive of Labor History in the United States. Special gratitude is due to the staff of the Immigration History Research Center at the University of Minnesota for guiding me through their rich Greek collections and for providing me with permission to quote from unpublished material in the Theodore Saloutos collection. I also thank Yorgos Kalogeras and the editorial committee of the journal *Gramma* for giving me the opportunity to publish earlier versions of parts of chapters 5 and 6 and for permission to reprint fragments of that material in this book.

Completion and revision of the manuscript took place between Athens and Volos. Working during the past two years with colleagues and students at the Department of History, Archaeology, and Social Anthropology at the University of Thessaly has been a learning experience. I thank them for cultivating a creative academic environment and for their generous willingness to share their experience. The members of the editorial collective of the journal *Historein* have provided me with a challenging space for intellectual exchange and collective work. I thank them for their support, criticism, and indispensable sense of community. To my professor, colleague, and dear friend Antonis Liakos I owe the realization that studying history makes sense for me subjectively, intellectually, politically, and ethically. I cannot thank him enough for his untiring support, sharp criticism, and intellectual courage. For as long as this book has been in the making, David Staples has stood by my side. Together we learned how to "hear voices" in the texts and to enjoy viewing the world from a transatlantic perspective. Without his help, his wonderful friendship, and his love this book would not be possible. Pothiti Hantzaroula and Ioulia Pentazou have generously offered me their friendship, support, and sharp insight into the continuously changing ways of our thinking and being. I thank Aris Alexopoulos for his companionship, for sharing with me his enthusiasm and his subjective view of reality, and for his caring yet unrelenting undermining of my certainties.

I am grateful to Douglas Mitchell at the University of Chicago Press for taking an interest in the manuscript and for his guidance during the early stages of the revisions. I am also grateful to Leslie Keros, who has been a responsive and caring editor, and to Lys Ann Shore, whose attentive editing contributed greatly to the materialization of this book. I thank Timothy McGovern for all his assistance and guidance. I am truly grateful as well to the two anonymous readers whose comments, criticism, and suggestions were indispensable to the revision of the manuscript.

Finally, I am grateful to my family for their support, confidence, affection, and love. This book is dedicated to the dear memory of my father, Nikos. Although his untimely passing still remains incomprehensible to me, I can acknowledge now, more than in the past, the deep impact that his commitment to life as such and his optimism have had on the way I understand the world.

From History to Subjectivity:
Migrants, Globality, and Culture in the
Twentieth Century

In 1945 Mary Vardoulakis, a second-generation Greek migrant in the United
States, published *Gold in the Streets,* a novel that narrated the story of a Greek
migrant community in Chicopee, U.S.A. One of the scenes in this book, which
takes place at Chicopee during the early 1910s, illustrates the complexity of the
processes through which migrant subjectivity was articulated and culturally expressed. In this scene three friends, Petro, George, and Michali, recently arrived
from Greece to Chicopee, have just tried to get a job at the mills. Their attempt
was unsuccessful; they were beaten and chased away by Polish migrants already
employed at the mills. Bitterly shocked and unprepared for this kind of con-
frontation, they stumble away from the factory and wander around the streets
of the town, perplexed and trying to make sense of their experience, explain the
reasons for the mistreatment, and regain a sense of themselves. Suddenly, they
stop in front of a store window and glance at their reflection in the glass.

> "Is this how we look?" scowled Petro, peering into the window of a hardware
> store on Exchange Street. They had passed workers, housewives, school
> children and storekeepers on the way, all of whom had given a second glance
> to the three men.
>
> George pressed his face against the glass and saw his reflection, black hair
> escaping from under his tasseled kerchief, dark eyes in a strong, handsome
> peasant face. His baggy blue trousers were tucked into his high leather boots.
> His shirt, woven by his sisters, was buttoned tightly under his chin, with the
> front part hidden by the blue felt vest with the elaborate lacings. He touched
> his black beard and gleaming moustache. Both needed trimming, he decided,
> for he didn't enjoy the shaggy effect. Well he had been on a boat where
> water for washing was limited. Was he expected to look as fresh and clean as
> when his sisters and mother sent him off to a feast or to Fortreza? Hardly, he
> decided with irritation. Hardly.
>
> Michali . . . had no beard to worry about, and only a small blond moustache.
> His curly hair looked tousled. While he was at school it was no trouble,
> because all heads were cropped before the term began. Now Michali car-
> ried a small comb with him, and used it when Petro and George weren't
> looking. . . .

> Petro complained that he was as pale as death. He was a slight man in build, and shorter than his friends. He had lost weight, with the result that he had to keep tightening his silk belt about his waist. His boots were dusty and muddy. He frowned as he looked at them, and the three wrinkles across his forehead deepened. Though he was twenty-seven years old, he had begun to stoop a little in the last few years. . . .
>
> An American passed by while the three men stood at the window, whereupon they turned to look at him. He was wearing low shoes, a broad coat, long trousers and a felt hat. His face was clean-shaven.
>
> "We're different," murmured George. "I see that."
>
> "If he came to Greece, he'd be different too, with his flat shoes," Petro declared. "But we look a mess just the same."[1]

The incident described by Vardoulakis vividly illustrates how migrant subjectivity was constituted at the intersection of glances, recognitions, reflections, and reminiscences. Migrant self-representations did not consist of singular images of the self, but included diffracted images of bodies and simulacra. The three friends did not know how they actually looked—they were unaware of their actual appearance and were forced to recognize themselves by the reactions of others (Americans in the streets, or Americanized Polish workers at the factory). They scrutinized their appearance through their reflection in the window of the American store, but they did not identify with the reflection (or with the American perception of them). Their current appearance did not resemble the image they had of themselves, the image they referred to when they mentioned how they used to look back in Greece. The reflection in the window was not they *themselves*, but represented the effects that the experience of migrating had had *on them* (shagginess and uncleanness, long hair, loss of weight and height). George's concluding remark in front of the window voiced the collapse of the distance between "what one is" and "what one has become." "We are different," George admitted. The bodily effects that migration had on the subject have already become what the subject's body was: *different*. This, however, was not a unilateral form of determination. The migrants' perception of themselves did not derive exclusively from the reflection in the window; the glances of American workers, housewives, schoolchildren, and storekeepers; the shouting of Polish workers. On the contrary, Petro, George, and Michali perceived *themselves* as migrants when they actively glanced back at the passing American man; his low shoes, broad coat, long trousers, clean face. "If he came to Greece, he'd be different too, with his flat shoes," affirmed Petro, showing at the same time how self-perception derives from a bilateral process of recognition.

The cultural archive that documents the history of migration and migrant communities during the first half of the twentieth century registers the new forms of subjectivity that emerged in the context of intensified flows of people, culture, and capital that marked the rise of globality in the politics and culture of that period. This cultural archive invites us today to rethink the interaction between the psychic and the historical forces that defined migrants as historical and social subjects with a central role in the transatlantic history of the twentieth century. Bringing subjectivity to the foreground of the study of migration entails a reconsideration of the complex interaction between the psychic and the social dynamics of historical process. It widens our vision of twentieth-century history and the ways in which that history was defined by the continuous interaction between nations and diasporas; empires and transnational communities; state, continental, and global conglomerations of power; centrifugal and centripetal forces of cultural and political formation.

Rethinking the history of the emergence of the migrant as a recognizable social subject is very important today, when migration is still at the heart of heated debates over security, cultural heritage, economic growth, education, environmental protection, economic development, globalization and antiglobalization movements, new internationalisms and fundamentalisms both in the United States and in Europe. There seems to be a consensus in contemporary public policy and opinion that Europe and North America are once again undergoing a massive invasion by non-European peoples who desperately seek a better future in the developed world. This consensus is very strong, although most of the experts in the field of migration studies would agree that it is difficult today to document with precision even the numbers of people who migrate from one European country to another, let alone those who migrate from third countries to the European Union or the United States. Often standing in the crossfire of social and political debates, the migrant is portrayed as a threatening outsider, invading otherwise secure borders. The invading migrant is a very powerful image, one that has been elaborated gradually in the course of the twentieth century. It is conceptually based on the assumption that migration constitutes an anomaly in modern and contemporary world history. This assumption also underlies the view that the countries that receive migrants are not active participants, but receptors in the process of migration. Although sociological, historical, and economic research during the last three decades has well documented the ways in which "push and pull" factors determine the trends of migration, the view that migration is exclusively the outcome of the individual's search for a better life remains dominant in contemporary political debates about migration. Researchers have demonstrated how countries of emigration and those that receive the migrants are inseparably connected within the international flow of people, capital, and ideas. Nonetheless, public opinion and policy still tend to view migration as an irregularity produced solely by the migrant's desire to partake in the advantages of life in the developed world. The migrants keep "invading."

Viewing migration as a form of historical irregularity leads to the association between migrants and different types of social, economic, cultural, and political crisis. This association is most strongly grounded in modern historiography's association of history with the acts of sedentary populations more or less permanently established within the territories of sovereign nation-states. Modern historiography has established an almost natural bond between national territories, on the one hand, and collective identities, culture, and politics, on the other. Assuming the universal normality of this bond has determined how we think—in both scholarly and political circles—about the history of the last two centuries. The close association between history and the nation-state has contributed greatly to the understanding of migration as a historical anomaly, possibly threatening the security of national history, politics, and culture. The problematic nature of this approach can be seen in how the development of transnational migrant cultures today is often attributed solely to the crisis of the political institution of the nation-state in the era of globalization. What would it mean for the ways we think about politics and culture, if we tried to reconceptualize movement and not stasis as the norm of modern and contemporary history?

During the last decade, the study of migration has been marked by the development of globalization theory and criticism, which has successfully undermined the prior dominance of nationalist conceptual frameworks over the analysis of transnational movements and diasporas. Theorists such as Arjun Appadurai have foregrounded the notion of the *transnation* in order to stress "the current crisis of the nation and . . . to provide part of the apparatus of recognition for post-national social forms."[2] Globalization theory and criticism has made us aware of how the *nation,* as a founding concept-metaphor that codifies economic, political, and cultural value, is itself produced on the level of the global flows of cultural production and interaction—a level defined by the intersection and diasporization of people and material as well as conceptual means and resources. Our lived experience of globalized cultural production has forced the realization that the nation is itself global and thus we have to analyze it beyond the territories of the modern (or postmodern) nation-states, as an intrinsically diasporic phenomenon.

Thinking about history and culture transnationally provides scholars of migration with the challenge of methodological and theoretical intersection. One could even argue that the concepts of diaspora and the transnation operate as mirror images of the concept of the social. As Avtar Brah has noted, transnationalism illustrates how power is exercised and articulated on differential, intersecting, and disjunctive levels of social experience.[3] Diaspora itself operates as a historical model of the figuration of power in its multiple modalities. However, the mirroring between the theoretical concepts and specific forms of historical experience (such as diaspora) has led many theorists to collapse the two sides of the reflection and to explode the category of migration so that it is made to contain the world and world history as such. One could argue that the terms *migration, diaspora,* and *transnation* are often used to describe the "world as migrant." Through an a priori diasporization of nativeness and sociality, all social experience, identities, cultures, interactions, conflicts, and struggles are then analyzed as phenomena of transnational migration.

There are many theoretical drawbacks in this expansive use of the notion of diaspora.[4] The introduction of concepts such as borderlands, diaspora, ethnoscapes, and deterritorialized nations in social studies during the 1990s satisfied the need felt by scholars in different fields to call into question the natural bond that is often presumed to connect community, culture, and place. However, the main discontent with the metaphor of the "world as migrant" is related to its complicity with neo-orientalist or neo-racist attitudes.[5] Images of the "world as migrant" often include a lamenting rhetoric of loss and nostalgia. Rhetorics of home-desiring and loss of roots, location and identity, often presuppose that actual roots, identities, and fixed homes did exist in past times, but were abolished by the contemporary conditions of life. The "world as migrant" rhetorics ostracize essentialist notions of identity and origin from the present by nostalgically projecting essentialism onto the historical past. Thus, discourses on rootlessness, displacement, and diasporization often presuppose and reestablish at their antipode essentialist notions of origins, location, homeland, and nationhood. Diasporic *pan-isms* often constitute essentialist and nationalist equivalents of discourses of displacement and diasporization. The same criticism can also be addressed to certain versions of globalization theory that were produced in the 1990s. The exaggeration of the novelty of globalizing forces during the last quarter of the twentieth century has falsely undermined the importance of transnational and global flows of culture, politics, and capital in previous historical periods. Depriving globalization of its historical depth and heritage presupposes that we exclude from our consideration the histories of peoples who have been experiencing and participating in the forces of globalization during the last two centuries. Today, historicizing globalization and its theoretical and historiographical articulations seems to be a necessary step in order to understand the complexity of global forces and the diverse and often local ways in which the notion of globality has emerged in politics and culture during the last two centuries.[6]

Second, the shortcomings of the metaphor of the "world as migrant" include the reductive association between diaspora and cultural difference. The obsession of Western academia with these concepts (as well as with other concepts, such as Third World, exile, or the margin) during the 1990s satisfied the need to give a name and identity to complex cultural and political expressions of otherness that emerged in the context of globalization. Diaspora, migrancy, and the Third World became proper names attributed to a seemingly generalized social and cultural margin. However, the generalized view of the "world as migrant" is an impediment to the study of migration and the relation among diaspora, postnational formations, and the nation-state, since it conceals the contextual and historical specificity of this relation. Seeing the "world as migrant" often permits academics and analysts to claim connoisseurship of global culture based on ethnographic research on migrant communities residing in the metropolitan centers of North America and Europe, as if migrant culture represents the essence of native national cultures. This approach blurs the distinction among diasporic, national, and metropolitan constructions of ethnicity and does not contribute to the understanding of the effects of global interplays on the transformation of culture and politics.

Finally, the argument that diasporization, exile, and migration are the model representations of modernity—an argument often encountered in contemporary academic discourses of displacement—describes only a part of the modern experience. Modernity has been marked by different kinds of voluntary and forced, violent and peaceful, movements of individuals and groups of people. These movements were made possible, or were forced, by social and political conditions that resulted from the expansion and the breakup of empires; the creation of modern nation-states, national territories, and economies; the development of technologies of transport that enabled safer and more affordable traveling; and the proliferation of different types of motivation that encouraged peoples to migrate. Displacements and migrations also resulted from the conditions created by the European expansion, exploration, and exploitation of the world and by the numerous European wars both within and outside the continent. Modernity was also marked by practices of confinement associated with the institutionalization of borderlines, reservations, concentration camps, and various technologies of segregation that conditioned social interaction at various levels of activity. The metaphorical understanding of the "world as migrant" often silences these aspects of modernity in the same way that it silences the deprivation of great numbers of people globally from access to the material means, structures, and institutions that supposedly have rendered the modern subject into a rootless and continuously drifting nomadic figure. Seeing the "world as migrant" can prevent us from grasping the multiplicity of modern experience. The same argument can be made about the exaggeration of the increased mobility of people, culture, and knowledge in the era of globalization and the association between increased mobility and the rise of postnational identities and institutions. This exaggeration overshadows the fact that a great part of the population of the planet is stranded at bounded locations—metropolitan, peripheral, native, or other—and deprived of any possibility of movement.

Let us then reconsider migration and its role in the history of globalization and global forms of power. Labor migrations have had a great impact on modern and contemporary Euro-American history. During the twentieth century in particular the numbers of migrants and refugees, and the variety of routes of migration, exploded. More important, the migrants as social subjects acquired a central role in both North American and European societies. Throughout the century, migration as a social, economic, cultural, and historical phenomenon has been at the center of all major debates that took place in the Euro-American world concerning issues of culture, citizenship, sovereignty and global control, labor, and development. During the first half of the century, transatlantic migrations had a great impact on the formation of dominant images of the migrant and political attitudes toward migration in the United States and in Europe. The questions that guide the historical exploration in this book and concern the role of migration in the history of globalization and global forms of power stem from a double realization about transatlantic migration: one concerning history and the other, subjectivity. Let us start with history.

Transatlantic migration is a central theme of study in American historiography, yet the impact of migration movements on the politics and culture in Europe and particularly in countries of emigration remained relatively unexamined until very recently. With migration viewed almost exclusively from the point of view of the receiving country, its transnational and transatlantic aspects were undermined.[7] Rewriting the history of migration in a way that widens our vision of its impact on contemporary politics and culture requires overcoming certain conceptual blockages that have conditioned historical understandings of migration. The first blockage concerns the rigid separation between emigration and immigration. We need to approach the movement of populations across borders as multidirectional flows, phenomena with local attributes but with translocal dynamics. In this respect, early twentieth-century migration should be reinvestigated not from a European or an American point of view, but within the context of multiple transatlantic flows of culture and politics. Viewing migration in wider continental contexts that supersede the nation-state—whether sending or receiving migrants—allows us to understand more fully the impact and structure of population flows without relating the phenomenon exclusively to separate national interests.[8] The disassociation of the analytical category of the nation-state and migration is important in order to avoid relating the history of migration solely to national histories.[9] This form of deduction partly explains why migration studies developed mainly in the United States and only much later in Europe.[10] As European historical traditions were grounded in a national perspective, European historiography of the last two centuries focused mainly on themes that concerned the multifarious augmentation of nation-states in historical time.[11] Viewed through the lenses of assimilation, migration was incorporated in U.S. historiography as a contributing factor to the history of national accumulation. The obsession of American historiography with almost identical case studies that documented the process of assimilation of different immigrant nationalities into the national culture of the United States can be explained from this perspective. The historical documentation of assimilation constituted a way of assimilating, since on the level of knowledge production assimilation requires the documentation of the particularities of each migrant group according to the conceptual framework and the cultural codes of the dominant national narrative. It is interesting here to note that migration never became part of mainstream historiography in European countries, mainly because the flow of migrants was viewed as a form of loss of national capital and was thus displaced in national historical narratives that celebrated mainly processes of national accumulation. As a result, European history of migration—both transatlantic emigration and intra-European migration—is often undermined and forgotten on the level of social and historical analysis. This also explains why European public attitudes and policies are often based on the assumption that migration is a *new* phenomenon in Europe, starting around the 1960s and increasing in numbers and volume ever since. European and national laws and policies are thus often driven by notions that associate migration with images of invasion and uncontrolled infiltration.

Let us now come to the issue of subjectivity and its importance for the understanding of migration history and global forms of power. As Saskia Sassen and others have argued, the origins of our contemporary understandings of migration and migrants can be traced to the years after World War I, the period when the formation of a rigid interstate system made it necessary to define with precision the status of people who transgressed national borders. In that period, most of the European countries and certainly the United States decided on comprehensive migration policies and instituted formal and technical means of border control.[12] The social portrait and the cultural images of the migrant and the refugee that emerged shortly after World War I and were related to the definitions of the Geneva Convention remained powerful until the 1990s. Only during the last decade did awareness of the transformation of the interstate system and of the nation-state lead to a reconsideration of who is the migrant and/or the refugee. For example, in Greece—a country that for a century has been a traditional sender of migrants—the arrival of migrants from Eastern Europe, the Balkans, and Africa during the last decade gave rise to a heated debate about the traits of the migrants as subjects in history, society, and culture. As migration researchers and policymakers alike often argue, international law, state policies, and public discourses on migrants and refugees are most often removed from the social, economic, and cultural realities of migrancy—that is, from the condition of being a migrant. This is the point where questions of subjectivity need to be addressed in order to view migration not only through the objectifying lenses of law and public reception but also through the subjective residue of the experience of migrating in the culture of migrant communities, receiving countries, and countries of emigration. Migration, and the social and cultural universe that develops in its process, produce and are produced by migrants—people with a certain understanding of themselves, of the conditions of their existence, and of their desires, strategies, plans, and fantasies of moving across borders and reestablishing themselves at a different place. The ways in which migrants become subjects of their individual, family, national, or community histories is a field that we need to study in order to widen our understanding of the role of migration and diaspora in the interplay of globalization, culture, and politics throughout the twentieth century.

Subjectivity is an overcharged and occasionally vague term, often used in migration studies to refer to the juxtaposition between the migrants' agency and the structural constraints that determine their decision making in the process of relocation. However, defining subjectivity as the space created between agency and structure is rather constraining, since this definition exaggerates the role of rationality and rational choices, and underestimates the importance of feelings, desires, and imagination in influencing how people conduct their lives. In the same vein, although toward a different goal, the term *subjectivity* is often used in studies that foreground the importance of autobiographical texts in the analysis of migration, ethnicity, and cultural politics. In these cases, subjectivity is associated with areas of experience that resist the interpellation by social and political forces and maintain a sense of authenticity in signification. Revealing the relation between this use of ethnic subjectivity and the modernist narrative of captivity and resistance, Rey Chow has criticized the "liberated culturalisms" according to which culture and subjectivity are "associated with fluidity and movement and thus with freedom":

> Emerging at the intersection between residual idealist assumptions about individual subjectivities and ever-intensifying processes of collective commodification (with inevitable effects of dehumanization and depersonalization), ethnicity continues, yet exceeds, the paradigm of the meticulous elaboration of the vicissitudes of the individual subject, on the one hand, and the paradigm of humanistic opposition against the rationalization and systematization of human labor under capitalism, on the other. Any consideration of ethnic subjection would therefore need to include not only the manner in which ethnics have been subjected to and continue to "resist" their dehumanizing objectification but also the psychological mechanism of "calling" (sense of vocation)—what Max Weber calls the "work ethic"—that gives rise, certainly, to compelling feelings of individual

resistance but is, arguably, already a dynamic built into the rationalist process of commodification itself.[13]

The term *migrant subjectivity* refers to ways of becoming a subject that emerged gradually in the context of migration and on different levels of politics, social and economic interaction, and cultural production.[14] This emergence was made possible through the dissemination of narratives of self that claimed to represent the experience of migration, being-in-migrancy, and thus migrant subjectivity itself. Of course, these narratives of self were produced at different social, cultural and political loci. The name *migrant* can have a different "calling," content, and cultural connotation, depending on the discursive, institutional, or geopolitical context in which it is used. For example, the name *Greek migrant* does not have the same signification in U.S. legislation as in autobiographies written by Greek migrants, although both the legislative as well as the autobiographical texts represent real subject-effects that institutions, history, and public discourses have had on those who migrated, as well as on those who did not. The characteristics and traits that are attributed to—or claimed by—the name *migrant* can thus be contradictory, reciprocally exclusive, but always historically situated. As Luisa Passerini has argued, subjectivity is always a historical process, a series of changes and not a static condition, a development although not necessarily a linear evolution. It is a narrative, although not necessarily a single story.[15]

The complexity of subjectivity derives from the term's use to describe the relation between the philosophical subject of knowledge and the subject's capacity to imagine, think, and decide about himself or herself. A coherent and universal form of migrant subjectivity does not exist, since the name *migrant* contains differential, situated, and contradictory elements. How can we then imagine the study of subjectivity and its history? At this point Foucault's concept of "genealogy" becomes useful, since it allows us to write a history of subjectivity by focusing on processes of subjectivation and moments of discontinuous articulation of situational difference. Foucault drew the notion of genealogy from Nietzsche and used it in order to define the relation between his own project of studying the discursive and institutional forms of subjectivation, and history. Following Nietzsche, he attributed to the concept of genealogy many different traits. Genealogy, as Foucault asserted, rejects the transcendental search for origins and the metaphysical reference to notions of continuity and evolution that characterize traditional historiography. "[Genealogy] must record the singularity of events outside of any monotonous finality; it must seek them in the most unpromising places, in what we tend to feel is without history—in sentiments, love, conscience, instincts; it must be sensitive to their recurrence, not in order to trace the gradual curve of their evolution, but to isolate the different scenes where they engaged in different roles."[16]

For Foucault, genealogy introduces difference where unification and identity are pretended. Genealogy thus does not establish foundations, but it disrupts continuities since, as Foucault argues, "knowledge is not made for understanding, but for cutting."[17] Genealogy permits a dissociation from the self, since genealogical inquiry does not seek to trace the origins and transcendental presence of the self in time. Far from that, genealogy is a form of effective history; it is concerned with the effects that different power relations, institutions, and discourses have on the body, the self, the individual, or the collectivity, and not with the metaphysical essence/meaning of the body, self, individual, collectivity themselves. The objective of this genealogical approach to subjectivity is to demonstrate the impossibility and the catachrestic character of metahistorical claims to essentialist and transcendental notions of self. Thus, the study of the content and the form of the name *migrant* in different processes of subjectivation and narrative articulation seeks to show that catachrestic *claims to identity* are also part of the processes of subjectivation and not the effects of the Subject's presence. Accordingly, Greek migrants' autobiographical life stories constitute aspects of the process of subjectivation and not expressions of already fixed migrant subjectivity. The same argument stands with reference to legislative texts, cultural representations, and images.

How can we study disjunctive processes of subjectivation in their diversity and simultaneity? How can we understand the simultaneous presence of the subject who thinks, feels, and decides, and the philosophical subject of knowledge in the context of migrant and national cultures? How can we conceptualize the simultaneous workings of agency and structure, sovereignty and subordination, that condition the realities of migrant life and culture? The process of subjectivation can be metaphorically understood as a type of *circuit*. Migrants *become* migrants in the context of their encounter with cultural traditions, racial stereotypes, and technologies of social integration in the countries they come from as well in the countries they arrive at.[18] The migrants' interaction with the political body of the country where they migrate constitutes a particular circuit of subjectivation. The actual presence of migrants in Western metropolitan cities, the preexisting cultural legacies and dominant cultural values, and the new codes of racial hierarchy that emerge in each period can all be conceived as moments within this *circuit*, although they are not starting points or ends.[19] Each of the moments influences the circuit, and none of the moments can be detoured. This circular framework is functional because it emphasizes that every point of the circuit is under constant transformation and negotiation, and that all the points are interdependent. Antimigrant discourses in Europe today subject migrants to a whole web of images of them that are produced and publicized by xenophobic information networks. However subjected the migrants are to racist imagery, the imagery does not operate as a form of identity that the migrants have to "wear"; rather, these representations operate as strong signifying forces, always intersecting with and depending on alternative signifying forces that seek to produce a different meaning of migrancy in contemporary European societies. The circuit of subjectivation is not a closed structure, since migrants are simultaneously implicated in many different and intersecting *circuits of subjectivation*. These circuits form a web of lines of (dis-)identification within which the subject is called to negotiate the recognition of his/her presence on the level of everyday life.

Many questions emerge if we employ the metaphor of intersecting circuits of subjectivation. Do all members of a migrant community engage in and have access to the same forms of negotiation? How does experience determine difference? For example, to what extent and in what ways do women migrants negotiate their presence and recognition, in the context of a *forced* dialogue with hegemonic perceptions of male migrant identity? How does a woman negotiate her *presence* within discourses and practices that include her only as *absence* (sometimes both inside and outside her own community)? Other questions concern the ways in which the migrant community itself perpetuates its internal fragmentation—and the unequal subject-positions this fragmentation produces—in an effort to deal with the "assimilating" forces experienced in the recipient country.[20] Migration represents an area of modern and contemporary history where different forms of *becoming,* in the way that Gilles Deleuze and Felix Guattari use the term, take place.[21] The migrants partake in flows of desire that break away from codes of signification determined by the dominant assemblages of power, including community, family, nationhood, tradition, and local belongings. Breaking away from certain familiar means—material, spiritual, mental, or imaginary—of making sense of the world around us is a necessary element of migration. In the same way, finding new practices of cultural recoding is also part of the process of migration, leading migrants through recurring stages of reterritorialization. The interaction among migrant communities and national as well as transnational contexts, and among diaspora, postnational identities, and nationhood, is marked by different points of de- and reterritorialization. One could even argue that migrant subjectivity constitutes a laboratory of cultural and political becomings that allows us to study moments of crisis of established majorities and minorities, strategies of articulation of new subject-positions, and alternative visions of self and community that do not necessarily historically evolve into fixed collective identities.

The effort to trace moments of becoming within the history of migrant subjectivity and to reconstruct a history of these points of tension and this crisis of representation presents the historian with questions that concern the nature of historical scholarship more generally. Quite often these moments of becoming, deterritorialization, and uprootings of cultural encoding lie outside historical inquiry, partly because historians have traditionally focused on the exploration of processes with fixed endings and the acts of subjects on the conscious level. Moments of becoming are not always recognizable parts of the main body of history; they are located within spaces of micropolitics that often do not find their way into mainstream politics, culture, and historical representation. Researching the history of migration from the point of view of subjectivity can be seen as a form of micropolitics that seeks to locate elements in collective histories that developed subjectively and did not necessarily become part of the existing claimed identities. Can we view the history of migration as an account of the ways in which social processes of differentiation, disjunction, and disidentification provided the basis for positive imaginings of self and collectivity?[22] Can we accordingly use the history of migration as a means of viewing disjunction as a positive and not as a subordinate form of historical being? Finally, can the history of migration and subjectivity operate as a laboratory for the invention of a language and a way of thinking that would enable us to represent in positive ways new forms of subjectivity that emerge out of processes of differentiations, movement, and shifting cultural and political environments?

Transatlantic Subjects

In this book I argue that the migrant as a recognizable subject related to distinct forms of sociality emerged during the first decades of the twentieth century within the physical and symbolic spaces created by transatlantic migration and transnational cultural processes. The book focuses on the case of Greek migration to the United States and traces the genealogy of migrant subjectivity through the analysis of narratives of self, practices of transnational cultural production, and discourses of culture and subjecthood that developed between Europe and America during the first part of the century. Shifting forms of nationalism and statehood, as well as rapid processes of integration between European and American cultures, economies, and politics, provided the background for the emergence of migrancy and transnationalism as a built-in *dangerous supplement* to hegemonic discourses on culture, subjectivity, and modernity. The early twentieth-century history of the Atlantic world was marked by the massive migrations from Southern Europe to the United States. These migrations constituted a formative moment in twentieth-century conceptualizations of subjectivity and culture on both sides of the Atlantic. The exploration of these conceptualizations shows that the historical event of the emergence of the migrant as a new subject of modernity was marked by the traces of early twentieth-century hegemonic cultural discourses on Europeanness and Americanism, and the technologies of subject-formation that derived from these discourses. The exploration of the history of migrant subjectivity offers powerful insights into the cultural, political, and ideological processes that produced the hegemony of twentieth-century Euro-American definitions of culture and subjecthood in the context of national as well as global politics.

The chapters that follow unravel histories of modern Greek migrations and bring into the foreground the historical interplay of cosmopolitanism, global integration, and nationalism. The exploration of Southern European and Balkan transnationalisms is instrumental for the study of the Euro-American discourses on culture and subjectivity, as Southern European and Balkan national identities to a great extent have been defined in terms of degrees of kinship to both Europe and America. Images and representations of Europe and America have operated as master-referents in the corresponding conceptualizations of Balkan and Southern European collective identities. The analysis of transatlantic imaginings of modern Greece—simultaneously Balkan, Southern, and, because of its classical heritage, quintessentially European—introduces a challenging twist in comparative approaches between Northern European and Mediterranean cases of transatlanticism.

The transatlantic crossings of Greek migrant workers, travelers, intellectuals, publishers, and politicians during the first half of the twentieth century constituted a dynamic encounter between a relatively new nation-state and America, at the height of processes of modernization and the intensification of global integration. Reciprocal images of homeland, America, and Europe (projections, identities, myths, and representations) produced entangled visions and definitions of culture, subjectivity, and nationhood in this period. Tracking these entanglements allows us to view the eventful social, political, and cultural history of the early twentieth century from a transatlantic perspective and through the lenses of those who occupied an "outside-in" position in relation to intersecting cultural settings. Through the history of transatlantic communities we can also view the interrelation between national politics and international affairs in this troubled period. How were forced migrations, ethnic conflict, the Balkan Wars, two world wars, and the continuous shifting of world hegemonies reflected in the life courses and the subjectivity of those who maintained multiple allegiances and cultural affiliations? By focusing on subjectivity, this work unpacks images of Europe, America, and homeland through the penetration of the structures of meaning that migrants gave to their experiences. Existing historiography often tends to reconstruct histories of migration and nationhood from within the conceptual framework that has grounded hegemonic representations of migrancy. In the following chapters I take a deconstructive turn and focus on the mechanics of cultural production and negotiation over hegemonic representations and conceptual frameworks. The analysis of the dynamic encounters between self-narration and cultural production leads to an examination of the interrelation among experience, self-conceptualizations, and hegemonic cultural discourses. These questions are approached through parallel readings of migrant autobiographies and anti-immigrant legislation, popular fiction, early sociological analysis of migration, migrant theater, and Americanization theories. These readings trace the retrogressive subject-effects of hegemonic cultural discourses and highlight the ambivalent relation between discourses and historical agency, illuminating the ways in which migrants, scholars, legislators, and state officials negotiated their own positions and politics in the context of rapid cultural and social transformations.

Race, gender, and class differences have had a critical impact on the formation of migrant subjectivity. The historical exploration of migrant subjectivity intersects with some of the vibrant debates that recent scholarship has opened up on the question of the gradual racialization and "whitening" of European ethnicities in the United States during the first half of the twentieth century.[23] By focusing on meaning production and processes of identification instead of finished identities, this book reveals processes of subject-formation that were rarely, if ever, predetermined by linear processes of "whitening," as some contemporary scholarship has claimed. Drawing on gender-specific and transnational perspectives, I foreground differentiated processes of racialization and explore the interrelation between "whitening," migration, and the rise of America as the center of what was already being heralded as a "truly global" culture in the first decades of the twentieth century. In this context, it could be argued that while the study of whiteness attempts to challenge the racializing process by naming it as such, it often results in effectively displacing this challenge back onto the self and other narratives of cultural nationalism and ethnic particularity. This book addresses the complexity of processes of racialization through emphasis on subjectivity. The exploration of gender-specific aspects of racialization focuses on male homosociality as an exemplary process of the gendering of history, rendering cultural nationalism another version of gynophobic subjective enclosure.

Cultural institutions and practices played an important role in the formation of migrant subjectivities. Reconstructing the cultural history of migration, the book points out the relation between subjectivity formation and cultural practices, including publishing, reading, acting, storytelling, consuming, imitating, parading, and traveling. The development of these practices is located within key sites and institutions of cultural formation, such as migrant and fraternal associations, educational institutions, state agencies and nongovernmental organizations, mental institutions, coffee shops, the church, steamship companies, banks, migration services, and chambers of commerce.

Part 1 deals with the political, legal, and cultural debates over migration that took place in the United States and Southern Europe (Greece and Italy), and traces the emergence at the turn of the century of the "immigration problem" as a central issue of public concern. Although massive movements of population in different regions of the planet had caused great political and social agitation in periods before the twentieth century, the systematic preoccupation of policymakers, legislators, politicians, scientists, scholars, political activists, and cultural producers with migration started during the last decades of the nineteenth century, fully developed around the turn of the twentieth century, and has remained a constant element of public affairs to our day. The "immigration problem" was a central issue of cultural politics on both sides of the Atlantic, on the national as well as the transnational level. Migration, I argue, had a great impact on the formation of twentieth-century nationalisms, notions of statehood, and political attitudes, both in the United States and in Southern Europe. Chapter 1 analyzes the role of the ideological discourses of Americanization and cultural pluralism in the production of migrant subjects in the United States. I argue that the "immigration problem," which basically concerned the need to invent productive ways of integrating the migrants into the labor market as well as into the cultural and political milieu of the United States, constituted a challenge for social engineering. I propose that we view ideological discourses of anti-immigrant nativism, as well as those of cultural pluralism and Americanism, as different visions of social engineering. Chapter 2 examines the impact of migration on conceptualizations of culture and nationhood in Greece and makes some comparisons with the case of Italy and the relation between migration and emerging notions of *italianità*. In Greece, the historical experience of early twentieth-century labor migration to the United States transformed older notions of Greek diaspora and was inscribed in differential and often contradictory ways in contemporary Greek culture. Dominant middle-class representations were based on the eventual suppression of stories of migration and the exclusion of experience and subjectivity from their representational order. Alternative representations were registered on different levels of cultural production, such as folk tradition and popular culture. Traces of these alternative representations were encountered in post–World War II representations of migrant culture with reference to the contemporary migrations to Western Europe and Australia.

Part 2 examines two aspects of the formation of diasporic imagination: popular fiction and public performances. We cannot think of subjectivity independently from the representations and the images that individuals and communities produce in the process of making sense of themselves as subjects of their lives and histories. The cultural production of migrant communities, including literature as well as other forms of popular culture, expressed a diasporic form of imagination and disseminated images and representations of migrants in diverse locations of the public sphere, including policymaking, international relations, humanitarian action, mass media, entertainment industry, and intellectual and academic production. Migrant subjectivity emerged within this circuit of cultural production where representations, claimed identities, forms of cultural production and consumption, and regulatory frameworks operate as passing moments in the process of cultural brewing that is the outcome of transnational migration. Chapter 3 focuses on practices of publishing and explores the relation among popular fiction, communicated experience, and the formation of migrant subjectivity. I analyze short stories of migration in order to trace the interactions between hegemonic discourses on culture (Americanism and cultural nationalism) and early stages of conceptualization of the migrant condition. In chapter 4 I enter the arena of cultural engineering of migrancy. Through an analysis of ethnic parades, theater, and commercial advertising, I explore the importance of cultural exhibitionism and parody in the formation of migrant subjectivity. Practices of performance played a central role in migrant culture mainly because they generated a sense of community and popularized particular images of migrant subjectivity. Many forms of migrant identification were in general performative, extroverted, and marked by a tendency to present (and defend) one's own identity to an external public. I argue that there is a subversive laughter echoing in the performances of migrant identity that we encounter in transnational forms of Greek popular culture, and that migrant self-representations were marked by the element of parody especially as far as significations of nationhood and national identity were concerned.

Part 3 examines the role of self-memory in the formation of subjectivity. Contemporary knowledge of past migrations derives from the generation, circulation, repetition, and diffusion of a specific body of narrative accounts of the migrants' life courses. One could even argue that the telling of a life story constitutes a central part of migrant culture. Chapter 5 focuses on psychobiographies, biographical accounts that were intended to regulate the representations of the experiences of migration by propagating ideal types of migrant life courses. Psychobiographies are juxtaposed to alternative types of biographies that promoted the values and contingencies of diasporic subjectivity. Chapter 6 analyzes autobiographical accounts and memoirs written by migrants in the 1940s and 1950s, and examines how autobiographical writing formed the first stages of historical writings as well as professional historiography of migration. This chapter traces the historicity of transnationalism as a form of sociality and the role of historical writing in representing it.

The exploration of the cultural mechanics of transnational subjectivity reveals complex as well as situational entanglements of migrancy, cultural nationalism, and the politics of self. Drawing on historical research in migration, this book traces the ways in which transnational cultural practices led to the emergence of new forms of subjectivity. Reading against the grain of hegemonic narratives of cultural and migration histories, I focus on particular manifestations of subjectivity in order to reveal how migrancy produced distinctive forms of sociality during the first half of the twentieth century.

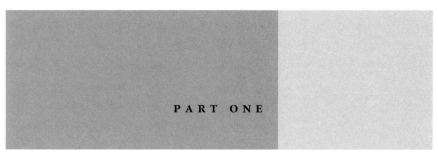

PART ONE

THE "IMMIGRATION
PROBLEM"

ONE

Technologies of Self: Nativism, Cultural
Pluralism, and "America"

In her comparative study on revolution Hannah Arendt argues that for the men of the American Revolution, "power came into being when and where people would get together and bind themselves through promises, covenants, and mutual pledges . . . it was, in the words of John Adams, the power of 'confidence in one another, and in the common people which enabled the United States to go through a revolution.' This confidence moreover arose not from a common ideology but from mutual promises and as such became the basis for 'associations'—the gathering-together of people for a specified political purpose."[1] According to Arendt, this characteristic differentiated the American from the French Revolution on the basis that the former was the deed of an already constituted body while the latter was the expression of the natural force of the "people's rights." Arendt also argued that the constituted body that participated in the revolution "was already an innovation born out of the necessities and the ingeniousness of those Europeans who had decided to leave the Old World not only in order to colonize a new continent but also for the purpose of establishing a new world order."[2] The centuries-long history of continuous migration, settlement, and colonization of the American continent contributed to the formation of the defining elements of American nationalism. Long before migration, its effects, and its implications for national prosperity became a central topic in political debates, the issue of the movement of populations to the American continent had already constituted a kernel for the consolidation of original narratives and discourses on national identity in the United States. Political, cultural, and legal discourses on nationhood in the United States were organized around the defining historical phenomenon of the continuous arrival of newcomers to the American continent. The imagination of national community was not based on myths of common origin, as in many other cases, but rather rested on the idea of mutual binding and commitment to the establishment of a new political order. As other scholars of American nationalism have argued, "the state articulates the ideological foundation for its existence and derives its legitimacy from the claim that, were everybody within the state to live by the principles and values of this ideology . . . the state would have realized its promise as a nation."[3]

In 1790 the national subject of the American polity, already defined by its role as a group of mutually bound communities of settlers, was further defined as a civil subject when the Congress affirmed the right to citizenship of "free white persons" who have or shall migrate to the United States.[4] Whiteness became at this point the synonym of citizenship and retained this role throughout the nineteenth century. The relation between whiteness and citizenship derives from the role that settlement and migration played in the formation of the American national imagination. As political scientists and scholars of the American polity have argued, the idea of citizenship was closely connected with the status of the landholder. Leon Higginbotham Jr. has suggested that "in practice the idea of citizenship had become thoroughly entwined with the idea of 'whiteness' (and maleness) because what a citizen really was, at bottom, was someone who could help put down a slave rebellion or participate in Indian wars."[5] In the context of American nationalism, race and nationhood were related to each other through the historical experience of colonization of the American continent. Settlement, economic exploitation of natural and human resources, and the need to protect these resources from the natives and the slaves determined the strong connection among American national identity, citizenship, and whiteness. During the nineteenth century race remained a biological and legal term more or less removed from any cultural or political connotation. Cultural distinctiveness—a trait often related to national uniqueness—did not constitute an important element of the American national narrative. Legal, social, and political expressions of U.S. nationhood throughout the nineteenth century promoted the claim to create a new nation on the basis of universal ideological principles that transcended cultural uniqueness and ethnic origin.

During the early twentieth century the relation among race, nation, culture, and politics in the United States was modified. New historical experiences, such as new types of migration, the eruption of World War I, and the gradual emergence of America as a global power, redefined the role that race and culture played in the construction of the national narrative in the United States. In the late eighteenth and nineteenth centuries national independence from the European empires and the foundation and consolidation of the political and constitutional national subject at the core of the American polity were the key points of the American national narrative. At the outset of the twentieth century, however, the emphasis was gradually but steadily shifting toward different questions, as the so-called social problem came into the foreground of political debates. Definitions of the social problem and the elaboration of social plans and programs aimed at solving it operated as a powerful circuit of subjectivation in this period, which historians have referred to as the "age of social politics" in Euro-American relations.[6]

The age of social politics was marked by the dominance of a new language of politics that was organized around the notion of the "social" and concerned a wide range of issues: labor, welfare, health and hygiene, urban planning, education, and family. The centrality of the social questions in this period was partly the result of worldwide transformations in the scale and structure of capitalist development. Metropolitan societies in the developing capitalist countries now faced problems that concerned regulation of different types of social relations in a context of sharpening differences, including differences in class, gender, race, ethnicity, and religioon. The social problem of this period sprang from the paradoxical concurrence of the rigid consolidation of the nation-state and its quest for monocultural homogeneity, on the one hand, and the proliferation and deepening of social differences within metropolitan societies, on the other. Envisioning ways of managing societies of difference became a priority in metropolitan politics on both sides of the Atlantic. Indeed, the age of social politics was marked by thickening transatlantic relations, as large numbers of social scientists, welfare capitalists, social and racial hygienists, reformers, and journalists traveled across the Atlantic in quest of ideas, plans, and new technologies of social reform. From the 1890s until the 1930s American progressives and reformers traveled to Europe in search of collaborations and exchanges with European counterparts that would provide them with working visions of social management. The transatlantic nature of the social question was recognized early on, as social reformers realized that national borders were porous to the differentiating effect of capitalist development. Thus, the forum of political debates and discussion about solutions became substantially transnational.[7]

The age of social politics was marked by the emergence of new technologies of social engineering across the political spectrum. Social engineering meant visions and methods of social planning that were aimed at the reorganization of social structures and institutions. Visions of social engineering relied on systematic efforts to understand social mechanics and to design interventions and planned transformations. The richness and variety of visions of social engineering in this period derived from parallel development in the social, physical, and natural sciences. Social engineering—related to urban planning, architectural design, and public administration, as well as to current ideas of eugenics and genetics—dominated the imagination of social reformers and scientists in this period when pressing social problems demanded solutions. The explosion of artistic expressions of this imagination manifested the deep cultural and political embeddedness of notions of social engineering.[8] Visions of social engineering were the main inspiration behind the utopian thought that developed dynamically during the first decades of the century and became popular through the proliferation of science-fiction themes in popular literature and early cinematography.[9]

The history of social engineering is directly related to the history of subjectivation, since it concerns the relation among subjectivity, sovereignty, and politics. The attempt to design social mechanics was grounded in the recognition of the sovereignty of the state, of social reformers, and of national and international agencies over the social order. In the case of social politics in the early twentieth century, the sovereign subject was constituted through its ability to produce the social order and thus produce the political and social subjectivities that in their turn invoked the subject's sovereignty. The political and social subjectivities that invoked—and were invoked by—the sovereign subject of social engineering were defined by the historical conditions that were referred to as the "social problem" in the capitalist metropoles at the outset of the day: labor, gender, class, race and ethnic relations, urban development, and war. Workers, women, children, domestic and foreign migrants, refugees, and the poor were invoked by the sovereignty of the reforming subject whose project included the social engineering of subjectivities. The history of labor, ethnic, race, and women's movements this period, and the often antagonistic relationship between these movements and the forces of social engineering, demonstrates the continuous interaction between forces of subject-formation and the ways in which people were subjects of their lives and of their collective and individual histories.

The early twentieth-century history of migration is closely related to that of social engineering. The concentration of large numbers of migrants from diverse origins in the developing metropoles in the United States provided social reformers, politicians, and scientists with a unique opportunity for experimentation in social planning. The "immigration problem"—a term that referred to the need to invent productive ways of integrating the migrants in the labor market, as well as in the cultural and political milieu of the United States—constituted a challenge for social engineering. Dissociated from native territorial sovereignty, the migrants were invoked as migrant subjects by the authority of Americanization programs, congressional committees, legislative bodies, fraternal associations, philanthropic institutions, and research centers. Migrant subjectivity was thus constituted in interaction with circuits of subjectivation whose prerogatives derived from projects of social engineering that did not concern exclusively the "immigration problem," but also envisioned wider plans of social reform. The migrant appeared as a socially and politically recognizable figure in the horizon of transatlantic politics and culture during this era. The appearance of the migrant as a transatlantic form of social and political subjectivity can only be understood in relation to wider projects of social engineering that transformed politics and culture on both sides of the Atlantic in this period. Antimigrant nativism and cultural pluralism were the two major political and ideological movements that inspired plans of social reform that concerned the migrants. Such plans for reform conditioned the transformation of American nationalism and the role that race and culture played in the constitution of political subjectivity in the United States during the early twentieth century.[10]

New Immigration: Defining the Immigration Problem

In the early twentieth century, migration in the United States was defined as a problem that epitomized all major aspects of the overall "social problem" that challenged social reformers and policymakers. State and reform agencies played an important role in defining migration as a social problem, with migrants as its subjects and thus as subjects of the reform policies that were envisioned in order to engineer a new type of social order. Experts, scientists, practitioners, philanthropists, state agencies and committees, journalists, and publicists played an important role in consolidating this definition of migration and of migrants as its subjects. This diverse community of professionals experienced great dynamism as its members delved enthusiastically into the "immigration problem" and the possibilities that it offered for experimentation with regard to social reform and the engineering of a new type of social order.

The first characteristic attributed to migration as a modern social problem was its newness. In 1912 the authors of an abridged edition of the results of the investigation of the Immigration Commission observed:

> A study of the immigration into the United States, from the time that our immigration records begin in 1819 to date, shows, as already pointed out, a change in the character of the immigration as well as in its extent. During the last twenty-five to thirty years so marked is the change in the type of immigrants that it is convenient to classify our immigration as the old, that is, the immigrants coming before 1883, and the new, namely, those coming since that date. . . . *Certain marked characteristics of the immigrants also emphasize strongly the fact that the new immigration differs much more radically in type from the earlier American residents than did the old immigration.*[11]

The term *new immigration* was introduced to distinguish between the migration that contributed to the building of United States as a nation, mainly migrants of Anglo-Saxon origin, and the new arrivals, mainly those from Southern and Southeastern Europe. The distinction was based on the assumption that the "new immigrants" differed radically from the populations that had historically constituted the "native" American society—that is, Anglo-Saxon American society. To decode the terms in which "native" Americans perceived these "new immigrants," we must unpack the concept of radical difference, as employed in the debates over migration in this period, and discern the parameters that politically defined and culturally consolidated "new immigration" as a *problem*.

The arrival of new migrants was perceived and experienced in public debates mainly as a problem that needed a solution. But before solving a problem, one should know its characteristics. To this end, in 1907 President Theodore Roosevelt founded the Immigration Commission.[12] The commission became popularly known as the Dillingham Commission, after its chairman, Sen. William P. Dillingham of Vermont. The task assigned to the committee was to gather trustworthy statistical material enough to enable a reasonably accurate judgment to be formed regarding the effects of immigration.[13] The commission worked for four years, until 1911, and it produced a lengthy report that constituted an actual mapping of the migrant presence in the United States as charted by government-appointed officials.[14] These reports compiled data concerning the distribution of migrants in the United States; the distribution of migrants in different industries and occupations; the education of children of migrants; the incidence of crime, insanity, and prostitution among migrant groups; and the fecundity of migrant women.[15] The commission favored on economic grounds a reduction in the supply of unskilled migrant labor and correlated the collected social and economic data primarily by means of a contrast between the Northern and Southern/Eastern Europeans in the United States.[16]

The appointment, the mode of organization, the constitution, and the political function of the commission indicate that migration from Southern and Southeastern Europe was perceived mainly as an information problem. Migration created the need to register new elements into the solidified cultural capital of social knowledge. The socialization of the migrant subject—both in terms of social policy and on the level of social consciousness and conceptual register—required the accumulation and systematization of a body of knowledge about the migrant. The integration of the new migrants into the native social body presupposed a stage of recognition; in other words, the new migrants had to be rendered identifiable according to the means of identification that were culturally meaningful and legitimate for the dominant native social subject. To explore the interaction between networks of cultural signification and circuits of subjectivation, we need to study the process through which migration took the form of an information problem. Producing knowledge about the migrants operated as a means of invoking the migrants as social subjects. The production of cultural meaning—representations, perceptions, images, and facts—about migration identified the migrants as subjects with the traits and characteristics of migration as a social process. Migration as a set of experiences generated by the massive movement of populations from a place of origin to a place of destination and reestablishment constitutes an exemplary topos of interactions between cultural signification and subjectivation. Committees of experts operated as political mechanisms for registering and policing elements foreign to the national body. The expert committees were temporary bodies, composed of individuals who combined expertise with social respectability. Such committees were politically appointed in order to manage an urgent public problem, a danger, or a catastrophe. They often requested consultation of individuals and organizations that represented the political bodies interested and affected by the given investigated issue. As a technology of subjectivation, committees combined the political legitimacy of cultural establishment with the dynamic agendas of interest groups that emerged in the context of transforming social conditions. The Immigration Commission Reports of 1911 included statements, opinions, and recommendations from organizations concerned with the issue of migration from a variety of perspectives and positions.[17] These reports portrayed the encounter between the host country's networks of political, social, and cultural signification, on the one hand, and the migrants, on the other. The reports constituted a summary representation of this encounter on the level of public official discourse. A closer reading of some of the issues raised by the Immigration Commission reveals the political and cultural force behind the initiative to produce accurate knowledge about the migrants. In the abridged edition of the commission's results, the authors defined the migration problem as follows:

> What is the immigration problem?
>
> The people of the United States stand for what, in their judgment, is the highest, best civilization in the world. Beyond question this judgment is often a narrow one. Few people know the best characteristics of the leading European nations, much less those of the more remote civilizations of India, Japan and China; but however biased the American judgment may be, their purpose is right: they wish the best. Moreover, in some ways, especially along industrial lines, it is generally conceded, the world over, that their judgment is correct, and that our country stands at the head. Americans undeniably wish to maintain their standard, and if possible to raise it. The problem becomes then, How does immigration affect American civilization now, and what is its influence likely to be in the future?[18]

Clearly, the problem of migration was defined according to the conceptual framework of civilizational superiority. Thus, the same authors declared:

> In order to solve a problem of this nature it becomes necessary:
> 1. To fix for ourselves a standard of civilization;
> 2. To secure all the facts about immigration that bear in any important way upon our civilization;
> 3. To measure as carefully as possible the influence of these facts upon that standard and
> 4. As a practical people, if immigration and the conditions brought about by it are affecting our civilization unfavourably, to suggest measures, either governmental or social, that will prove to be a sufficient remedy.[19]

The modernist vocation of this elaboration is quite powerful, especially in its reliance on the solid ideological substratum of the "standard of civilization" narrative. The notion of the standard of civilization was systematically employed in international relations in the early twentieth century and reached its zenith during the 1920s as an essentially regulative principle concerning interstate relations. As Roland Robertson has noted, the notion of the standard of civilization in this period was interrelated with the issue of the right to national self-determination, as well as with incorporation into the community of nations.[20] In the context of migration debates, the same notion was also employed with reference to the native society's right of self-determination and the integration of migrants into the recipient country. Migration as a social problem was closely tied to international relations and the worldview of those involved in the debates. The massive arrival in the United States of people whose origin was out of the geo-cultural territory that had nurtured the superiority of Anglo-Saxon civilization created the need to restate that civilization's qualities; migration from Southeastern Europe created the need for a redefinition of the borderline between superior civilization and others.

Safeguarding the civilizational standard presupposed knowledge about it and about the people who threatened it with degradation. The native society, as the sovereign subject that invoked migrants as subjects, could register information only through the mechanisms established in its already accumulated cultural capital. From this point of view, we can explain the urgent need expressed in this period "to fix for ourselves a standard of civilization." The acquisition of knowledge about the migrant and the fixation of the knowledge about the native self were almost indistinguishable parts of the same project. As Jeremiah Jenks and his fellow authors noted in their 1912 summary, "for the purpose of this book it is . . . desirable that at the beginning the principles be summarized on which the standard of civilization of our country may be affected by immigration."[21] In the following section, under the title "Principles upon Which American Civilization Is Based," the authors acknowledged that "it is extremely difficult to analyze a civilization so complex as ours," thereby revealing the crisis in self-definition that the lack of knowledge about the migrants had produced.[22] The process of perception of the migrant subject required a cultural translation performed by institutional bodies such as the Immigration Commission, whose agents had to acquire knowledge of the migrants' activities, practices, organizations, and community institutions. The commission had then to codify these practices in ways that were culturally intelligible to the dominant native community. Thus, making the migrants into an object of study required a simultaneous refixing of national identity in the United States. In this context, "knowing the migrant" proceeded through a process of epistemic violence by means of which the conditions of the migrant's socioeconomic and political existence in the recipient country were solidified as defining traits of migrant subjectivity.

The aim of the commission's investigation was to discern the physical, mental, and moral characteristics of the migrants and to classify them in the system of established relations between peoples and racial groups.[23] The retrieval and employment of this old division of human characteristics indicated the need not just to know about the migrant, but, even more, to position the migrant in established types of physical, mental, and moral hierarchy upon which civilization was thought to depend. This is a central point, because it introduces one of the main elements that defined the perception of Southeastern European migrants in the United States. The triple division of human characteristics (physical, mental, and moral) referred to equally old characteristics of *racial* differentiation and categorization. The problem of lack of knowledge about the migrants derived from the difficulty inherent in the encounter between Anglo-America and the new migrants who were not yet racialized. One of the first tasks that the commission undertook was to produce the *Dictionary of Races and Peoples,* a work that identified over six hundred races or peoples and explored their physical characteristics, history, and civilizational status.[24] Early on the commission expressed its dissatisfaction with the existing racial classification that was used by the Bureau of Immigration since 1889. A proper study of the problem of migration required a more sophisticated system of racial classification. The commission therefore proceeded to hire two anthropologists, Dr. Daniel Folkmar and Dr. Elnora C. Folkmar, and appointed them to produce a more elaborate account of racial classification that would serve the needs of the committee's investigation.[25] As John Higham has observed:

> The evolution of white supremacy into a comprehensive philosophy of life, grounding human values in the innate constitution of nature, required a major theoretical effort. It was the task of the race-thinkers to organize specific antipathies toward dark-hued peoples into a generalized, ideological structure. To the development of racial nativism, the thinkers have made a special contribution. Sharp physical differences between native Americans and European immigrants were not readily apparent; to a large extent they had to be manufactured. A rather elaborate, well-entrenched set of racial ideas was essential before the newcomers from Europe could seem a fundamentally different order of men.[26]

Faced with the need to identify the migrants, the commission reverted to the already existing, dominant system of social identification: white supremacy. This would accommodate the presence of new European migrants.[27] More than manufactured, the racial differences were retrieved as the *sine qua non* condition for the social recognition of the new European migrants. The old division of human characteristics into physical, mental, and ethical was employed in order to introduce the migrant to the sociocultural territory of the racially *known.* The commission's conclusions on this point reveal the ways in which this mammoth institutional investigation echoed and further elaborated the ruling, supremacist racial anthropological criteria. The three categories of human characteristics were studied as "subjects treated in determining effects of immigration upon American standards."[28] The migrants were never studied independently, but always in terms of the effects that their interaction with the native racial stock might have on the latter. The migrants were therefore perceived as agents of a series of activities with important implications for the native subject, and were not viewed independently as objects of investigation. In this sense, the native subject subjectified the migrants, by recognizing them only as far as they were implicated in intersubjective and racial interactions. Aspects of migrant culture that did not seem to have repercussions for the national culture of the United States remained completely unattended.

Concerning the migrants' physical characteristics, attention was drawn to health and sanitation. The commission's basic conclusion on these issues suggested that the migrants' health condition when they arrived in the United States was very poor. This constituted a threat for America' s human stock, since it could result in the biological, physical degradation of the dominant Anglo-Saxon element. Under the impact of eugenics and social Darwinism in this period, low physical state was considered a feature of racial inferiority. The same argument had already been used to prove the racial inferiority of African Americans.[29] The issue of sanitation was very important, especially because of the explicit conceptual and symbolic connections among cleanliness, purity, poverty, and civilization. The extensive statistical data collected by the commission offered further grounding for the notion of Anglo-Saxon civilizational superiority with an impressive precision. For instance, in the study of the sanitary condition of the migrants' households,

> an attempt was made to classify the care of the apartment into four different grades: good, fair, bad, and very bad. . . . The American ranking is higher still if the distinction is made between the whites and the negroes in the native-born, 58.3 for the whites, and 34.5 of the negroes having their apartments being rated as good. . . . Among the foreign-born there seems to be all through a very marked distinction; in this regard the Swedes rank the highest, 75.7 per cent. of their apartments being rated as good. The Germans next with 65.8 per cent.; then the Bohemians and Moravians with 65.8 per cent. Among the lowest were the Greeks, with only 12.2 per cent.; the Syrians, 26.1 per cent.; the South Italians, 30.9 per cent.; Slovenians, 30.2 per cent. The North Italians again ranked above the average, with 49.3 per cent., and the Russian Hebrews barely above with 45.5 per cent.[30]

This passage illustrates the kind of racial ranking that informed the commission's investigations. Racial ranking was repeatedly reinforced through a long series of measurements. The position of each of the "racial units" in the racial hierarchy of the civilizational standard was thus solidified, being now apparently grounded on scientific research and endowed with institutional authority.[31] The employment of scientific authority was one of the ways in which racial hierarchy was solidified. Another method was the use of the symbolic order that was deeply embedded in the native subject's treasured forms of cultural heritage. For example, the migrants' dwellings were often compared with the "Indian tepee."[32] The report proved the inferiority of new migrants by means of an iconographic association with the American Indians; an already naturalized signifier of racial hierarchy was employed in order to attribute to the migrants an inferior social position.

The report raised many issues that referred to the migrants' "mental characteristics," but the first and foremost concerned literacy. At the end of the 1910s much of the debate over the need for legislation to restrict migration revolved around the famous literacy tests, so this part of the commission's report was of vital importance.[33] Illiteracy was considered an indication of the migrants' low level of intelligence and thus a characteristic of racial inferiority. The commission advised in favor of literacy tests, as a requirement for entrance into the country.[34] Additionally, the commission stated the need for detailed documentation of the developing migrant cultural activities, such as "the papers, books and associations founded and supported by the migrants."[35] The preoccupation with the migrant culture revealed the rising force of American nativism in this period. This preoccupation has to be understood in the context of World War I politics, the rise of national and international conspiracy theories, and the impact of the "Red Scare" on American political attitudes.[36] The hostility toward the particularity of migrant national cultures was related to the proclaimed inaccessibility of the migrant presence. The rapid development of the foreign press in the United States was considered dangerous since the anglophone American public could not have access to it.

Finally, the commission argued for the connection between the migrants' occupations and their mental characteristics.[37] The study of the occupations of the migrants proves in part the commission's strong interest in the economic aspects of migration. However, the association between occupations and mental characteristics was also part of a popular belief in the migrants' parasitic presence within the native body politic. A feature of the migrants' social position and condition in the recipient country was thus naturalized as an inherent racial trait. The racial ranking was verified once more, since the general result of the investigations indicated that the foreign-born appeared mainly in unskilled labor and in trade professions. The implicit association between trade and parasitic earning was very important with regard to the connection made between trade and specific ethnicities. For example, the report noted that "the tendency of Syrians, Greeks and Hebrews is clearly to engage in trade."[38] Although the association

between trade and parasitic presence was more apparent and powerful in popular writings than in official documents, the appearance of the argument in the
commission's reports reveals the degree of complementarity between different
spheres of public discourse on the issue of migration.

The exploration of the migrants' moral characteristics was also driven by the
need to detect and measure the "effect of immigration upon the morals of the
American people."[39] This exploration emphasized the migrants' criminal nature,
for "the moral characteristics of the various races may be indicated by the number of crimes and the character of the crimes committed by them."[40] The results
of the two previous inquiries (on the physical and mental characteristics) were
used to support the representation of the "criminal migrant" whose presence
threatened to insinuate criminality in the native American body. The migrants'
physical and mental characteristics determined the nature of the crimes they
committed. Despite the great variety of crimes attributed to the migrants, their
criminal nature was most clearly shown in their incapacity for civil social interaction. The lack of sociability referred mainly to the seclusion of each migrant
community and the lack of communication between different communities.

> Each gang is a racial unit, living in separate cars and usually in a separate
> camp. Sometimes Bulgarians and Croatians, Croatians and Rumanians
> and Italians, were found in the same camp, but it seemed that Greeks
> could not live peaceably with any other race. Croatians and Bulgarians,
> speaking practically the same language, fraternize readily; but Bulgarians
> and Rumanians must be kept apart from Greeks, both of the former being
> secessionists from the Church of the Greek Patriarch, with tendencies
> anti-fraternal in high degree.[41]

The inability to coexist in a civil way was attributed to the migrants' sense of
national loyalty. That quality, along with lack of sociability and the existence
of interethnic violence, framed the migrants' moral character from the commission's perspective. The proclaimed need to protect the migrants from their
own people and other migrants called for the intervention of the U.S. government in the communities' internal affairs. This claim provided grounding for
paternalistic attitudes toward migrant communities and echoed gender-specific
prejudices, since migrant women were often represented as the weakest members of the racially inferior migrant community. The association between racial
inferiority and criminality historically has been one of the constitutive elements
of supremacist discourses.[42]

Yet, from the commission's point of view, the migrants' criminality was harm-
ful because it could be transmitted and diffused to the native society. The commission expressed not the fear that the native subject would suffer from the
migrants' violent acts, but rather the fear that the native society would be
contaminated by the criminal migrant nature and would itself become violent.

Migration was thus studied according to a conceptual framework that was systematically reproducing the political and scientific rhetoric of miscegenation. This rhetoric provided the main framework of social analysis of migration in the period; consequently, the issue of migration was politically articulated mainly in terms of racial purity, intactness, and stability.

The investigations of the Immigration Commission represented the first large-scale attempt to register information on migration to the United States. These investigations are very important for our discussion of how migration was perceived as part of the social problem and how migrants were evoked as subjects in the context of projects of social reform. The commission's investigators and political authorities organized and presented the accumulated data on the basis of the radical difference between old (Anglo-Saxon) and new (Southern and Southeastern European) migrants. The commission defined difference according to the conceptual apparatus of racial thinking, and therefore the content and the political connotation of this difference between old and new migrants can be understood only in the context of the transformation of discourses of Anglo-Saxon supremacy in the late nineteenth and early twentieth century. As scholars in the field have noted, "Before the Civil War, much discussion had taken place concerning the 'superiority' of white men over non-whites. After the Civil War, however, as an increasing percentage of migrants began to arrive from the non-Anglo-Saxon countries of southern and eastern Europe, more and more attention began to be paid to the differences within the white race."[43]

As the reports of the Immigration Commission indicate, the process of racialization involved the production of means of scientific management of racial values and differences. If the racial order was to be socially maintained, the commission and all subsequent authorities that addressed the "immigration problem" needed the means of control over the terms of interaction between the migrants and the native society. The commission expressed the urgency of this need through its consistent preoccupation with "measurements of effects" and the "fixity of standards of civilization." Many researchers have argued that the Immigration Commission approached migration predominantly from the economic point of view.[44] However, the reports also gave expression to what seemed to be the major political claim in the period: the necessity of sophisticated monitoring of racial interaction that would include definition, fixation, and regulation of circulation and exchange of racial and cultural values. In this context, economy and race became very proximate categories.

American Eugenics as a Project of Subjectivation

The need for the articulation of an elaborate system of racial classification that would provide the means of maintenance of the racial order was served in this period by the scientific movement of eugenics. Francis Galton, Charles Darwin's cousin, introduced the term *eugenics* in 1883.[45] Galton defined eugenics as "the study of agencies under social control that may improve or impair the racial qualities of future generations either physically or mentally."[46] In essence, eugenics was a science and a social program of racial improvement through selective breeding of the human species. Galton was a geographer who, impressed by the implications of evolutionary thought for social reality, decided to dedicate himself to biology. His project was to apply the evolutionary doctrine of natural improvement by means of rational management and protection of the naturally inherited physical territory of racial supremacy and domination.[47] Its supporters propagated eugenics—its principles and its implications for social policy and practices—as a technology of self-improvement. As it has been noted, "what gave eugenics its force in the modern period was its association with Darwinian evolution whose essence was the natural selection of inherited variations."[48] In this sense, eugenics as an ideology of self-improvement took on different content and political connotation in different sociopolitical and cultural contexts.[49]

The American eugenicist movement played an important role in the formation of the conceptual framework within which new migration was perceived in the United States. Eugenics "migrated" from Britain to the United States during the first decade of the twentieth century. Through an emphasis on unalterable human inequalities, American eugenicists confirmed notions of Anglo-Saxon superiority and sounded a warning about the multiplication of the unfit and the degradation of the superior stock; this was the contribution of eugenicists in the conceptualization of unrestricted migration as a form of "race suicide" for the Anglo-American racial stock. By 1910 eugenics had penetrated public debates on migration in a remarkable way. This was the year when Charles B. Davenport, a pioneer of American eugenics, founded the Eugenics Record Office, a foundation devoted to the study of the hereditary traits of American populations. In the same period, the Immigration Restriction League, an organization founded in 1894 and devoted to the propagation of anti-immigration ideas and to lobbying for anti-immigrant policy, considered renaming itself the Eugenic Immigration League.[50]

Eugenics was a distinct phase in the history of racialist thought. In the long historical process of the transformation of racialist thought, eugenics has to be understood in the context of the late nineteenth-century obsession with the study of physical differences between different races, and more specifically with the delineation of European peoples into distinct types.[51] This trend in racial thinking has been attributed to the intensification of national rivalry in Europe in the second half of the nineteenth century. As Elazar Barkan has argued, "the increasing number of racial categories around this time reflected an eagerness to use primordial affinities as modes of justification for nationalism sanctioned by the growing repute of biology and evolution theory."[52] The historical and intellectual heritage of eugenicist discourse in its European version determined its character as an internal racial discourse. As a stage in the history of racial thought, eugenics was characterized by its emphasis on the need to elaborate fine distinctions between racial units; eugenicist discourse was developed as a discourse on racial proximity and the dangers it posed.

In terms of political agenda, American eugenicists were engaged exclusively with two main contemporary political issues: the "American Negro problem" and the massive arrival of migrants from Southern and Eastern Europe. In this sense, American eugenics developed as a racialist discourse of social engineering. The aim of eugenicists was not to exclude the racially inferior, but to engineer forms of social relations and organization that would define and control the terms of interaction between different racial stocks. Their political agenda was organized around the need to protect and cultivate the superior white racial stock *at home*. The aim of this racialist political program was to internalize difference by engineering subjects and social relations according to the principles of eugenics. Eugenics, a means of subject-formation, relied on strict definitions of normality and deviance, as well as conformity and tolerance. In this sense, the physical, cultural, and mental differences that characterized migrant peoples when compared with the native Anglo-Saxons were perceived as deviance and were investigated and measured in terms of effects on the native social body. The preoccupation with effects indicates how migrants were seen only in the context of binary interrelation, between normality and deviance, conformity and tolerance, subjectivation or extinction; in this case, extinction took the form of deportation, social rejection, and juridical and coercive penalization. Difference was thus internalized through its representation and stigmatization on the map of already existing cultural and anthropological geography.

The process of acquiring and systematizing knowledge and information about the new migrants necessarily took the form of a constant translation of ways of sociocultural being into the dominant symbolic codes of the host country. The need to appoint a social face to the arriving migrant population from Southern and Southeastern Europe required the elaboration of a new code of racial classification by means of which the migrant presence would be socially and culturally classified and made recognizable. In response to the new social conditions, eugenics reorganized already existing elements of supremacist racial and social thought. The massive migration of "racially inferior" European populations before and after World War I, the rise of antiforeign sentiment during and after the war, and the social crisis of the same period called for a reorganization of the constitutive elements of racial and social thought. The "preconceptual plane" of racial discourse was thus modified in the context of shifting social conditions.[53] Eugenics played an important role in this process.[54] Based on their belief in the inheritance of the characteristics that determined racial distinctions, the eugenicists formulated their primary principles—namely, systematic racial distinction and classification as a means to avoid miscegenation and to protect and improve the naturally superior racial units. Miscegenation in particular was considered a great threat to the stability of the racial order. Eugenics constituted a code of racialism as well as a plan for social reform. The political circumstances to which eugenics responded were marked in the United States by the need to incorporate in the social body sizable populations whose location in the racial hierarchy was vague and ambiguous. The new migrants had to be positioned in this racial hierarchy in a way that made sense culturally and was in accordance with perceptions already existing in the native consciousness. This positioning had to be adequately theorized; furthermore, it had to be endowed with the legacy of scientific rhetoric, since at the time this constituted one of the most powerful tropes of political discourse. The eugenicist movement, in its scientific as well as its political expressions, provided the code that dictated the migrants' subjectivation.

The inward character of Anglo-American racial discourse was intensified during the period of mass migration of inferior, but nevertheless European, races during the last part of the nineteenth and the early part of the twentieth centuries. The popularity and the political impact of eugenics expressed this intensification. The rational kernel of eugenicist political discourse was the need to propagate and to graft onto social consciousness a body of knowledge of all the fine and irreducible differences that characterized naturally distinct racial units. In this sense, the acquisition and popularization of knowledge concerning the racial traits and divisions of the populations of European origin became a first priority. The European origin of groups of people that had to be socialized in racial terms, and thus had to be identified as racially inferior, helped render the dominant racial discourses of this period even more inward. As Nancy Stepan has noted, "eugenically, the lesson was not that the lower races outside Europe should be prevented from breeding. Nature herself ensured that, through competition, the less fit races would be displaced and eliminated. Eugenics instead was to be directed inward towards the dominating, civilizing white race, which was spreading itself across the globe."[55]

According to this argument, eugenics was as a technology of the racial self, regulating, guarding, and administering the territorial proximity of the dominant Western native subject. In the case of the American Negro, white supremacist discourse stressed the "far away," the irreducible distance between the white world and the black world. Quite differently, as far as the new migrants were concerned, the Anglo-Saxon supremacist discourse was articulated in terms of proximity and closeness: a peculiar closeness, so close as to be the most threatening and repelling, yet not so close as to be recognized as part of the self. Proximity constituted a nodal point in the articulation of eugenicist discourse on the migrants, since it represented a danger against racial order based on the principle of biological segregation between races. It was in this context that eugenics was employed as a form of biological and anthropological knowhow to prevent miscegenation and destabilization of the racial order.

The study of eugenics is important for our discussion of how new migrants were evoked as subjects in the United States. First, eugenics constituted the code underlining the racial conceptual framework according to which new migrants were perceived. Second, there is a close interrelation among migration politics, public perception of migrants, and eugenics—an interrelation manifested by the formation of eugenicist circles of political intervention and antimigrant propaganda. As we will see later, eugenicist ideas also influenced the ways in which migrant subjectivity was evoked in the context of migrant communities themselves. Eugenics as a movement within science and politics constituted a reorganization of already existing elements of racialist and social thought. This does not mean that it was merely a temporary expression of elements of supremacist ideology, whose impact was annulled after the decline of the eugenicist movement. Movements that express the convergence between different intellectual traditions and between politics and science have the capacity to generate legacies of truth and principles whose durability is much longer than that of the movements themselves. Although eugenics was not endorsed by the entire scientific community and definitely did not appeal to all contemporary political circles, it introduced into both spheres conceptual and discursive elements that can be traced throughout the decades that followed the decline of the movement in the late 1920s.[56] The active participation of eugenicists in public debates over the issue of migration led to the irreversible dissemination of their principles in the public sphere and to the popularization of racial perceptions of new migration and of native self-superiority, reworked within the frame of eugenicist codification of difference. Eugenics contributed greatly to the elaboration and the politicization of racialized elements of migrant subjectivity in the United States.[57]

Images of New Migration, Nationhood, and Europe

The popularization of racial and social discourses was achieved through the diffusion of narratives and images that depicted the migrant as a new social and racial figure. Scientific discourse and popular images were complementary. The consolidation of networks of people and institutions that had a great influence on policymaking, as well as on public opinion, enhanced the connection between scientific knowledge and popular representations of the migrants. Scientists became public figures through their participation in policymaking committees; publications in newspapers, magazines, and popular journals; and the formation of associations with clearly political objectives. Lobbyists, journalists, fiction writers, and social commentators also participated in the debates over migration and its impact on society. These networks of influence created a field of micropolitics among the scientific community, the political community, and society at large.

In 1920 George Horace Lorimer, editor of the *Saturday Evening Post,* assigned journalist Kenneth Roberts to travel to Europe to work on a series of articles on migration. These articles were compiled two years later in a book under the title *Why Europe Leaves Home: A True Account of the Reasons Which Cause Central Europeans to Overrun America; which lead Russians to rush to Constantinople and other fascinating and unpleasant places, which coax Greek royalty and commoners into strange by ways and hedge sand, which induce Englishmen and Scotchmen to go out at night.*[58] During the early 1920s Roberts played a very active role both in popularizing antimigrant racial theories and in lobbying for antimigrant policy and legislation. He was one of the public figures called to appear in front of the Immigration and Naturalization Committee, the successor committee to the Immigration Commission whose recommendations resulted in the Immigration Restriction Act of 1924, also known as the Johnson-Reed Act.[59] As John Higham has acutely remarked, "Kenneth Roberts practically camped in the committee's offices while working on his immigration series for the *Saturday Evening Post.*"[60]

In his introduction, Roberts explained the reasons "why Europe leaves home." He put emphasis on the issue of national culture, and he reflected on the ways in which nationhood and nationality were experienced at that time in Europe. His reflections on these issues showed mystification over the intense loyalty that Southern and Eastern Europeans retained and publicly performed for their national cultures, after their arrival as migrants to the United States.

> The United States Immigration Commission proved conclusively that the bulk of the more recent immigrants from the Central and Southeastern Europe hived up in settlements of their own, where they retained their customs and their languages and the ideals of the countries from which they came, and failed utterly to become Americans. They had their own publications and occasionally their own laws. . . . In the cant phrase of the day, the majority of the more recent immigrants didn't assimilate. . . . Most of them seemed to have been inoculated against assimilation before leaving home.[61]

Patriotic devotion was considered a positive quality for Europeans who remained in their homelands. For example, Roberts admired the strong national sentiment of the non-Jewish Poles, while he believed that Jews were the most dubious of all European figures, since they had no commitment to any national cause at all. Jews were not just potential migrants, but also nomads.[62] Yet for the migrants who established themselves in America, devotion to their native land was considered suspect—almost a conspiracy against Anglo-America. According to Roberts, migrants treasured and often concealed their national culture and did not allow it to become known to Anglo-America. As a result, although migrant national devotion was apparent and striking, migrant national culture was inaccessible by Anglo-America. The invisibility of migrant national culture made the socialization of migrants very difficult. According to the political vocabulary of the times, this was understood as a failure to assimilate. "[The immigrants] are not interested in seeing the people of this country get all the facts about their mother country. They only want them to have the *favourable* facts. This is the common failing of many immigrants who have become naturalized citizens of the United States. Their first love is their mother country. They forget that in becoming American citizens, they 'absolutely and forever renounce all allegiance and fidelity to any foreign country.' "[63]

The perceptions of migrant national cultures within the conceptual framework of Anglo-America at this time manifested the contradictions of modern subjectivity, especially as far as migrants themselves were concerned. Perceptions of migrants as social subjects were caught between the worship of national culture and the perceived need to forget national culture for the purpose of civilizational advancement through assimilation. In this second respect national devotion was considered an impediment to progress and thus a sign of inherited racial inferiority. The split character of modern subjectivity was also manifest in the contradiction of a highly territorial modernity that was at the same time offended at the sight of the ghetto territories and frightened at the feeling of concealed and incomprehensible, ghettoized national culture. In reference to migrant establishments, Roberts observed, "If they are allowed to live in the slums and Ghettos and foreign settlements in which they are now living, they can not be assimilated. There isn't a chance of it. . . . The people of these foreign settlements work all day by the side of other aliens. When they leave their work, they go back to crowded homes in which the only atmosphere is one of dirt and Europe."[64]

The anger against the inclusive and secluded character of the ghettos and foreign settlements was a consistent element of popular representations of migrants. On the one hand, seclusion was desirable, since it served to exclude the migrants from the social body. On the other hand, seclusion was attacked fiercely as an impediment to the native society's will to control the migrant communities. The iconographic representation of the "new ghettos" in the United States was accomplished by means of reference to Jewishness.[65] A considerable part of Roberts's introduction was dedicated to descriptions of Jewish ghettos in Poland and Warsaw as the sites of human degradation and depression. "Jew has always exploited Jew so remorselessly in Galicia that the majority of the inhabitants of that vast Jewish reservoir are and have been perilously near the starvation-point."[66] As Roberts observed during his visit to Europe, "the ghettos themselves are depressing spectacles . . . and the standards of life in them are the standards of life which their residents bring to America with them."[67] The iconographic material assembled for these representations was used identically in the representations of Jewish, as well as non-Jewish, migrant settlements in America. The ghetto was portrayed as a basic characteristic of migrant self. It was presented not as the site of oppression, but as a symbol of racial inferiority.

> Between ninety and ninety-five per cent of our immigrants from Poland at
> present are Jews; and the conditions under which the Jews of Poland live are,
> to put it conservatively, very bad indeed. They herd together in cities, and
> the overcrowding and the filth and the squalor of the Ghettos of Poland are
> terrible. . . . The sentimentalists declare that the Ghetto is kept in existence
> by oppressors so that the Hebrews can be segregated and controlled. New
> York's Ghetto, however, is almost on a par with Ghettos of Lodz or Warsaw as
> far as overcrowding goes. So is London's Ghetto and Vienna's Ghetto; but in
> none of these cities is any effort made to segregate and control the Jews. They
> segregate themselves.[68]

According to Roberts and other commentators of the time, segregation was an essential characteristic of the European culture that was transplanted in the United States. It was an inherent European racial and cultural trait that did not depend on historical and political conditions. As Roberts concluded, "our climate may, as some claim, change the stature of immigrants, but nothing can alter the shape of their skulls or the distinct racial traits that have characterized them through the centuries."[69] As I have already suggested, Roberts's account insisted on the particular connotations that nationhood had in Europe, as he perceived it in the areas he visited. Roberts's views about nationhood in Southern and Eastern Europe evolved gradually to a negative representation of European culture with reference to its potential impact on America. For Roberts, nationality in Southern and Eastern Europe was primarily associated with violence, since "each nationality had a bitter, passionate and unwavering hatred for at least one adjoining nationality; and all of them want to go to America."[70] Of course, Europe was not studied for its own sake; rather, every characteristic attributed to Europe, and to European forms and expressions of nationhood was necessarily conceptualized in terms of the potential impact on America. Accordingly, Europeans desired to migrate to America as violently as they experienced their own national selves.

> Their longing for America is so violent and poignant and all-pervasive that
> they would willingly permit themselves to be kicked all the way from Warsaw

to Paris or from Belgrade to Danzig—both of which trips would require a vast amount of kicking . . . if the final kick deposited them aboard a ship bound for America. They would do anything to go to America. They would lie with a fluency that would cause the bones of Baron Münchhausen [*sic*] to rattle feverishly in his grave; they would steal anything which could be stolen by human hands; probably they would willingly commit murder; for human life is not highly valued in Europe at the present time, what with several years of war, and the menace of Bolshevism, and the low rate of exchange.[71]

Hatred and violence were presented as the main constitutive elements of the migrant's psyche. Hatred and desire for America sprang from the same psychic domain. It was the desire for America that fed, as much as it exposed, the migrant's violent nature. Moreover, it was the migrant's violent desire for America that sublimely transformed pain to pleasure and enjoyment. This aspect was manifested mainly through references to the ways in which migrants conducted their everyday lives in America. In the following description, even starvation and absolute economic degradation were presented as involving a certain degree of enjoyment, since they represented a seemingly desired state of being: "Great numbers of men, accustomed all their lives to living on starvation rations, come to America and take jobs at low wages and then, in their determination to save money, crowd into wretched quarters and live in squalor and filth and darkness on a fraction of the money which an American workman must spend in order to live decently. Such a proceeding lowers the standard of living in America."[72]

The imaginary references used subsequently in Roberts's account of foreign enclaves in New York and Boston were borrowed from representations of Jewish ghettos, as the overall image of Southern and Eastern European migrants was articulated on the basis of anti-Semitism. Jewishness was thus incorporated in popular American perceptions of Europe, as the Europe of migrants who deprived America of a surplus of enjoyment, which they transferred back to their homelands through the channels of interaction and communication established in the process of migration. In economic terms this surplus referred to the wealth that the migrants sent to their relatives who remained in the homeland; on the psychic level it referred to the combination of desire and hatred that constituted the migrant psyche and that was also transferred to the European homelands through the same channels of interaction. Referring to the causes of migration, Roberts illustrated the process of abduction and transference of the surplus of enjoyment:

Part of them went [to the United States] because the agents of steamship lines painted glowing pictures of the ease with which money could be made in America; part of them went because agents of big manufacturing concerns circulated through the crowded districts and offered jobs in American mills at wages which seemed fabulous to the poor peasant; and by far the largest part went because relatives and friends and acquaintances who had already gone to America wrote back to their home towns telling of easy money and bright colours and fine clothes, and filling the minds of the stay-at-homes with a red-hot, sizzling desire to be up and doing in order to participate in the delights of America—especially in the easy-money part.[73]

The notion of enjoyment is fundamental for understanding the ways in which the subject is able to recognize itself as such through the subjectivation of its "others." As Slavoj Žižek has explained in his psychoanalytic treatment of enjoyment as a political factor, the subject comes to terms with the impossibilities that characterize its social existence only through the attribution of these impossibilities to the other's enjoyment.[74] Through a process of inversion, what the subject lacks is enjoyed by the other (the Jew, the migrant, the black, the woman, the homosexual). This inversion is functional only because the other's enjoyment is abducted, "stolen" from the self.[75] The intervention of the notion of enjoyment in representations of new migrants led to metonymic associations of America and Europe. According to these associations, America and Europe become the two aspects of the migrant's psyche: America as "desired," "longed for," "painted [in] glowing pictures of ease," "fabulous," "[filled with] bright colors and fine clothes"; and the Europe of hatred and envy, of "dirt" and the "ghettos," of "sly Jews" and "unruly Slavs."

The images of Europe that were circulated in the context of the debate about new migration marked a shift in the relation between Europeanism and Americanism in the years around World War I. Nineteenth-century perceptions of Europe in America developed around supremacist principles that propagated the treasured European origin as a constitutive element of Anglo-American superiority over American Indians, Africans, and Asians in the process of national formation of the United States. In perceptions of the new migrants, this European origin was certainly acknowledged as a shared origin, creating a need for the distinction between old and new migrations. However, the acknowledgment of a shared origin with racial and ethnic groups that were perceived as inherently inferior was quite conflicted. The negotiation over the shared European origin in the beginning of the twentieth century led to the emergence of counter-images of the Europe of dirt, of political decadence, and of moral decline. This was certainly not the first or last time that negative images of Europe became popular in the United States; in the period after World War I the notion of Europe became almost synonymous with violence, political turmoil, and moral decadence. However, it was probably the first time that this negativity was conceived and expressed in terms of racial inferiority.

In the conceptual framework of scientific racism, counter-images of Europe were supported and propagated through elaborations of hierarchical internal distinctions among the different stocks of the "white race"—namely, the Nordic, the Alpine, and the Mediterranean. Racial thinker Henry Fairfield Obsorn offered a very colorful insight into Europe's other face, as perceived in the context of Anglo-America in the early 1920s.[76] Osborn was a paleontologist, born in 1857 to a prominent and wealthy family. In 1879 he went to England, where he studied comparative anatomy under Thomas H. Huxley. There he was introduced to the circle of the most prominent people in the field, including Darwin himself. In 1908, he became president of the American Museum of Natural History, a position he held for twenty-five years.[77] Osborn wrote articles on Americanism in which he addressed the issue of religion in an attempt to defend Protestantism as a racial tradition of civility and morality. He was preoccupied with the impact on American public life of the proximity of Judaism, Catholicism, and Protestantism:

> I love the ideals of our founders. I cling to the preservation of their interpretation of the magic watchwords of democracy. At the same time I recognize that splendid qualities may be found in other racial stocks and splendid contributions made by them to human progress, but I do not confuse this dispassionate admiration of the fine qualities of people of other races, other origins, other religions than my own, with the notions that true Americanism was derived from these other stocks or races, or that true Americanism can survive wherever its original principles are *alienated* by the influx of foreign elements which have different definitions for each of the great watchwords of human freedom.[78]

The issues of proximity and origin were recurrent in articles opposing the new migration. The appreciation of the civilizational achievements of different racial stocks was not troubling when distances were kept. However, in the case where distance was transgressed, the very same elements of admiration were transformed into sources of alienation. Admiration of differential racial features lapsed when it raised genealogical claims to the heritage of "true Americanism." In this sense, civil proximity threatened the foundations of American subjecthood, since it potentially introduced into it elements other than itself. From this point of view, it was exactly the initial admiration that rendered these different racial stocks dangerous when geo-cultural locations were shifted because of migration. The admiration of Europe as the colonial motherland, as the claimed origin, and as the source of differentiation between the Anglo-American self and its territorial and racial others was transformed to repulsion when Europe was viewed not from afar, through the mist of the Atlantic ocean, but immediately at hand, in the urban landscapes of New York, Boston, and Chicago.

It was in this context of transformation from admiration to repulsion that the counter-images of Europe emerged. Osborn quite vividly presented some of these counter-images as he observed Europe as represented on the theater stages, in the movies, and on the newsstands of New York:

> In face of the increasing tide of Oriental and decadent European influence in current literature, in some sections of the daily and weekly press, in the "movies" and on the stage, we witness with alarm in all the smaller as well as the larger social centers in America the decline of original American standards of life, of conduct, of Sabbath observance, of the marriage relation. The entire control of the "movie" industry and the larger part of the control of the stage industry in the United States are now in the hands of people of near or remote Oriental origin. It is no exaggeration to say that there has been a complete revolution in the standards of the popular stage in fifty years. Ridiculing religion, modesty and chastity, substituting European for American ideals of love and marriage, grossly decadent and dissolute librettos saved only from obscenity by the occasional hand of the censor, ridiculed as Puritanism the original American standards are all insidiously tending towards moral decadence.[79]

It is not clear if Osborn was referring here to the growing migrant theater of the 1920s or to the development of the movie industry. In either case, it is interesting that he chose the world of spectacle and public performance as a point of reference in his attempt to show the dangers that derived from the migrants' cultural activity and presence in the metropolis. In his opinion, the danger seemed to derive from the creation of different poles of cultural subjectivation and of civil and moral commitment, poles that emerged in conflict with the dominant Anglo-American Protestantism. The differentiation between Europe and America was expressed by means of the categories of race, culture, nationality, and religion. In the process of conceptualization of counter-images of Europe, these categories often overlapped, in a way that undermined proper categorization itself.

In Osborn's article, the fear of "ridicule" emerged when the new migrant's gaze—the Oriental and decadent European gaze—was directed to Anglo-America and produced counter-images of the American culture. The migrant's gaze reformed American culture since it produced images of the American self as seen by "decadent Europe." Ironically, Osborn, in his effort to find solutions to the threat facing Anglo-America, turned back to European imperial discourses for counter-examples.

> The American people, partly through sad experience, have become conscious of their own great heritage and determined to maintain the high standards

of that heritage. We are avoiding the same insidious sources of national decadence and decline which undermined the great ancient republics of Greece and Rome. From their downfall we have learned what we now feel compelled to avoid despite the appeals of false humanitarianism and of false sentimentality. . . . The benefits of this awakening of the national consciousness will not be instantly visible, but years hence we shall see the rebirth of America.[80]

The retrieval of the notion of empire reveals the ways in which images always appropriated material derived from the representational traditions within which they were inscribed. The idea that the European empires declined because their structure and administration permitted cultural and racial intermixture to the extent that all the superior elements that had led to the building of the empires disappeared was an already existing and powerful counter-image of Europe. Osborn invoked this traditional element in order to supplement the counter-images that emerged in the process of negotiation between Anglo-America and the new migrants over their shared European origin. Counter-images of Europe constituted a dynamic element in the cultural genealogy of European identities and Europeanness. The itineraries of this genealogy can be traced both inside and outside the European continent. The colonial setting of the United States was one of the territories where the memory of Europe played a very important role in the formation of the politically dominant Anglo-Saxon American national and political subjecthood. Yet the emergence of new forms of migrant subjectivity shared by Southern and Eastern Europeans and the popularization of racial ideological discourses that stressed the internal differentiation of whites complicated American cultural and political reference to a shared European origin. Counter-images of Europe were reappropriated by migrant cultures in the United States as the new migrants conceived themselves as Europeans through the process of cultural interaction between Anglo-America and other "Americas."

Difference and Cultural Pluralism between Europe and America

By the end of the 1920s the doctrines of cultural pluralism were gradually winning over antimigrant nativist discourses, following the general ideological and political shift from scientific to cultural racism on both sides of the Atlantic.[81] As World War I was seen as a symptom of the crisis of Western modernity—a crisis associated mostly with Europe, political turmoil, and moral decadence—American narratives of national identity shifted toward liberal versions of universalism. Cultural pluralism was seen as the best way of applying the principles of universalism in domestic politics.[82] According to the advocates of cultural pluralism, the Americanization of the newcomers was not only possible, it was also desirable since it was compatible with the fundamental ideals and principles of true Americanism. Those ideals and principles were mostly associated with the notion of American democracy. As Horace Kallen, a prominent supporter of cultural pluralism, argued, democracy was an intrinsically American characteristic, more particularly a characteristic that differentiated the United States from Europe.[83] Kallen suggested that America was politically superior, though culturally inferior, to Europe, but nevertheless he based his idea of cultural pluralism on the convergence between American and European political cultures. Both Europe and America, he argued, were marked by sharp internal cultural, political, and social differences. Thus, both faced the problem of finding ways and political practices that would make it possible to manage difference. However, Kallen argued, cultural, political, and social differences in Europe as well as in America were not radical and disruptive, but compatible. He related the differences among the European nations to the differences among the American ethnicities, as deriving from the same order of cultural and political value. Following this definition, he argued that interethnic solidarity under the flag of American nationalism was possible, desirable, and necessary for social stability and democracy in the United States. In the same way, cooperation among the European nations was necessary for the establishment of international peace. For Kallen, as for other supporters of Americanization, ethnic hyphenation was a natural phenomenon and did not imply that the migrants had to reject their ethnic heritages in order to become true Americans, in the same way that one could be a father, a brother, and a son at one and the same time.[84] The prevalence of cultural pluralism and the advancement of the process of the migrants' Americanization gave rise to notions of transnationalism and transethnicism that were supported and mediated by reference to Europe as a metaphor of a community of nations. Advocates of cultural pluralism and Americanization argued that the lack of cooperation and of democratic treatment of national differences had led to the Great War and had resulted in political, cultural, and moral decadence. The times called for pluralistic, rather than antagonistic, understandings of difference, as a guarantee of peace internationally and of social order domestically.

From the point of view of subjectivity, cultural pluralism was very closely related to essentialist notions of identity. As Walter Benn Michaels has noted, culture here provides the technology through which subjects are bound to identities. "Cultural pluralism is thus committed to principles of identity essentialism, which is to say that in cultural pluralism, culture does not constitute identity, it reflects or, more precisely, expresses it."[85] The discourse that developed in the United States in the interwar period in favor of transnational and transethnic communities relied greatly on pluralistic conceptualizations of both Europe and

America, and promoted the idea that difference had to be seen more as variation of the same than as radical difference. Interwar transnationalism tended to obliterate the notion of antagonism that characterized the relations among different nations, ethnicities, and races, and the ways in which these had emerged historically. Already in 1916 Randolph Bourne described America as "the world-federation in miniature, the continent where for the first time in history has been achieved that miracle of hope, the peaceful living side by side, with character substantially preserved, of the most heterogeneous peoples under the sun."[86] A loyal supporter of internationalism, Bourne recognized the transnational character of migrant culture and allegiance, and warned his fellow Americans that "in the migratory Greek, therefore, we have not the parasitic alien, the doubtful American asset, but a symbol of that cosmopolitan interchange which is coming, in spite of all war and national exclusiveness." The recognition and cultivation of transnationality of all nations was for Bourne America's hope and promise in the context of world history.

The images of war and migration that fueled popular and political imagination in the United States also transformed the idea of Europe into a symbol of internal diversification. Europe became a way to talk about national, ethnic, and social difference, and about how modern postwar societies should deal with difference and conflict. Thus the project to Americanize the migrants rested on a pluralistic vision of domestic as well as international politics.[87] Kallen and other advocates of Americanization shared the idea that the American democracy could contain European national differences in a peaceful and civil way that would shape diverse migrant cultures into ethnic varieties of the American social ideals. The belief in the potential of American democracy to overcome the causes of conflict, war, social unrest, and revolution in Europe was also an expression of America's confidence in its new role as a rising world power. The project to Americanize the migrants was a response to the need felt by social planners on both sides of the Atlantic to manage the emerging societies of difference and diversification. Americanization was thus inspired by pluralistic visions of transcendence of radical difference and conflict on the national as well as the international level. This goal was pursued in the postwar years domestically through cultural and pluralist management of ethnicity and corporatist management of class and gender difference. Internationally, it was pursued through projects that supported the articulation of transnational communities and political identities, and the operation of international organizations, companies, and institutions. In either case the success of Americanization as a major project of social engineering depended on the elaboration of new types of political and social subjects that would be able to perform socially in pluralistic ways. It thus provided a dynamic context for the emergence of transnational forms of subjectivity during the first half of the twentieth century. Transnationality, however, was envisioned by intellectuals, Americanization pioneers, and the migrants themselves through the lenses of cultural pluralism, which generated essentialist forms of identity and eventually promoted the idea that each person had to *be* his or her identity.

There is a direct relation between Americanization and definitions of nationalism in the United States, as Americanization concerned both the foreign-born and the native-born, and was often understood as a more general program for the cultivation of national consciousness. As many of the contemporary scholars of the project would agree, "the Americanization movement had its primary, or immediate, origin in 1914 when the World War broke out and the renaissance of nationalism occurred throughout the civilized world."[88] The arousal of national consciousness of both the native-born and the foreign-born as a result of the war created the need to reconsider the different varieties of Americanism that were supposed to be transmitted to the new migrants. In a sense, Americanization had to begin at home. Many of the writers on Americanization described that period as one of "mental crisis" in which the American people realized the need to develop an ideology of the nation as a union of all. For some, this mental crisis was due to "the stimulation of group consciousness among immigrants."[89] If public opinion had been more or less indifferent to the Americanization process until the war, after 1914 the realization of the importance of migrant nationalisms led to a mental crisis and the awakening of the national consciousness of the native-born.[90]

The doctrines of eugenics and assimilation that were prominent before World War I were marked by a preoccupation with genetic purity that implied the need for the elaboration of sophisticated means of social control with the goal of managing the process of genetic mixing and "amalgamation." After the war social regulation became the cornerstone of national vision in the United States, since the goal of Americanization was to exercise control over the institutions and culture of migrant communities. As Julius Drachsler has noted, "to tamper with social institutions, to interfere with the 'natural' unfolding of group activity by artificial control is still regarded as fraught with hidden dangers . . . and yet, more and more is the imagination of students of American life coming to busy itself with the idea of conscious creation of a new and rich civilization that shall combine within itself the culture-values of the various ethnic stocks represented in the American people."[91] Americanization involved the elaboration of methods of social control that would manage transcultural interaction and exchanges.

Exercising social control presupposed a deep knowledge of the mechanics of migrant communities and culture. Drachsler argued that the first period of Americanization had ignored this factor and had dealt with migrants on the individual level. He noted that "led astray by this atomistic view of the immigrant, the eager Americanizer failed to take account of another striking fact—the rise and growth of immigrant communities. Not immigrant *colonies* merely, but *communities* in the true sociological sense."[92] Rather than analyzing the mechanics of Americanization, Drachsler urged scholars to examine the mechanics of migrant communities and to redefine the principles of Americanism. American sociologists showed a great interest in the study of migrant communities during the 1920s and 1930s. The systematic work of sociologists such as Robert Park focused on the investigation of the mechanics of migrant communities. Park studied community institutions with an emphasis on the role that the migrant press could play in the process of Americanization.[93] The study of migration marked the research orientation of the Chicago School of sociology in its early years and offered some definitive approaches to questions of social engineering in the context of migration policy and Americanization.

Apart from institutions and public culture, the project of Americanization also concerned more intimate aspects of migrant life. Molding the traits that constituted migrant subjectivity according to the civil and cultural ideals that composed American democracy was the goal of the project to Americanize the migrants. In the context of cultural democracy Americanization should not result in the rationalization of habits since everyday life activities are not organized around principles and conscious beliefs but around feelings, preferences and desires.[94] Americanization should be planned also as a micropolitical process aiming at the cultivation of particular subjective qualities. Drachsler argued in the 1920s that it was necessary "to direct the [migrant's] instinct of curiosity and to convert into an active search for the new and the unique, thus fostering not only tolerance but developing a 'passion' for uniqueness and distinctiveness."[95] As the psychic world was brought gradually into the foreground of projects of Americanization, subjectivity acquired an important role for cultural and ethnic politics in the United States. The interest that the pioneers of Americanization showed in the subjective aspects of migrant life proves that what was at stake was not just the nationalization of political identities, but the engineering of a new type of social subject that would think, feel, and imagine the world according to the values of American pluralism.

The Migrant Remitted

It is impossible to conceive the history of European modernity independently from the centuries-long history of movements of European populations across the globe. The massive movements of Europeans during the last five centuries set the necessary conditions for European expansion and colonization, and for the consolidation of European world domination. The labor migrations from Europe to the Americas and other continents during the nineteenth and twentieth centuries constitute a distinct stage in the history of the transoceanic movements of European peoples. As I have already argued, the close connection between European historiography and the history of the nation-state resulted in the marginalization of migration as a subject of historical inquiry in Europe. Not until very recently did the history of European migrations and their impact on European cultures and politics become a subject of interest for European historians, whose research suggests that migration constitutes an integral part of European history, as well as of national histories of the various European nation-states. This shift in focus was related to the reorientation of historical studies toward issues of subjectivity and culture, and to its impact on the study of nationalism and national identities. Historians have started exploring how notions of nationhood were historically formed in social and geographical spaces that exceeded the borders of the nation-state, and have traced the history of European nationalisms as well as phenomena of ethnic absolutism across the Atlantic world. The transnationalization of historical studies has put migration in the foreground of historical research, a process that may also influence contemporary discussions over the impact of migration and migration policy on European societies. As Saskia Sassen has remarked, the exploration of "the history of migration and refugees in Europe over the last two centuries might lead to an interpretation which sets us free from the imagery of 'mass invasion.'"[1]

The European South

Migration has been a constant phenomenon in Southern and Southeastern Europe throughout the modern era. Unlike the case of Western European countries, in Southern Europe migration has played a central role in the formation of national self-image. This is most evident for Greece and Italy, as both countries were affected by intra-European as well as transatlantic migration. In the late nineteenth and early twentieth centuries migration caused great national debates in both countries. These debates continued for decades and related migration to all the major political issues of the period, including national integration, state consolidation, cultural homogenization, economic development, and global integration.

In Italy, migration was politically associated with the "southern question." Among the numerous and complex problems that emerged after national unification, the new Italian state had to bring uniformity to a territory marked by great political and economic diversity. The indiscriminate application of the administrative, judicial, and fiscal structures of the old Piedmont created a further divide between Italy's more economically developed northern and central regions and the poorer southern region. The discussion about migration started as early as the 1870s, as officials, intellectuals, and public figures noticed the dramatic increase in the numbers of people migrating to the Americas. Although most of the Italian migrants in the nineteenth century went to other European countries, Italian social imagery was constructed around the experience of overseas migration. This paradox can be related to the clear difference between the geographic origin and the social background of Italians who migrated to Europe and those who left for America. Following a long tradition of seasonal migration, northern Italians chose the European route and moved toward Switzerland, Germany, France, and Austria. In contrast, southern Italians migrated almost exclusively to the Americas.[2] The difference between seasonal and more permanent migrations also explains the hegemony of overseas imagery over the cultural representation of Italian migration.

The association between migration and major political problems played a very important role in the formation of the cultural representation of migration in Italy. At the end of the nineteenth century the debate over Italian migration focused on three major political issues: political integration, economic development, and the "southern question." In the late nineteenth century, many European countries considered whether to adopt particular migration policies or instead trust the labor market to determine the numbers, the origins, and the destinations of the migrants. The official preoccupation with migration was manifested at the International Conference on Governmental Intervention, which took place in the context of the Paris World Fair, held in 1889. In that conference, delegates from both Old and New World countries discussed the costs and benefits of government regulation of migration and decided that the market would be the best regulator. In Italy, however, the question of regulation became more complicated when it was related to the "southern question." The greatest change in Italian official attitudes toward migration happened around

1900 and was summed up in a lengthy survey that was published the same year and documented the impact of remittances from the United States on the Italian South. The authors of the report argued that besides remittances, migration was promoting social and cultural change by transforming the migrants themselves. American money was expected to integrate the Italian South with Italy and with the rest of the developed world. In 1907 Sen. Eugenio Faina submitted a parliamentary report that became know as Inchiesta Faina and was considered by many as the final demise of the Italian South. The report suggested that there was no need for the Italian government to invest in development of the Italian South since the market—and by that he meant migration, as a natural mechanism of the labor market—would regulate economic development in the best possible way.

Despite occasional conflict between liberals and nationalists, migration was in general considered as a sociopolitical safety valve—with the exception of communists and fascists, who were both against migration, though for different reasons. Although the fascist regime introduced the first formal legal restrictions on migration, at the same time it addressed a large part of its propaganda toward the Italian communities abroad. Mussolini himself hosted the International Migration Conference held in Rome in 1924, where Il Duce argued that "emigration is a physiological necessity for the Italian people."[3] Migration was politically related to the issue of population and economic development. From this point of view, it was also related to the debate over colonialism. The nationalists especially found in mass emigration the justification for Italian colonialism. The supporters of Italy's colonial projects suggested that the massive exodus of Italians would benefit Italy the most if the migrants were directed to overseas locations that would still be administered by the Italian government. However, this idea did not become dominant. As migration was gradually seen more in economic rather than in cultural and political terms, it also became clear that colonial expansion and administration required a considerable investment of capital, while modern migration returned capital to the country.[4]

The relation among migration, the political process of unification, and the position of the Italian South in this process attributed a specific cultural meaning to the term *migrant* in Italy. The negative connotation of the term reflected the southern origin of the majority of emigrants, which carried with it "the prejudices that historically surround the South within the Italian national context."[5] The southern origin of the migrants carried a social as well as a national meaning. The economic underdevelopment of the Italian South associated the migrants with the difficulties and obstacles that Italy faced in the process of economic growth that followed the national unification. For most of the late nineteenth and early twentieth centuries the migrant was often excluded or marginalized from the cultural universe associated with the notion of *italianità*.

The northern origin of the content of *italianità*, as well as the higher social status that it connoted, excluded Italian migrants from positive representations of national cultural identity. Further, a great part of the migrants had not participated in the nationalization process since they had left their homeland earlier. As a result the Italian migrant communities abroad—especially those established at overseas locations—developed their own versions of *italianità* in diaspora.

The interaction between diasporic and national versions of nationhood in Southern Europe is in general understudied. Research in the cultural and political remittances of migration to the Southern European homelands requires the exploration of official as well as popular and cultural discourses on migration. These discourses run though representations of migrants as culturally discernible social subjects in Southern Europe during the first half of the twentieth century. The intertwining of nationhood, territoriality, and diaspora in modern discourses of political subjectivity is manifested in the case of Greek transatlantic migration and its cultural remittances in Greece. In the period 1890–1924 transatlantic labor migration was a massive phenomenon in Greece: nearly 7 percent of the total population had migrated, and thus almost the entire population was affected by migration.[6] Demographic data for that period suggest that between 1908 and 1930 more than 60 percent of the migrants had returned to Greece (although in most cases migrants would return to Greece only for a short period of time and then migrate again to the United States).[7] Transatlantic labor migration had a forceful impact on Greek society and culture. The public debates and reactions to the phenomenon of migration and the cultural "remittances" of migrancy show that contemporary conceptualizations of migrant subjectivity were interlocked with hegemonic—as well as alternative—notions of national identity and history.

To understand the public perception and cultural impact of early twentieth-century migration, we need to position the emergent representations of Greek migration within the long tradition of Greek debates over nationhood, territoriality, and diaspora.[8] Diaspora and territoriality have constituted key concepts in discourses of Greek nationhood and its political expressions from the eighteenth century to the present. The emergence of Greek diaspora in the early period was mainly a result of Ottoman imperial administration and economic organization. The latter encouraged the creation of Greek (as well as Jewish and Armenian) merchant communities in different parts of the Ottoman empire and in Europe.[9] The economic advancement and intellectual development of these communities during the eighteenth and early nineteenth centuries and their active involvement in the ideological and material preparation of the Greek War of Independence (1821) contributed to the consolidation of the importance of diaspora in Greek politics and culture even after the creation of the Greek nation-state. After all, at the time of the creation of the Greek nation-state only a part of the population who were self-identifying as Greeks were actually residing within Greek national territory. The continuous antagonism between nativism and irredentism determined Greek politics and culture throughout the nineteenth century and into the early twentieth century.

The political vision of irredentism, known as the "Great Idea," constituted a plan to enlarge Greece's territories and liberate areas that were predominantly populated by Greek populations but were still parts of the Ottoman empire.[10] Despite its political persistence and ideological impact, the "Great Idea" was never unanimously accepted and caused vivid conflict and political disagreement between Greeks residing within the Greek nation-state, Greek communities residing in neighboring territories that were targeted by official Greek irredentist politics, and Greek communities located in the wider area of the eastern Mediterranean and Southeastern Europe (Greeks in Russia, Egypt, and the Balkans). The "Great Idea" found numerous supporters as well as enemies within and outside the Greek nation-state. The linkage of the formation of the homeland state to an irredentist program conditioned the political and international claims of Greek nationalism and consolidated a very strong relationship between homeland and diaspora. The transterritorial conception of the national subject was a constitutive element of modern Greek nationalism from the moment of its genesis and thereafter.[11] This relationship between nation and diaspora was expressed politically in antagonistic terms, which generated crucial questions and points of ambivalence that haunted political debates for many decades. These questions concerned the metaphysics of politics, as they constantly referred the issue of political sovereignty and historical agency to a meta-level of definition based on abstract definitions of the state and the nation. What is the relation between the nation and the state? Is the latter merely a political representation of the former, according to the dominant international political system of nation-states? Do state and nation coincide in one political and cultural entity? Is there a possibility for transnational nations and transnational politics that supersede, overrule, or determine state politics? Does the state contain the nation, or does it constitute the nation's political "workshop"?[12] These were a few of the common questions that marked political debates in Greece at the outset of the twentieth century.

The debate around the Greek "Great Idea," essentially a foreign policy issue, produced well-defined cultural representations and ideological inscriptions of the intersection among territoriality, diaspora, national identity, and political subjectivity. The first two decades of the twentieth century were marked by historical developments that accentuated the political importance and cultural vitality of these concepts and representations. Two such developments— the transformation of national geography with the territorial expansion of the Greek state and the massive movements of populations across the new borders—

took place within a larger context: the rise of Balkan and Turkish nationalisms, the popularization of the notion of ethnically homogeneous nation-states in the area, the Balkan Wars (1912–13), the impact of World War I on Near Eastern politics, the Greek military expedition in Asia Minor (1919–22), the violent expatriation of over a million Greeks from Asia Minor and of hundreds of thousands of Muslims from Greece, and the imposition of the practice of compulsory exchanges of population as a condition of peace according to political objectives of the Great Powers. Within this context, scholars of the Greek diaspora have affirmed that 1922 marked the end of the "Great Idea" as a valid political vision and that this termination led to the diminution of the importance of diaspora in Greek politics. In the interwar period, the Greek state followed a less interventionist attitude toward diaspora affairs and viewed Greek communities abroad as economic auxiliaries rather than as organic parts of the Greek nation. The territorial expansion and stabilization of the Greek state was a precondition for the reorientation of Greek politics toward domestic issues. The consolidation of statehood; the modernization and liberalization of politics; the formation of social, educational, and economic policies; and the establishment and institutionalization of a homogeneous form of national identity became key political aims.[13]

On the level of cultural production, particularly as far as representations of self and conceptualizations of subjectivity were concerned, a chain of catalytic transformations marked the interwar period. Notions of territoriality and diaspora that were already well defined over a century of active irredentist and diasporic politics were filtered through the traumatic experiences of war, ethnic purification, and refugeeness, and through their mutation they played a primary role in the formation of dominant as well as alternative narratives of nationhood during the interwar period. In this context, phenomena of transgression of the national borders became key points of reference for cultural definitions of nationhood and national identity. As almost one and a half million ethnic Greeks were expelled from Turkey and came to Greece as refugees and about three hundred thousand Greeks migrated to the United States during the first two decades of the twentieth century, territoriality became a less urgent issue on the level of cultural representation. On the contrary, the content and defining elements of nationhood acquired urgent importance as the movement of Greek populations in and out of the consolidated territories of the Greek nation-state led to parallel movements and flows of cultures, customs, beliefs, and everyday life identities.[14] As the political vitality of older notions of diaspora was diminishing, new historical experiences of deterritorialization sparked different conceptualizations of migrancy, nation, and Hellenism. Emerging forms of political and social subjectivity in Greece inspired perceptions, reflections, and discourses on transatlantic labor migration. Official and popular representations of migration mirror central aspects of the modern Greek cultural history of the period. At the same time migration generated dynamic cultural processes and introduced new elements into the symbolic order of collective self-identification.

Migration as a "Multifaceted Phenomenon": State Concerns and Official Definitions

Social scientists and analysts of the time perceived migration as a multifaceted phenomenon that touched upon the most central areas of public interest. In 1923 Ioannis Tournakis, a prominent commentator on the issue of migration, declared with confidence that Greece had to be considered a preeminently emigrant nation. In his view, since 1920 Greece had acquired a position within the international economy as a country of emigration par excellence since it received more profit from the exportation of labor than from the exportation of material economic goods.[15]

In the early 1920s there was great disagreement concerning the causes and effects of migration, as well as over the need for official state policy that would regulate migration. Official reports, articles, and social/political commentaries of the time indicated that migration was registered as an economic, demographic, statistical, moral, and national phenomenon. Prominent Greek economists speculated on the multifaceted character of migration.[16] Apart from the economic advantages and disadvantages, the debate had other important aspects, demographic, hygienic, national, and military. Economists were addressing questions such as these: Does migration result in a decrease of population, or does it even make the rate of increase drop? Does migration have an impact on national health through the dissemination of unknown or rarely encountered diseases? Does migration deaden national consciousness for the migrants and their descendants? Does migration put Greece into a disadvantaged strategic position in relation to its Balkan neighbors since most of the draftees would not present themselves for military service?[17] The complexity of migration as a social phenomenon prompted Andreas Andreadis, a leading economist of the day and a professor at the University of Athens, to organize a research seminar devoted to the study of contemporary migration as part of his general course on "Public Affairs, Economics and Statistics." This research project involved fieldwork in Greek provinces that were most affected by migration. The results of this research project were published in a book that constitutes the first systematic exploration of Greek migration through case studies and with the use of questionnaires.[18]

In the early twentieth century migration was often perceived as a "natural" phenomenon. The naturalness of migration was based on two assumptions.

First, migration was presented as a natural demographic phenomenon. The migrants were considered to be an excess of the population. Since national resources were not enough to support the population, a percentage had to migrate in order to survive. The most optimistic advocates of this position argued that migration was profitable for the nation since the remittances that migrants sent to their families constituted the largest part of national export earnings. Less optimistic commentators referred to migration as a symptom of the country's economic underdevelopment and political chaos. The subject of migration was frequently brought up in parliamentary debates, especially when members of the Parliament who were critical of the government's policies wanted to stress the economic, social, and political malaise that overran the nation's rural areas.[19] Either way, political commentators and analysts found it difficult to draw conclusions about the overall positive or negative role of migration based solely on economic or demographic factors. As Andreadis pointed out, migration was a social phenomenon that could not be analyzed exclusively from a single perspective.

Tournakis summarized the ways in which one could assess the phenomenon of migration.[20] In a lengthy article on migration and related policy issues, he argued that the phenomenon affected so many aspects of social life and could be approached from so many different perspectives that an overall judgment was impossible. He argued that as an economic and demographic issue, migration could be viewed either from a national or from a global point of view. It could also be viewed either as a problem of political economy, or as a social and biological problem. As far as political economy was concerned, Tournakis argued, migration was a natural and positive development. Given the scarcity of the Greek nation's natural resources, the departure of a part of the population at a period of great influx of population (due to the massive arrival of refugees from Asia Minor) operated as a safety valve that permitted the social organism to survive and to develop. Accordingly, from the perspective of the global economy, migration represented a natural movement from places with fewer economic resources toward places with abundant resources. However, he argued that a phenomenon that is natural from the point of view of international political economy is not necessarily positive from the point of view of national politics and interests. This argument was based on the assumption that there is not one global economic system, but many, which correspond to ethnologically defined territories, and that each of these systems pursues its own interests, which are in conflict with the interests of the others.[21] Thus, migration should also be studied with reference to its effects on the Greek national economy specifically. Tournakis supported the position that migration was at the time the main source of wealth for the nation. Human labor was thus represented as a form of export good that guaranteed the survival of the national economy. In this view, migration was considered as a natural phenomenon on the international level and as a trade enterprise on the national level.[22] However, society could not be considered solely as an economic organism; social, moral, and national aspects also had to be considered. One had to study in depth the effects that migration had on the national character and consciousness, in order to assess the whole phenomenon and decide on the appropriate official policy. Although from an economic point of view migration was "naturally" and undoubtedly a positive development, its cultural and national effects should be assessed with great attention. More important, political initiatives should be taken in order to manage its impact, and thus state intervention was necessary. Greek public debates over migration show that two issues were central to all confrontations and disagreement: the impact of migration on national character, and its effect on the strength of national consciousness. In the political vocabulary of the period, *national character* referred to the defining elements of Greek identity, culture and tradition, while *national consciousness* referred to the subjective as well as political forms of identification with Greek identity. National consciousness signified the predominance of national over other types of civil and cultural identification.

Tournakis expounded on the idea that given the circumstances of the time, migration had a positive effect on Greek character and psyche. He did not expect the Greeks who migrated to the United States to be assimilated by the Anglo-Saxon culture, because of "the great difference in culture and national character between the countries . . . mainly due to the naturally great difference between southern and northern civilizations."[23] According to his argument, the difference between Anglo-Saxon and Greek culture rendered the Americanization of Greek migrants very difficult. The Greek migrants' national consciousness was not endangered because of the great degree of difference between their culture and the dominant culture in the United States.[24] On the contrary, Greek migrant communities were expected to operate as physical links between the homeland and the United States. Greek migrants would be representatives of their national culture abroad. Tournakis argued that migration policy should be part of the state's efforts to propagate Greek culture abroad and to create relations between the Greek nation and the outside world.[25] This perception of migration assumed an understanding of national culture as a fixed and permanent entity and was grounded on the undermining of subjective experience in favor of solid forms of identity. The actual experience of migration was disconnected from the identities of the social agents, the migrants. This disconnection was a precondition for the purification of migration as a social phenomenon, and it was compatible with a certain political tendency toward the propagation of the homogeneous images of Greek nationhood that privileged objective representations of present history and excluded differential forms of subjectivity from the symbolic order of the nation.

Tournakis criticized the state for its failure to modernize its attitude toward migration due to a "parochial idea that migration is a symptom of morbidity which results in the weakening of the social organism."[26] Indeed, in the early twentieth century the Greek state remained a passive observer of the phenomenon of migration. In the same period intellectuals, analysts, and politicians maintained an ambivalent attitude, while on the level of popular culture the themes related to migration and migrants were often treated in a satirical way that ranged between fascination and malevolent contempt. Political and popular reactions to migration were often contradictory and conflicted. Contradiction, however, offers insight into the cultural terms and references through which indifference, passivity, distancing, ambivalence, or satire were culturally and politically expressed, and thus reveals the position that debates over migration held within the cultural context of the time.

In the period between 1905 and 1912 state officials appointed by the Greek Parliament compiled and submitted detailed reports concerning the phenomenon of migration from Greece to the United States.[27] The purpose of these reports was to discern the defining characteristics of the phenomenon, inform the government about it, propose appropriate legislation, respond to popular reactions to the matter, and defend the state against public accusations of indifference to the emergent "national menace." One of the primary issues addressed in these reports was the state's authority to legislate with reference to the right of its citizens to migrate to another country. Crossing the national borders was a constitutional right for all Greek citizens. Accordingly, the Greek state did not have any authority either to encourage or to forbid migration to another country. From this point of view, migration was an issue of international relations and was regulated by international law. Accordingly, when parliamentary appointees approached migration as an issue of domestic politics, they defined it as a social phenomenon that concerned the needs of Greek citizens who were deciding to migrate and their social and financial relations with other Greek citizens who remained in the homeland. This definition legitimized the state's authority to intervene in order to regulate the process of migration through legislation.[28]

According to the suggestions made by different committees, a migration bill was submitted to the Greek Parliament in 1912. This bill proposed that the state should play a managerial role, aiming not to encourage or discourage migration, but to regulate the processes and practices of migrating. The reports indicated that the Greek committees drew lessons from the study of older legislation of other European states on this matter. The Italian case in particular was used as an example, because of the similarities that the phenomenon presented in the two countries. In 1911 S. Balanos, an official representative of the Ministry of Domestic Affairs, visited Italy to gather information about the ways in which the Italian state was dealing with migration to the United States. Following the

recommendations provided by Italian officials, Balanos suggested that a distinction should be made between the phenomenon of migration to the United States
and other, prior migrations in the history of the Greek and Italian nations. What
was important about Balanos's report was his insistence that the government
should take some initiative to prevent migration to the United States. During his
visit to Italy, Balanos became familiar with U.S. policy toward migration through
a report that the U.S. government had submitted to the Italian government in
1907. This early report stressed that the U.S. government did not welcome South
European migrants for cultural and racial reasons. Balanos's report echoed the
views expressed in the same period by American nativists opposing the arrival
of "new migrants" in the United States. He reported:

> The United States is a place with a type of organization, legislation, politics
> and culture totally different from the Latin and Slavic nations and this is why
> the present increase of migration presents itself as an issue for the legislators
> of this country; in this context, two issues are the most urgent and important:
> to what extent and for how long a period can these races mingle? To what
> extent and through what kind of legislation is it possible to prevent the
> wave of migration, encourage the migrants to be assimilated, prevent new
> migration and transform the migrants into good American citizens as soon
> as possible?[29]

Balanos's recommendation to prevent migration did not convince the committee that submitted the migration bill a year later. His recommendation, however, was grounded on an official acknowledgment that the migrants were not
welcomed in the recipient country, an acknowledgment that contributed to the
consolidation of the idea that migration to the United States was a case quite different from preceding Greek migration movements. Balanos also depicted in his
report the harsh conditions of traveling and the dangers that the Greek migrants
faced after they abandoned their homeland, due mainly to poverty, exploitation,
and discrimination against migrants based on their social class and their race.
Distancing itself from Balanos's report, the committee suggested that the only restrictions that should be applied should regard persons who had not completed
the compulsory army service or who were bound to their land because of debts.
Although migration represented a constitutional right of every Greek citizen, the
state eventually applied particular restrictions that indicated an official acknowledgment of internal differentiations and inequality among groups of Greek subjects in relation to gender and ethnic background.[30] The only legislation that
the Greek state issued to restrict migration applied to women and underage girls
and boys older than sixteen. According to a royal decree that was published in the
government gazette on February 18, 1921, it was determined that underage boys
older than sixteen were not allowed to migrate, while "women and underage

girls older than 16 years old are allowed to migrate only if they are accompanied by a husband, parent, adult brother, uncle, son, son-in-law, brother-in-law, or any other close relative, or if they are invited by one of the above mentioned persons or by fiancés who reside in the country of migration and declare their responsibility for the migrant women in front of the local authorities at their place of residency."[31]

This amendment provided legal support to the popular contention that migration was mainly a male expedition and that women participated only to the extent that their participation would serve the male migrants' needs to create a family in the United States. By prohibiting women from migrating freely, the state created the legal basis for the social dependency of Greek women migrants on male members of their families. This type of legislation was also supported by organizations such as the International Labor Office as a means to "fight against prostitution and exploitation of women."[32] In 1922 the International Service for the Protection of Migrants was founded in Athens. The service sought to study and provide information on the practices and results of migration from an international perspective and to protect the rights of women migrants and children who were traveling in order to reunite with their families abroad.[33] The 1906 committee had also suggested the foundation of the Migration Council, which would be composed of ten members: the director of the Migration Office; representatives from the Ministries of Foreign Affairs, Finances, Education, Military, and Navy; one academic expert in political economy; one academic expert in public law; the president of the Athens Association of Commerce; and one important banker.[34] The committee suggested that strict control should be exercised over the activities of migration agents. Migration agents were allegedly responsible for instigating migration by means of false advertisement in the nation's rural provinces and concealment of the dangers and hardships that were involved in migration. Migration agents were thought of as a great menace, especially since in many cases they defrauded poor villagers into mortgaging their land in order to obtain a boat ticket to the United States—a ticket that in some cases was useless since many of these villagers were promptly deported from the United States for violating American laws, especially laws against underage or contracted labor.

Communication between the homeland and the emergent migrant communities was also an issue that caused official concern. Different migration committees pointed out the need for more frequent and quicker transportation between Greece and the United States. The government was prompted to support and encourage Greek steamship companies as a way to cultivate closer relations between the nation and its migrants in the United States. Steamships became an object of fascination since the possibility of direct, frequent, quick, and relatively pleasant transportation to the other side of the Atlantic captured the popular imagination. If America signified an extraordinary remoteness (both in geographical and in cultural terms), the steamship signified the possibility of mastering distance and dominating geography and culture. As a journalist noted in 1911 in his report on steamships:

> The boat is the bridge that connects the foreign land with the homeland, it is the link that binds the migrants to the idea of homeland. When they board the boat at Piraeus . . . our migrants have the impression that they are not separated from their native land . . . they feel that they stand on Greek territory not in the abstract sense of international law, but in reality. . . . We do not want to examine here if the massive Greek migration to the United States that is increasing in our days benefits the country or not. It is however beyond any doubt the fact that as long as migration is continued transportation to and from the United States by Greek steamships not only will decrease the dangers and the detriment, but it will also benefit the nation in material ways.[35]

The Greek government was very cautious in deciding on migration legislation. In the early decades, numerous committees were appointed to study the phenomenon, and reports were duly submitted to the Parliament. In 1913 Emmanuel Repoulis, the minister of domestic affairs, submitted a migration bill to the Greek Parliament and gave a lengthy speech on the issue. With the intervention of the Balkan Wars, however, the bill was not enacted until 1920.[36] Apart from defining the ways in which the state was responsible for managing and supervising the practices of migration and exercising control over those who were profiting from these practices (such as migration agents and steamship companies), the Migration and Expatriation Law offered an official definition of the "migrant" as a discrete social figure.

The issue of definition had emerged early on in the various reports on migration. Although it was clear that those who were migrating shared some social and economic characteristics, state officials were eager to give inclusive definitions that would describe the migrants and indicate the difference between migration to the United States and other kinds of movements of populations. As this period was marked by different kinds of movements and resettlements of populations, the word *metanastes*, "migrants," was often used to describe Greek refugees from Asia Minor and other places in the Balkans and the Near East. However, the character, practices, duration, and destination of migration to the United States made it a novelty, and so did the social profile of the modern migrants. The Migration Bill that was submitted to the Greek Parliament in 1913 defined the profile of the Greek migrant in the following way: "Article 5. According to this law a migrant is a citizen who goes to countries outside the European Continent and beyond the Suez Canal and the Straits of Gibraltar and travels third class. . . .

The natives who are traveling . . . are not considered to be migrants, if they are less than fifty."[37]

According to this definition three characteristics were attributed to the migrant and used to describe migration: transcontinental movement, social and economic disadvantage, and collective character. These three elements rendered migration to the United States an indisputably distinct category of movement. The migrants were thus differentiated from the earlier diasporic Greeks who had decided individually to pursue their economic interests in a place other than their native land. Labor migrants were considered objects rather than subjects of history, since they were individuals caught in the collective movement of history; history acted upon the migrants who were forced to migrate by factors beyond their own agency. Labor migrants also belonged to the lower classes of Greek society, since they had to be people traveling "third class." They were deprived of the social, political, and cultural privileges that were enjoyed by the Greeks of the diaspora in previous eras. Labor migrants migrated because of economic necessity and not as a result of economic strategy. Finally, labor migrants moved to a country that lay outside European and Near Eastern social and political settings. Twentieth-century labor migration was by definition transcontinental and transoceanic. Greek labor migrants were thus defined as subjects who transgressed the borders of the world that defined the natural, historical, and geo-cultural landscape of Hellenism. The Greeks of the diaspora in previous periods crossed the borders of Greece, a nation-state that was not in any case considered to contain the whole of the Hellenic nation; they were, however, moving and acting within the broader territory of Hellenism as charted by centuries-long history and heritage. The labor migrants of the twentieth century crossed the imaginary borders of this broader cultural territory of Hellenism, and in this sense they also transgressed the borders of their own national history. A prominent Greek intellectual who wrote extensively on Hellenism at the outset of the twentieth century noted that "in some countries the Greeks are natives, in others they are colonists, resident aliens, metics, migrants, expatriates. In Eastern Romilia Greeks are natives. In America they are resident aliens."[38]

The United States as a recipient country of migration was seen as exotic in relation to Hellenism. Reports, articles, and monographs on migration published in the 1920s and 1930s were increasingly marked by a preoccupation with the United States as a transatlantic, metropolitan nation-state that aroused the curiosity of commentators and fueled their imagination. American infiltration into the public imagination of the day was certainly related to the increasing expansion of U.S. political influence in the Near East, the gradual awareness that the United States was developing into a world power of first order, and popular representations of American life that repatriated migrants were propagating in Greece.

Migration, Subjectivity, and the Greek "National Character"

Political positions on migration were initially inspired by reflections on Greek national character and the character of the developing Greek migrant communities on the other side of the Atlantic. Early reports on migration were rich in Greek self-representations that were elaborated in the context of changing social conditions. Self-representations distilled conceptualizations of nation, territoriality, historicity, culture, and subjectivity. At first, the connection between migration and Greek national character was discussed in relation to the causes of migration. In the early 1880s various commentators started reporting on the beginnings of the migratory movement. The first reports on this issue showedsurprise, curiosity, and initial reservation toward a phenomenon that was gradually becoming an epidemic. The following passage is a typical portrayal of migration in this early period:

> Five years ago 12–15 men from Tsintzina went by chance to America and there they devoted themselves in different professions, confectionery in particular; after a short time these men sent money back to their relatives and by doing so they made other people jealous of their luck and in their letters they encouraged four hundred people to migrate also to the prosperous country of the United States. . . . Nobody can refute the fact that this is the first incident of so massive a migration from Greece since prehistoric times and nobody can foresee the extent to which this migration will increase.[39]

This passage addresses three points that later became standard elements of commentaries on migration. First, the author pointed out the endemic and "contagious" character of migration. The psychological factor of jealousy and the performance of mimicry were seen as the main explanatory causes of migration. Later commentators often related migration to pathological or psychological causes. The letters sent by the migrants to their relatives back in Greece were often represented as the means of contamination of the popular imagination and the spread of the epidemic desire to migrate.[40] In the 1890s commentators who were opposed to migration had stressed that the depopulation of Greek provinces was a threat to the nation. Migration was depriving the nation of its natural resources (that is, human labor) and impeding agricultural and economic development. For these critics, migration had pathological and psychological causes. Many contemporary journalists referred to a form of "collective psychopathy" that had taken over young Greek peasants and led them to abandon their native land and migrate to the United States.[41]

Commentators often attempted to position the contemporary phenomenon of migration in the overall history of the nation and thus to explain it as an aspect or a symptom of national identity. They attempted to render the phenomenon historically familiar and to exorcise the newness that characterized modern migration as a symptom of social change. From this perspective, two main elements were presented as basic characteristics of Hellenic identity: the inherent desire to migrate *(philapódimon)* and the innate ability to adapt culturally. The inherent desire to migrate had been culturally established as a defining element of Greekness well before the beginning of the twentieth century and with reference to issues quite irrelevant to migration. The conceptual coordinates of the notion of *philapódimon* can be traced to two points of the ideological chart of modern Hellenism. First, it was conceptualized in relation to modern popular images of the glory of Greek antiquity, the archetypal figure of Homer's Odysseus and the history of ancient Greek colonialism. Second, the stereotype of the forever itinerant Greek had been deeply embedded in social and political consciousness at the outset of the twentieth century, especially since the Greek diaspora in the eastern Mediterranean migration had been conceptually and indissolubly related to national and civilizational progress. These stereotypes were so deeply embedded in self-conceptualizations of Greekness and Hellenism that they were almost considered to be geographical and biological traits. In 1923—a year after the defeat of the Greek army in Asia Minor that caused the violent expatriation of several hundred thousand Greeks and the considerable cultural and geographical shrinkage of Hellenism—a prominent historian and university professor, Konstantinos Amantos, attributed the diasporic desires and history of the Greek people to the Aegean Sea: "The Aegean Sea gave Hellenism a certain orientation . . . the easiness of transportation through the sea resulted in the dispersion and final disappearance of millions of Greeks . . . and most important it impeded any expansion towards the interior of the Balkan Peninsula. Although Hellenism came from the North, when it encountered the calmness of the Aegean Sea, it was so seduced by it, that it followed its direction blindly."[42] The Aegean Sea operated as a signifier of the seafaring character of the Greek nation. This characteristic was also related to the desire to migrate, although the emphasis in this case was on the Greek people's tendency toward trade and commerce. The two-centuries-long history of the Greek diaspora in the East had led to the cultural inscription of the figure of the cosmopolitan Greek merchant as a dominant representation of Greekness. This inscription was deeply embedded in popular consciousness and widely accepted across the spectrum of political positions. In his book *The Contemporary Problems of Hellenism* Yeoryios Skliros, a renowned socialist thinker of the time, noted: "Greeks have always been an urban, commercial, maritime, cosmopolitan, mobile people with many connections with Europe, whereas the Slavs and Vlachs have been an agricultural, quiet, slow-moving and conservative people, like all the agricultural people; they lacked the historical traditions of the Greek people."[43]

The commercial and seafaring identity constituted for Greeks a treasured self-representation, since it portrayed them as superior to other peoples of the same geopolitical region and manifested the cultural proximity between the Greek people and the civilized nations of the time. As another author noted, referring to the history of Greek diasporization and commercial expansion, "Like the English of today our ancestors sought to discover new lands and to establish themselves there in order to disseminate their civilization, to create commercial centers for the trade and the consumption of their goods and to provide their native countries and their own hands with sources of wealth."[44]

Stories of the "ever seafaring" nation of Greek merchants linked national history to the contemporary meta-narrative of historical and civilizational progress as revealed in the histories of the leading imperialist nations of the time. It is not surprising that this identity was evoked when social commentators attempted to place twentieth-century migration within a "comfortable" narrative of national history. Early monographs on Greek transatlantic migration to the United States devoted extensive chapters to the ancient period of Greek expansion around the Mediterranean coasts as well as the eighteenth- and nineteenth-century diasporization of Greek merchants in the Near East. The multiplicity of Greek words used to refer to migration reveals the conceptual framework of representations of the national self in relation to the phenomenon of diasporization. The terms *apoikismós* (colonization), *diasporá* (diaspora), *xenitiá* (migrancy), and *apodimía* (expatriation) were used interchangeably to describe migration; the term *apoikies* (colonies) was also often used to refer to the Greek migrant communities in the United States. These terms are not precise synonyms; the variations in their use mark the shifts of emphasis in representation and also reveal how migration was placed within the historical narrative of the nation.

In 1919 Michalis Dendias published a book under the revealing title *The Greek Colonies around the World*.[45] In this book the ancient and inherent desire of the Greek people to migrate was combined with the image of the seafaring nation in a narrative that presented the history of the Greek diaspora as a history of Greek colonialism. In narrating the histories of Greek communities in Asia, Egypt, and Russia, Dendias stressed that Greeks not only retained their own culture and identity but also propagated Hellenic culture in the host countries. The edifying and civilizing mission of Greek diasporization was particularly emphasized. This approach was modified, however, in the chapter that dealt with the Greek migrant communities in the United States. The low educational and social profile of the Greek migrants was mentioned as a factor that made it difficult to maintain the Hellenic culture in the United States. Greek migrants were considered likely to assimilate because of the superiority of the American culture. The migrants' efforts to maintain their nationhood and national consciousness in the United States and their struggles to advance socially and financially were acknowledged and encouraged. In the end, Dendias admitted that the migrant communities in the United States could constitute a significant part of the Greek diaspora, but that remained to be proved. Other scholars of the time did not take up this colonialist interpretation of the Greek diaspora. As S. Vlavianos, a prominent psychiatrist, suggested in his article "The Psychology of Modern Greek People," "the Greek people do not seek to enslave and oppress free peoples, nor do they seek to form colonial states, or to fill the national treasuries with gold which is derived from the sweat of inhumanely slaving peoples."[46]

According to Vlavianos, the Greek desire to migrate was rather an expression of patriotism and natural inclination toward progress and development. This opinion touched on a very interesting point. As I have argued, the desire to migrate was a key element in dominant Greek self-representations at the time. Paradoxically, this element was always combined with references to Greek patriotism and devotion to national causes. Within national self-representations elements of national identity operated in antithetical dyads: the desire to migrate versus patriotism, the inherent inclination toward change and progress versus traditional ideals and principles of national culture, cultural adaptability versus strong national consciousness. The ancient instinct to migrate was often related to the Greek people's ability to easily and successfully adapt to different cultures and to survive.[47] Ion Dragoumis, a prominent Greek intellectual at the time, suggested that cultural adaptability and strong national consciousness represented the feminine and the masculine aspects of Hellenism. "Like the female that she is, the Greek race is always ready to accept the nesting of old and new civilizations, no matter what their origin is. But as a male that he also is, the Greek race reacts and exudes something of himself and in this way he transforms the alien elements that he accepted."[48]

The issue of cultural adaptability became central in debates over the impact that modern migration would have on the nation. The following passage from the report submitted by the Migration Committee in 1906 is extremely evocative of the ways in which already dominant representations of Greek culture and national subjectivity were invoked to inscribe culturally the new phenomenon of modern labor migration according to the historical, cultural, and social sensibilities of the time.

> The Greek's susceptibility to all civilizations is a known fact. Ever since antiquity the Greek race was marked by a unique feature; despite the solid preservation of its particular character and the reaction to any kind of assimilation by any other race, the Greek race easily appropriates progress and processes quickly any other civilization which it reproduces as its own product. It is true that this phenomenon, which . . . in ancient times resulted in the elevation of Greek civilization, has not yet happened in this

period of transition that our country is undergoing from the time of its national resurrection to nowadays. Because nobody could argue that we have completely assimilated the invading civilization to our own culture, and indeed this is the cause of all the anomalies and irregularities that lead to agitations, since it is often considered that we are running the danger of losing our national character. . . . There is no danger. The natural agitation that is caused by the fact that we have not yet assimilated all the new elements that have been introduced into our culture can be attributed easily to the extreme volume of these elements due to the orgasmic progress of the Greek race. Gradually and slowly this assimilation will be completed . . . and we will achieve complete harmony . . . the character of the Greek race will leave its mark on the whole of these new elements; the Greek race will render this new civilization its own and through this civilization it will follow the direction towards which the race's constituting powers are pushing it. . . . The contribution of those who migrate—particularly those who migrate to the United States—will be great during the process of progress. Since the migrants live in the midst of a great civilization, inspired by the highest principles of freedom and equality which guarantee success for all of one's own intelligent and honest acts, they are under the influence of this environment which educates them so that they become able to regulate their own inherent strengths and inclinations. . . . If they assimilate the culture within which they live and they return to Greece, they can then elevate the level of our contemporary assimilated culture and contribute undoubtedly to the rapid ending of the period of transition that we are undergoing today.[49]

The fundamental elements of Greek nationhood and migrant subjectivity are all present in this report. First, cultural adaptability as a national trait indicated the nation's commitment to the principles of civilizational progress as already defined by Western European culture and politics. The acknowledgment of cultural adaptability presupposed the acknowledgment of cultural backwardness and civilizational in-betweenness, as well as the need to change and adapt to the new world conditions. However, it did not assume a tendency to cultural assimilation. Strong national consciousness and devotion to traditional cultural principles were also claimed as treasured elements of Hellenism. Conceptually, the combination of cultural adaptability and strong national consciousness guaranteed the nation's agency within the sphere of history and politics. The antithesis between the two poles, however, was grounded on the cultural validity of the double assumption that *history equals progress* and *nationhood equals political subjecthood.* The cultural validity of the equation of history with progress was based on the belief that the leading point of progressive historical process was located in geopolitical areas other than Greece. This cultural validity was thus

grounded on the acknowledgment of the nation's backwardness and civilizational time-lag. The only way in which the Greek nation could follow world
progress and survive was to develop organic links with those countries and
cultures that were at that time at the leading edge of historical progress. This
was the role that the migrants were supposed to play in the process of national
modernization—the role of the organic link between Greece and the leading nations. This type of collective self-representation internalized established cultural
hierarchies and assumed the hierarchical canonization of peoples and cultures
globally. An aspect of this cultural entrapment was that the internalization of this
value-system positioned the nation itself at a position of inferiority on the scale
of progress and civilization. The validity of the second equation—nationhood
equals political subjecthood—operated as an auxiliary of cultural entrapment,
since the very idea of nationhood constituted the political grounding for discourses of unequal civilizational progress in history. As illustrated in the passage
quoted above, civilizational time-lag became a defining and quasi-inherent element of Greek national identity itself.

Public debates over migration led to a re-elaboration and distillation of already existing representations of national identity. However, the introduction of
the theme of migration into the cultural imagination of nation and subjecthood
caused a twist within already existing narratives. The discussion of migration
forced self-conceptualizations that stressed identity as a process of continuous
becoming, one that led not to annihilation but to an enrichment and consolidation of national culture. And once again, the debates over migration shifted the
emphasis toward the importance of the subjective aspects of cultural developments. As the committee report stated, the agent of historical change was not the
abstract force of the nation, the state, or the race, but a specific form of sociality,
the migrants. The migrants as a new social subject were expected to become the
agents of cultural and historical change by themselves *subjectively* undergoing
transformations that were related to their actual experience of migration. Early
approaches to migration were based on previously defined concepts of Greek diaspora and nationhood. The connection between modern migration and older
forms of diaspora served to integrate the former into the dominant narrative of
Greek national history. However, this integration was not an unimpeded process,
since the "remittance" of the experiences of migrancy to the homeland introduced radically new elements into older definitions of nationhood and diaspora.

The Other Side of the Atlantic: Early Transnational Politics

The official Greek state showed a vivid interest in the formation of Greek communities in the United States. The gradual increase of these communities forced

the creation of Greek consulates in cities where considerable numbers of Greek subjects were residing. Initially the mission of these consulates was to facilitate the migrants in their communication with the homeland. The early consular reports to the Greek Ministry of Foreign Affairs almost exclusively concerned responses to requests for investigation of missing persons. The consuls also requested funds to cover the expenses for the repatriation of destitute Greek migrants who were crowding the Greek consulates in many American cities pleading for financial aid to return to Greece.[50]

The Greek state was interested in statistical and demographic information concerning the Greek migrant communities. Different projects were launched that sought to register migrants by city of residence, profession, or income.[51] This project did not exclusively concern the Greek communities in the United States, but all the countries where Greeks resided. On different occasions the ministry submitted questionnaires to the consulates seeking particular information on local migrant communities, such as the number of Greek subjects residing there, their citizenship, ethnicity, language, and religion. The ministry expressed particular interest in the number of slavophone Greek subjects, Muslims, Bulgarians, or "foreigners originating from Greece" and residing in the United States, and the politics and disposition of these "special" categories of Greeks with regard to the Greek state. The ministry was also interested in the number of years that each subject had been residing abroad, the history of each particular community, the migrants' reasons for remaining in the United States, their occupation, their level of patriotic feeling, schools and number of students, number and size of Greek families, financial situation, degree of assimilation and Americanization, numbers of workers participating in corporations, numbers and frequency of mixed marriages, interracial relations and reciprocal perceptions, property owned by Greeks, commerce between Greece and the United States, and the state of the Greek language press, newspapers in particular.

The collection of information was aimed at the construction of an official cartography of transnational Hellenism. This cartography would enable the state to use the different migrant communities as resources in the service of national interests and politics. The state was also keen on monitoring the political activities related to foreign propaganda within the Greek migrant communities. During the Balkan Wars (1912–13) the Greek state was particularly interested in monitoring Bulgarian propaganda within the Macedonian migrant communities in the United States.[52] The state was interested in the politics of the migrant communities because state officials foresaw the impact that migrants could have on local politics after their return to Greece. State transnational politics were closely connected with the expectation of the repatriation of the migrants.

The Greek state also attempted on different occasions to exercise administrative control over the Greek subjects residing in the United States. On one of these occasions the state took the initiative to create the Panhellenic Union, an organization with branches in different American cities that had as its aims the protection and welfare of Greek migrants. On another occasion the state attempted to impose a special "residential" tax on Greeks residing in the United States. Both attempts were eventually unsuccessful, due mainly to antagonisms and conflicts between different political groups within the migrant communities. However, both attempts generated lively debates within the migrant communities, where the authority of the state in the context of transnational politics was often questioned and doubted in many respects. The residential tax constituted a special tax that Greeks residing in other countries (particularly the Ottoman empire) had been paying to the Greek state for services and legal protection offered to them by Greek consular authorities. The need for these services sprang out of the special status that foreign subjects had been enjoying in the Ottoman empire according to the system of capitulations. Under this special status the Ottoman authorities did not have the right to arrest or put to trial a Greek subject since the latter was legally responsible to the local Greek consulate and not to the Ottoman Porte. The attempt to impose residential taxation in the United States caused a great reaction on the part of the Greek migrant communities. The terms in which this reaction was expressed are indicative of the transformation of Greek conceptualizations of the notion of diaspora following the experience of migration to the United States. As the editor of *Atlantis,* a major Greek newspaper published daily in New York, put it:

> The taxation of the Greeks in America through the method of residential taxes is altogether inapplicable and likewise most dangerous so far as regards our relations with the American people, coming in the internal regulations with the American Republic. The United States considers, and rightly so, that the migrant who comes here, comes for the purpose of establishing himself here, and as a first footing and proof of sincere intention of establishing himself here, considers that the migrant has a duty to become a citizen. Moreover when he makes this fact known he becomes entirely less desirable and in addition to this he is hated by the American people, and particularly by the working classes. . . . Because what else does the payment of "Residential Tax" mean, but that we are Greek citizens, and that it is our intention to remain as such? What else does it mean but that we disdain the principles of the American Federation by acknowledging the fact that we must ask "permission" to reside in this country—not from the American Government, but really the representatives of Greece?

> What else would the payment be but an acknowledgment on our part that
> the American Government is unfit to protect our lives and our property, and
> that consequently we are paying a "residential tax" in order to have, as by
> right we will then have, the protection of the Greek Government?[53]

The Greek state's unsuccessful attempts to exercise administrative control over
its migrant subjects residing in the United States opened a channel of communication through which these changing forms of conceptualization of self,
subjectivity, nationhood, and diaspora found their way back home. Conflicts
between migrant communities and state authorities were often publicized in
Greece, and this facilitated the "repatriation" of migrant self-representations.
The Greek Ministry of Foreign Affairs attributed the failure of its attempts first
to the practical difficulties that jeopardized the whole project and second to the
Greek citizens' unwillingness to cooperate due to their "inherent mistrust in state
initiatives."[54] Already in this early period the issue of jurisdiction appeared, as
the Greek state agencies were often obliged to claim their authority over overseas national subjects whose rights and obligations were subject to international
rather than national legislation and jurisdiction. The contemporary conditions
of labor migration and migrant life in the United States led to the gradual consolidation of the idea of transnational political subjectivities whose legitimacy
transgressed strict definitions of state nationhood, even though they retained a
certain degree of compatibility with it. Given these circumstances, the creation
of the Panhellenic Union with the aim of maintaining the ties between homeland and migrant communities, and steering the Greek migrants' patriotism and
national consciousness, was also doomed to failure exactly because of the close
connection between the organization and the Greek state. The general laws of
the Panhellenic Union indicated that the organization would have the form of a
mutual-aid fraternity with many branches in different American cities. Its primary objectives were described in these terms:

> a. To cultivate among its members and through them among all Greeks
>   residing in the United States and Canada the spirit of mutual aid and of
>   love for their nationality.
> b. To instill veneration and affection for the laws and institutions of their
>   adopted country and the cultivation of friendly relations between the Greek
>   and American citizens.[55]

The Panhellenic Union was promoted by state representatives—in particular by
Coromilas, the Greek consul in Washington, D.C.—as an organization seeking
to arouse the migrants' interest in Greek national causes and irredentist politics. The union's monthly bulletin was dominated by articles that supported the
"Great Idea" of irredentism and propagated the notion of unity among different

Greek diasporas, and thus the unity of Hellenism.[56] The end of irredentist politics and the diminishing need for mutual-aid societies led to the decline and
final disappearance of the Panhellenic Union branches. Already in 1912, the
Greek legation in Washington was advising the Greek Ministry of Foreign Affairs that the authority most suitable to operate as a national nucleus within the
Greek migrant communities was not the state so much as the church.[57] Several
years later, Ioakim Alexopoulos, a clergyman, popular intellectual, and publicist, expounded on the idea that the national character and consciousness of
Greek migrants were in danger and that a political intervention was needed to
overcome the crisis. In his opinion, however, because of the particular social,
cultural, and political conditions that marked life in the United States, the agent
of this intervention should be the church and not the state.[58] The social organization of American society and the forced movement toward Americanization were making transnational state politics impossible and detrimental to the
position of Greek migrants within their adopted homeland. The imperative of
cultural integration within a society that was trying to regulate cultural difference and subordinate differential political allegiances forced diasporic modes of
identification away from political and toward more spiritual, cultural, and moral
notions of nationhood. In the transnational context, nationhood was thus dissociated from statehood and referred primarily to the domain of consciousness and
subjectivity. This does not mean, however, that nationhood became less political
and more cultural in definition. Migrant notions of nationhood were politicized
according to the transatlantic imperatives and principles of modern statehood
and social politics.

Repatriation and Generation of New Representations

In the context of migration, consciousness clearly became an issue of foreign
policy. The Ministry of Foreign Affairs showed an interest in the moral, spiritual, and social character of Greek migrants and the impact that their behavior
could have on Greek-American international relations. Many of the reports that
were submitted by consulates commented in detail on the migrants' living conditions and social profile. Early reports made references to nativist antimigrant
perceptions of early Greek migrants as "barbaric" and "unworthy citizens."[59]
In the years before 1924 the Greek legation in Washington often informed the
Greek government about antimigrant nativist political campaigns taking place
in the United States. In most cases the underlying implication was that the migrants' low social background led them to the kind of behavior that provoked
nativist reactions and disgraced the Greek name in the United States. Other
reports stressed the moral decadence that characterized migrant life. In 1907

the consul of San Francisco described the local Greektown between Third and Fourth Streets:

> This place is mostly frequented by the Sons of corruption and dissipation
> who avoid honest work because they do not like it and they devote themselves
> to other indecent activities of their preference, like gambling and other
> unspeakable acts, and indeed many of these people happen to have big
> families in Greece, and they inherit incurable Syphilis at the price of a dollar,
> and when they return to the Country they offer it [syphilis] as an inherited
> paternal right. If one questions them about their immoral activities they reply
> impudently that what they have in America they would never get in Greece.[60]

The political interaction and communication between the homeland and the migrant communities, as well as the conflicts and antagonisms that emerged in the context of transnational politics, created the "channels" for the generation and dispersion of representations of Greek migrant subjectivity that were soon culturally inscribed in Greece. One major aspect of migration serves to show how images of migrant subjectivity were remitted to the homeland—repatriation. Even at the peak of Greek migration to the United States, the numbers of those returning to Greece were high. According to official statistical records for the period 1908–30, around 60 percent of the migrants returned to their homeland after spending a few years in the United States.[61] The discussion over the possible impact that migration would have on the Greek nation was quickly focused on the impact that Greek returnees were having on Greek society. Repatriation remained a crucial issue and continued to provoke debates even in the post–World War II period.[62] Repatriation also caused official concern. The ministry invited Greek consulates to submit reports on the causes of repatriation. The responses referred to the pressure of Americanization, which was imposed on Greek migrants during and after World War I; the return of American soldiers to their previous professional occupations, and the consequent exclusion of Greeks and other migrants from the jobs that they had held during the war; and nativist antimigrant campaigns. The reports also noted that many migrants, having accumulated a small amount of money, preferred to return to Greece before an upcoming economic crisis in the United States would force them to spend all their savings. Furthermore, a great percentage of the migrants were originally from areas that were still under Ottoman control when they migrated, but had recently become part of the Greek nation-state. The new political situation and the hope of better living conditions inspired many migrants to return to their native land.[63]

State officials proposed that the government follow a specific repatriation policy. Their premise was that the repatriated migrants could benefit their native homeland only if their reestablishment was planned according to national needs.

Free and uncoordinated repatriation would be detrimental to national interests. The state should thus encourage repatriation by offering the returnees temporary exemption from military service, and easy transportation. The proposal for a direct steamship line that would connect Piraeus to New York had already been launched as a means of facilitating contact between the homeland and the migrant communities. In the context of repatriation the idea became very direct and timely.[64] Other proposals suggested that the repatriated migrants should be directed to establish themselves in the newly acquired province of Macedonia in an effort to strengthen the Greek ethnic element in certain areas there. Repatriated migrants were considered the most suitable for this role, since the conditions of migration had strengthened their national consciousness.[65] If the reestablishment of migrants was left to chance, the government feared that after a short stay in Greece they would spend all their savings and would be forced to return to the United States. The state should thus undertake to help the repatriated migrants adjust smoothly to the conditions of Greek life. Such an initiative was taken in 1919 by the Ministry of Domestic Affairs, which informed the Ministry of Foreign Affairs that a committee had been created to study whether repatriation should be encouraged, in which sectors of production in Greece repatriated migrants should be employed, and to what extent the repatriates could be absorbed in agriculture and husbandry. In order to fulfill the policy plans the ministry requested information on the number and the current occupation of repatriating Greek migrants.[66] Many of the repatriation plans were put on hold due to the unstable political situation in Greece at the time and the pressure imposed by the military expedition to Asia Minor. After the 1922 defeat and the influx of almost one and a half million destitute refugees from Asia Minor, official concern about migrant repatriation diminished, if it did not disappear.

Apart from its economic and political aspects, the issue of repatriation also had serious moral and cultural implications. A report submitted in 1920 by the Greek consul in Seattle to the Ministry of Foreign Affairs indicated the importance of cultural issues related to migration and repatriation:

> Unfortunately, regarding his social relations the repatriated Greek is a foreigner also in his own country. He is an "American" in the cities and even in his own village, although in America he is a Greek. Apart from his relatives everybody else keeps away from him, as if he were a total stranger; in some cases he is despised. . . . His eagerness to return to his homeland . . . is curbed by the cultural difference and inferiority of the ways of life there. These problems could be overcome, were he able to achieve the emotional happiness that is impossible for every Greek in America since he cannot even speak his own language in front of Americans without being scorned and ridiculed.[67]

Popular images of the Greek migrant had been consolidated in Greece by the 1920s to such a degree that the repatriates constituted a discernible type of Greek or American identity and were treated in their homeland as such. The report also indicated that the migrants themselves were conscious of the reception by their compatriots and that to a certain extent they performed the imagery that was attributed to them. The migrants' self-conceptualization as Greek and American subjects was twofold: it included an internalized belief in the social inferiority of their native country, a belief based on the migrant experience of self-degradation and ridicule of ethnic background in the United States, as well as a sense of self-inferiority within their homeland. The author of the report related this contradiction to the paradoxical double estrangement and cultural alienation that the migrant had undergone: the migrants are "more Americans in Athens, than Greeks in America." In the consul's opinion the reason for the scorn that repatriated migrants suffered was their poor, rural social background. Their integration in Greek society required a reformation of social mentalities in Greece. The migrants, whose mentalities had already been reformed, were seen as the force for a more general reformation of Greek society and morals.

Negative representations of repatriated Greek migrants were consolidated during the first two decades of the twentieth century. The genesis of these representations can be traced in articles published in the daily press at the turn of the century, reporting on the return of destitute Greeks who had mistakenly hoped to find a better life in the United States. In 1911 an Athenian newspaper published this description of the arrival of steamships from New York to the port of Piraeus:

> The passengers' faces as they were disembarking were different according to their emotional state and the conditions under which each of them was returning to his homeland. There were some sick or recovering people among them, who had fallen sick while they were in migrancy and they were returning to their place of birth in order to restore their health in the mild and familiar climate of the homeland and under the sympathetic attendance of their own people. There were also those who had been unlucky in finding jobs and making the money that they had dreamt and they were returning exhausted, disappointed and ready to content themselves with the piece of bread that their homeland can offer them. They were those who failed in their enterprises, victims of bad luck, defeated and discouraged, unable to resume the laborious struggle all over again.[68]

Even references to migrants who had succeeded financially were clouded by the implication that successful Greeks in the United States had become more American than Greek in terms of consciousness. Negative representations stressed the notion of the migrants' inability to transcend their own fate and improve their

lives and lot. In this category we encounter images of defeated subjects who experienced bodily the forces of impossibility of progress and advance. These images
emphasized the notion of physical degradation through the representation of the
migrant body as the carrier of diseases contracted while in migrancy. Syphilis
and tuberculosis were the main contagious diseases related to migrants and migrant life in the United States.[69] The main reason for this physical degradation
was considered to be the migrants' tendency toward moral degradation—a tendency that was related to the migrants' low class background. In a popular med-
ical book dedicated to the study of syphilis we read the following remark: "As
the young girls from the villages who migrate to the cities in order to find jobs
for the most part become prostitutes, in the same way foreign men who come to
America in order to find a job become so-called male prostitutes, in other words
they become depraved."[70]

Within this imagery migrant subjectivity became the signifier of a class-
defined notion of nationhood. Negative images of repatriated migrants were
based on the association made among low social background, poverty, and
Greekness. These images thus operated as personifications of the nation's inability to transcend the structural conditions of its own underdevelopment and
civilizational delay. Nationhood operated as a denominator of the nation's inherent inferiority and structural deficiency in the international scale of progress.
Within this representational order the migrant subjects were presented as being
self-conscious of their position within the international system of movement of
labor, capital, and culture. The migrants' self-consciousness represented a notion
of nationhood that internalized the impossibilities of the nation's present and future history. If we relate this representational order to the historical conditions of
the time, we can explain how images of migrant subjectivity functioned as a cultural means of representing the nation's gradual integration within the increasingly consolidated world order that emerged from World War I and from the
remapping of European and non-European geographical, political, and cultural
territories. Transnational and transatlantic migration was the process though
which the notion of the "world" was engraved onto cultural representations of
the nation and the self.

In this context, cultural representations were marked by internal contradictions of form and signification. Popular representations of migration and
migrants illustrated a multiplicity of content and signification. In this period
depictions of migrants were often found in various forms of popular art and
entertainment, theater and theatrical political satire in particular. The revue became the most popular theatrical genre in Athens during the first three decades
of the twentieth century, addressing an audience of diverse social backgrounds
and propagating new ideas of bourgeois modernization.[71] As historians of modern Greek theater have noted, the revue was an early form of mass media as it

popularized certain cultural and political ideas over a wide range of audiences.[72] In the period 1907–23, one of the most popular revues was the *Panathínea*.[73] After 1923, the *Panathínea* was mounted again in 1931, 1936, and 1940, but by then the genre of revue was already in decline. *Panathínea* represented a form of political, social, and cultural satire and commentary. The play was rewritten every year since one of the main characteristics of the revue was its political timeliness. Only scarce traces of the original texts have survived.[74] The character of the Greek migrant to America often appeared in *Panathínea*, while the skit "*Ο Αποχαιρετισμός του Μετανάστη*" [The migrant's farewell] was one of the longest lasting skits. The characters changed every year, although certain characters were presented in different stories each year. One of these stock characters was Nikoletos, a Westernized Greek from the Ionian island of Zante. In the 1907 *Panathínea*, Nikoletos was presented while in Athens, where he had come in order to accompany his sister and brother-in-law who were both migrating to the United States.[75] In 1908 Nikoletos returned to Athens to welcome his relatives who were returning from the United States. While waiting at the port of Piraeus, he was surrounded by wretched beggars. The following exchange between Nikoletos and the beggars illustrates powerfully the popular perception of migrants and migration in Greece in that period:

> NIKOLETOS: Who are all these bearded men? Look at their wretchedness, ill-fated men they are!
>
> FIRST MIGRANT: Spare me your charity, boss!
>
> SECOND MIGRANT: Help me, sir!
>
> THIRD MIGRANT: Give me something, may God bless your dead people!
>
> NIK.: They are all beggars. . . . Wait a minute, I will give you something.
>
> FORTH MIGRANT: Give me something as well, boss!
>
> FIFTH MIGRANT: Give me something as well!
>
> NIK.: Hey, there are so many of you! Why have you all gathered here? Are you planning on making an association?
>
> FIRST MIGRANT: We are migrants! Boss!
>
> NIK.: Migrants? Oh, I see. You are gathering money for your tickets to America?
>
> SECOND MIGRANT: We just came back from there!
>
> NIK.: Are you coming back from America? What are you saying now? Are you saying you are coming back from America and you are begging for money? But you should be loaded with money!
>
> FIRST MIGRANT: Where are we supposed to find the money, Boss? We were stricken by poverty and desolation and we came back.

NIK.: What are you saying now? And why weren't you grabbing some of this money that is wandering around the streets in America and fill up your pockets and as this agent was saying to me last year the streets are paved with them for you?

FIRST MIGRANT: What are you talking about, Sir? That is what we were told as well, that there is money wandering around in the streets . . . but later we realized that we were the only ones who were wandering around without jobs. And fortunately there was that blessed boat *Moraitis* and the government took care to bring us back.

NIK.: Oh, it was the government who withdrew you from foreign currency and brought you back to circulate in our land? Let's say, you are the new currency. Okay![76]

The representation of destitute migrants stressed the contradiction between popular images of America as the land of wealth and the actual experience of migration. The juxtaposition between popular representations of American prosperity and migrant destitution became a marked element of the internal contradiction of representations of migration. Nikoletos and the migrants shared vain hopes and expectations of wealth. The experience of migration, which was communicated to Nikoletos via the migrants' repatriation, proved the impossibility of altering one's own conditions of life. When in a later scene Nikoletos met with his relatives, he was in the beginning unable to recognize them. Migrant life had wrecked his sister's body and had drained from her all the life and the vivacity that she had previously possessed. Poverty was depicted as an inescapable fate, and struggle against one's own fate as fatal. Both Nikoletos and the migrants were conscious of this impossibility. The symbolic collapse between the physical bodies and money illustrates this impossibility. The migrants could not own wealth, since they *were themselves* the American wealth; American streets were paved with human bodies, not with gold. According to this metaphor, the migrants represented a form of rejected currency. They had to be withdrawn from circulation as if they were counterfeits or devaluated banknotes. Images of devaluation and forgery were thus associated with the repatriated migrants. As Nikoletos remarked, the migrants represented a "new currency" that was "circulated" in the national economy. This remark indicates how the migrants were viewed as a new social subject whose identity was just being introduced in the nation's social and cultural economy. Nikoletos himself, however, represented the new dominant social subject of the Westernized middle class. As historians of modern Greek theater have noted, in that period the theatrical figure of the modern Greek who dressed in Western clothes, spoke the dialect of the people from the Ionian islands, and breathed an air of cosmopolitanism, replaced older representations of traditional and provincial Greekness and was depicted as the typical form of the national character. Nikoletos represented the new dominant national subject at the time. The encounter between Nikoletos and the migrants at the port of Piraeus operated as a symbolic encounter between the new dominant national subject and other emerging forms of social subjectivity. Cultural in-betweenness, social intermingling, and fusion between the old and different types of the new marked the topos of the encounter, the port.

However, theatrical representations of migrants did not always depict the negative aspects of migration. In the *Panathínea* of 1910 we encounter also another character: the American.[77] Although the extracts of the surviving text are somewhat ambiguous, it is clear that the American represents the type of the successful cosmopolitan repatriate. In the play the American engages in discussion with Athenians, to whom he describes his arrival in Athens by airplane. The Athenians reply that they had mistaken the airplane for a comet that was expected to fall in Athens those days. The American was the central character in many scenes of this play, observing and commenting on many different aspects of Athenian political and social life. The American represented the cosmopolitan and modernized subject, an authority on politics and on life in general. The airplane operated as a symbol of future technological achievements and modernization, and underlined the association between the American character and the formidable paradoxes of American life.

Popular representations of migrants and migration were rarely one-sided or coherent. They included contradictory and antithetical elements. This makes sense if we consider that cultural representations in general do not have the character of a verdict; they do not serve the purpose of approving or disapproving history. On the contrary, cultural representations register the traces of the processes through which societies and individuals make sense of their present history. Representations thus bear the input of historical experience as well as the impact of dominant ideological discourses that police processes of "making sense" historically. Representations of migration and migrant subjectivity illustrate the contradictions between these different kinds of input, which are essentially the contradictions of history itself. Thus, popular representations of migration illustrate the conceptual space within which certain aspects of historical experience were made culturally intelligible. Studying the history of representations of migrant subjectivity allows us to trace out this conceptual space, although we cannot pronounce its coherence. The migrant as a social category that emerged in Greece during the first two decades of the twentieth century remained incessantly open.

American Imagery and Reformed Subjects

Negative representations of Greek repatriates were often coupled with representations of Greek migrants as *reformed subjects*. The notion of the reformed subject was based on the contention that acquaintance with American culture would reform the migrants, who would then spread the ideals of a higher culture in their homeland. In 1934–36 Vasileios Valaoras, a Greek doctor, visited the United States and studied at Johns Hopkins University as a Rockefeller fellow, and then published a book dedicated to the Greeks in the United States. In this book, he referred to the impact that migration would have on Greek culture:

> Apart from the economic benefit, migration also brought the large rural populations of Greece into contact with the more civilized environment of the United States; under the impact of this environment the Greek migrant was transformed into a better human being. The benefit of good climate and better nutrition creates healthier people and the fast pace of work stirred industriousness and awoke the Greek spirit of collaboration and enterprise. The Hellenism of America was formed in this way and was led by powerful national organizations and became thus not only a useful national resource, but also superior to the equivalent class of the Greek population that constituted the migrants' social background. . . . The migrants' children undergo a progressive biological transformation which distances the young generations from the original type of the Greek from Greece and comes closer to the still forming new human type, the common type of the white American. The higher educational background, the broader horizon of individual freedom, and the process of growing up within the context of relative abundance of means and pleasures, produce a different psychological make-up and a different mentality about life and duties.[78]

This type of positive representation of Greek migrants stressed the possibility of cultural reform under the influence of American culture. Positive representations of the reformed subject were grounded on the premise of the superiority of American culture and the inferiority of modern Greek culture. These representations concerned mostly the migrants who decided to remain in the United States and even more so the second-generation migrants who were supposedly becoming alienated from their parents' native national culture. Positive representations of reformed migrant subjectivity were generated in Greece during the interwar period, at the same time that images of the United States as an emerging world power were becoming increasingly popular. We cannot decode positive representations of migrant subjectivity in Greece unless we associate it with contemporary images of America. Reports on the wonders of life in the New World and the paradoxes of American life can be traced in the Greek popular press even before World War I. America excited the imagination because it was depicted as the land where different kinds of social, economic, and moral restrictions were revoked, especially with regard to practical aspects of everyday life, gender relations, technological experimentation, and national intermingling. America was associated mainly with modernization. After World War I U.S. political influence in the Near East increased. In the same period popular representations of America were gradually modified: it was not the paradoxical, but the superior nature of American civilization and culture that stirred the imagination.

The gradual increase of American prestige in Greece was certainly related to the establishment of high-profile educational, cultural, and philanthropic American institutions in Athens, including the Near East Relief Foundation, the American College, the Gennadeios Library, and the Greek branch of the YMCA. Most of these institutions were founded in the late 1910s and early 1920s, and their activities generated images of American superiority and resourcefulness.[79] The distance of the United States from European politics up to that period had contributed to the production of images of America as immune to the moral decadence and turmoil often associated with Europe in the interwar period. America was thus treated as a treasury of high civilizational principles and a guarantor of progress. For Greeks America was also becoming a treasury of the highest principles of Hellenism. In 1922 Ioannis Gennadeios, a prominent Greek intellectual, collector, and state representative abroad, decided to donate his personal collection of books and manuscripts to the American School in Athens. His donation led to the foundation of the Gennadeios Library, one of the most famous libraries in Greece to this day. Gennadeios's decision to donate his collection to the American School caused some negative publicity, and the donator was accused in the proceedings of the Greek Parliament of "not donating the collection to his country as any real Greek would have done."[80] The ways in which the donation and the foundation of Gennadeios Library were justified and reported in the press indicate the prestige that was associated with America at the time. As a reporter noted in 1924, "the ancient Greek spirit has survived in the souls of Americans . . . the waves of dirty and repellent Asia have altered so much the face and morality of Greeks that we do not value, or recognize each other. Gennadeios's donation has such a value and was done in such terms that it is very probable that in the future we will learn how to recognize ourselves in better ways."[81]

America was represented as the most appropriate guardian of the essence of Greek national identity. American culture represented the treasury where the remnants of the highest forms of Hellenism had been deposited. The same view was propagated by American associations, such as the American Hellenic Educational Progressive Association (AHEPA), that strengthened their relations with Greece around the end of the 1920s. Tourism was one of the ways in which migrant associations started making public appearances in Greece. In the late 1920s Greek migrants started visiting Greece for vacations and tourism. Many Greek associations in the United States were organizing group visits to Greece. In April 1928 the AHEPA made its first official visit to Athens. During this visit the association's representatives held meetings with Greek officials and made official statements that illustrate the process of merging representations of migrant subjectivity and images of the reformed Americanized subject. In his speech, attended by Greek officials and members of the government, the president of the AHEPA, Dean Alfange, declared:

> The AHEPA today seeks also the Americanization of its members, but this Americanization does not mean the same with Bulgarization, or Turkization. Americanization means that you preserve intact and you respect your own religion, the worship of your country of birth, your morals and customs, your language. You should preserve your church and your schools according to the laws, you should adhere to your national and religious celebrations, but at the same time you should be always actively participating and be interested in the political and social life of the country where you reside. It urges you to become citizens and enjoy the privileges of citizenship, and if you have the qualifications, it encourages you to advance to the highest political positions beyond all religious or racial prejudices. The AHEPA today represents in America all the noblest Greek principles and works systematically for the revival and propagation of the high and immortal Greek ideals.[82]

By the late 1920s, representations of Greek migrant subjectivity were embracing images of Americanness. Images of migration were gradually fading away and were being replaced by images of reformed Greekness. The American Greeks represented a distinct version of Greekness that had been grafted onto American cultural elements and political principles. Valaoras had pointed out this possibility of cultural grafting in an elaboration that appears similar to the principles of social eugenics:

> It is well known that, after Greece, America is the place where the second largest number of Greeks reside. . . . When the Greek of America came to this new world, he *changed*. But this change was for the better. His educational level was *elevated*. His life and social relations *improved*, and his heart was filled with more civilized and noble feelings. . . . A new human type was formed within the new environment, *the type of the White American . . . Heredity* is a conservative element, and supports the passing of the paternal characteristics to the descendants in the ways that these were formed in the homeland. The *environment* tends to annihilate the differences between peoples and as it affects all of them in the same way tends to form a single human type, a new variety of humanity that has never before appeared on Earth. This constitutes a progressive element. . . . It is, however, possible that a third factor intervenes. And this would be *human will*. . . . Today the civilized world has created a new science, *Eugenics*. This science aims

at the refinement of the human race, the abolition of sub-humans and the
construction of a better society.[83]

Images of reformed Greek migrant subjectivity represented the possibility of a
general reformation and elevation of Greek culture and identity according to
the principles of white American superiority. Although representations of reformed subjectivity included positive images of migrants and migration, they
also indicated internalized images of Greek cultural inferiority. The gradual dissemination of popular images of America during the 1940s and 1950s was paral-
leled by the spread of representations of the migrants as reformed subjects. The
role that the United States played in the fight against Nazism in Europe during
World War II consolidated popular images of American culture after the end of
the war. In the 1950s various Greek intellectuals visited the United States and
were given the opportunity to reflect on American culture, politics, and state
of civilization.[84] Many memoirs and essays on this topic were published in this
period. Books on the United States always included references to the Greek migrant community. These commentaries indicate how by the 1950s the history
of Greek migrants had been registered in national consciousness as a history of
cultural reformation of subjectivity. In 1952 Manolis Triantafyllidis, a prominent
Greek linguist and intellectual, published a book that documented his impressions from a visit to the United States. In this book, he treated the Greek community as an American rather than a Greek phenomenon. He lamented the loss
of the migrant culture and tradition, and stigmatized the indifference that the
Greek had supposedly shown toward the Greek migrant communities. According to Triantafyllidis, this indifference was ultimately responsible for the fact that
the present history of the Greek communities in the United States constituted
part of American history rather than the history of the Greek diaspora.

> In general we lacked here the *consciousness of the migrant Hellenism* ,
> wherever the latter is to be found; we also lacked the kind of intellectual
> stamina that would otherwise permit the voice of Greek art, literature,
> education to reach the migrant Hellenism wherever the latter is located,
> across the continents. . . . Some consideration on our part would have been
> useful. Not only as a retaliation to those to whom we really owe so much,
> but as a movement . . . as a self-evident radiance, as an ethical position. Also
> as the duty of a people that in no era of its history ever conceptualized itself
> within the narrow borders of Greece, a people that has always attended with
> sympathy to the fate of all of its Diaspora.[85]

Triantafyllidis associated the lack of migrant consciousness with the Americanization of the Greek migrant communities. He argued that Americanization was
a self-conscious decision on the migrants' part; a decision that the migrants were

forced to make in order to survive within a cultural environment that underval-ued and culturally persecuted their Mediterranean ethnic background. He sup-ported the idea that in the context of imposed self-degradation and internalized belief in Anglo-American superiority, the relations between migrant Greeks and Greece had taken at best the form of philhellenism.

> Because of the education that they acquire in their new environment the children easily develop—directly or indirectly—a feeling of inferiority, as they try to reconcile the culture of their ancestors with the newly acquired native culture of the place where they live; this feeling of inferiority was also intensified in previous years by the not so flattering image that had been created in the United States about Mediterranean migrants, the kind of people that they were, the culture that they were bringing with them, their professions and their ways of life. The Greek children were then ashamed of their homeland and were hesitant in revealing their origins. . . . On this ground only Philhellenism could flower.[86]

The internalization of American perceptions of Greeks in the United States—especially in terms of class and ethnic background—led to the suppression of different histories of migration in Greece. For example, aspects of the expe-rience of migration that were related to labor exploitation, ethnic and racial discrimination, or gender-specific marginalization were suppressed in favor of stories of individual reformation and betterment through Americanization. These privileged stories were treated as treasured memories of self-becoming. Most of the Greek intellectuals who visited and wrote about the United States in the 1940s and 1950s focused on the second generation of Greeks in the United States and tried to understand and to position the identity and consciousness of that generation within the context of American life. In his book *An Essay on America* Yiorgos Theotokas, another prominent intellectual and man of poli-tics, described contemporary American Greek characters in a way that reveals the impact of the suppression of histories of migration on the formation of sub-jectivity.[87] According to Theotokas, there were two types of second-generation Greeks in the United States. First, there were the young men who had been born and raised in the United States as American citizens, but who maintained vivid memories of their ethnic background and their personal histories of migra-tion, the "heavy residue of the lives and the souls of migrants." These memo-ries were impediments to the subjects' personal balance, happiness, and social survival.[88] Theotokas regarded the memory of migration as a form of "psycho-logical pathology" and the main cause of self-inflicted inferiority complexes. In opposition to this pathological type, Theotokas discerned the second type, the liberated Greek American. This type represented the subject who had based his self-conceptualization on the suppression of migration stories that referred mostly to the experiences that their parents had had as migrants in the United States.

According to Theotokas, the history of migration represented a form of traumatic memory in the post –World War II period, and thus the migrant subject was forced to suppress this memory in order to survive. Histories of migration also seemed to represent a traumatic memory that had to be suppressed in the context of Greek national history. In the conclusion of his chapter on Greeks in America, which was also the conclusion of his book, Theotokas returned rhetorically to the decades-old question: had migration benefited or harmed Greece? After stating that the question was really outdated, he stressed that from a historical point of view migration represented Greece's contribution to the European adventure of creating the United States of America:

> The United States of America is a European artifact. The American nation constitutes a composition of old European nations that was accomplished on the wonderful English base and continued enriching itself with new elements. Today we can argue that Hellenism partook in this process of composition: this is finally the historical importance and moral justification of the Greeks' migration in America. Even though we've had less power [than other European nations] we too contributed our blood and human energy in order to build America the way it is in the twentieth century. From now on, the American people will also be—to a small, but considerable extent—descendants of the Greeks also.[89]

The historical experience of migration was thus purified of its subjective aspects and disconnected from any notion and experience of class relations, labor exploitation, ethnic and racial discrimination, gender-specific exclusion, moral intimidation, and degradation. In terms of representation, this purification was possible through the symbolic intervention of America as the signifier of difference and Europe as a symbol of historical progress. Thus, migration—purified of subjective historical experience—was smoothly integrated in a historical narrative that described the Greek nation's possibility to be "on the right side of history" and to follow the historical teleology defined by the forces of Euro-American world domination.

Histories of migration, however, were not eliminated from representations of America, American Greeks, and Greek nationhood. Histories of migration—especially the subjective aspects of the experience of migration—were registered in different forms of cultural representation, such as folk tradition, songs, and later popular music and cinema.[90] Popular tradition and culture transformed memories of uprooting, separations, hardships, discriminations, and bodily pain and disease into representations of Greece as a nation of migrants. These representations referred to histories of collective struggles against the

impossibilities and the constraints that defined one's own life. These historical narratives illustrated the ways in which the migrant was seen as a social and
historical subject that acknowledged structural constraints and impossibilities
while being in a position that did not allow one not to struggle against them.

Greek folk poetry has constituted a long-term cultural register for the experience of migration. The tradition of the songs of migrancy, *ta tragoúdia tis
xenitiás,* covers a chronological period from the fifteenth to the twentieth century and has registered a multiplicity of historical cases of Greek migration to
Central and Western Europe and the United States. Folksongs registered the social and psychological impact of migration on the migrants' homelands. These
songs offer unique insights into the ways in which migration was associated with
the most inevitable forms of separation within the histories and the lives of local communities: marriage, death, and migration seem to belong to the same
representational register of subjective experiences of separation and loss.[91] As
Michel Saunier has pointed out, over the centuries and in the context of different historical experiences of migration, popular imagination related migrancy,
xenitiá, to death, as both these phenomena seemed to represent forms of ultimate separation and loss. As Saunier put it, "in the language of folksongs, the
word 'foreigner' becomes a synonym for the desolate, the underprivileged, the
innocent victim of the evil forces."[92]

The folksongs that referred to the experience of migration to the United States
constitute a distinct category. The common characteristic that differentiated
these songs from the long tradition of folk poetry dedicated to migrancy was
that they always included specific references to America and to different cities in
the United States. Older songs of migrancy did not always include specific references to the places where the migrant lived. On the level of popular tradition, the
symbolic intervention of the concept of America differentiated the experience
of twentieth-century labor migration from all previous cases of migration. The
themes of these songs included the hardships of travel, the humiliation that the
migrants had to undergo during their examination by the U.S. Immigration
Service, and the sense of loss, loneliness, and anonymity in the foreign place.
They also referred to the ways in which women experienced migration when
they were left behind in the villages to take care of the elders, when they were
forced to marry aged migrants and follow them to America, or finally when
they decided themselves to migrate. Many songs were dedicated to the migrants'
return and their failure to escape poverty and to become rich in America. These
last songs were marked by sarcasm and scorn against the Greeks in America, a
sense of self-addressed bitterness expressed toward the Greek nation as a whole,
a self-ironic and transcending laughter at the inevitability of poverty.

Folksongs of migrancy are marked by a satirical mood as they describe the
misfortune of Greek migrants who return to Greece poor and destitute.[93] These

songs indicate the community's sympathy for the migrants' hardships and misfortunes. There is a tone of ridicule against the repatriates who try to hide their
poverty by flashing American watches, trousers, collared shirts, and so on. Folksongs of migrancy indicate that the community self-consciously denied fake images of success and wealth accumulated in America. The returnees' poverty was
gradually revealed, and this revelation caused laughter and self-irony—laughter
at the community's constrained conditions of life. The folk tradition maintained
and preserved histories and memories of subjective experiences of migration.
Popular representations of migration did not undergo the process of purification
that I have described in reference to official and mainstream representations. Another element that distinctively marked folk representations was the importance
that they attributed to the ways in which women experienced migration. Many
of the songs about migrancy represented women's negative attitudes toward migration and described aspects of life in communities dominated by women after
the mass departure of men.[94] They also referred to the women's refusal to follow
elderly migrants to the United States as picture-brides, and their struggle against
the invasion of their villages by American Greeks who were offering money and
seeking young brides. The following song depicts these reactions toward the phenomenon of migration.

> Mother, Turks, mother, Francs
> Mother, three Americans came
> They came to take me
> To bring me to Chicago
> I'd rather drop dead
> Than go to Chicago.[95]

Folk representations of women's reactions to migration often stressed that women
valued personal relationships and feelings more than the wealth that could be
gained through migration. Folk tradition represented women as the advocates
of that part of the community's beliefs according to which migration was against
traditional morals and values, and maybe not the wisest decision that one could
make. In fact, these representations indicate that for poor rural communities,
migration, like death, was not a matter of choice, but an unavoidable end. De-
nial, contempt of migration, and the implication that only the inevitability of
death can compare to the inevitability of migration as a social and historical
phenomenon are the main elements depicted in the following song.

> Mother, don't send me to America
> I'll be wasted away, I'll die there.
> I don't care about dollars, how can I explain to you?
> I just want olives and onions and the man I love,

He has kissed me by the gulley
And he has hugged me under the willow trees.
Yiorgo, I am leaving you, I'm going away
They are getting me married in the foreign land. Like a lamb getting
   slaughtered
Buried in my sorrow.[96]

Representations of women's reactions to migration depicted the ways in which in popular imagination migration represented those moments in life when social subjects are "caught" by history. Such histories of migration represent a form of subjectivity that is conscious of the self's entrapment *by* and *in* history. Consciousness of one's position in history constituted already an act of resistance, although it also acknowledged one's inability to escape history. In popular culture migrant subjectivity was associated with this type of conflictual consciousness.

The historical experience of early twentieth-century labor migration to the United States was inscribed in different and often contradictory ways in contemporary Greek culture. Cultural representations of Greek migrants in the United States appeared in the context of developing transnational politics. The web of transnational politics between Greece and the United States developed in the early twentieth century and involved, on the one hand, the Greek state's initiatives to exercise control over the communities abroad and, on the other hand, the migrants' claim to maintain a political and cultural presence on both sides of the Atlantic. The image of the Greek migrant that emerged in this transnational context radically transformed older notions of diaspora that had played a very important role in Greek national politics throughout the nineteenth century. Transatlantic migration introduced new social subjects into the political and cultural universe of Hellenism and triggered processes of redefinition of nationhood, history, and subjectivity. The multiplicity of cultural representations of migration offers insight into the continuous exchange between hegemonic discourses of nationhood and the lived experiences of migrancy, repatriation, territorial consolidation, global integration, and cultural transformations, including the gradual emergence of American global cultural hegemony. During the first half of the twentieth century representations of migration continually shifted. Early public reactions to migration were overdetermined by hegemonic definitions of national identity, according to which migration was seen as an expression of national identity. In this sense, it was the nation that determined the history of Greek subjects abroad. The proliferation of migration stories in the following decades brought certain aspects of hegemonic notions of nationhood into crisis. Cultural representations of migrancy in the interwar period reveal the emergence of the Greek migrant as a central figure in the Greek social milieu as it was gradually understood that migration was resulting in the transformation of national identity. The history of transatlantic movement was determining the nation itself. The proliferation of migrant stories of hardship, failure, discrimination, and struggle contributed to the portrayal of the migrant as a subject who embodied the nation's inability to transcend history. Toward the end of this period and more clearly in the years after World War II, hegemonic images of America overdetermined narratives of migration. The "Americanization" of migration histories in Greece was followed by the reconsolidation of fixed definitions of national culture. These definitions were based on the introduction of notions of "reformed" subjectivity into accounts of migrancy, transnationalism, and history. During the 1940s and 1950s stories of migration were assimilated into the rise of hegemonic notions of America as a cultural and political force. America appeared to determine both history and the nation. In post–World War II Greece, the subjective aspects of migration were marginalized, and the profile of the Greek migrant was associated with images of reformed subjectivity. Alternative representations were registered on different levels of cultural production, such as folk tradition and popular culture. Traces of these alternative representations were encountered in post–World War II representations of migrant culture with reference to later Greek migrations to Western Europe and Australia.

The genealogy of representations of migration in Greek culture reveals the ways in which the intervention of images of migration in national culture introduced the elements of ambivalence, contradiction, impossibility, and change in representations and expressions of self and subjectivity. In Greece, the "migration problem" that made its appearance in the early twentieth century was predominantly a cultural and later a political problem. It was a cultural problem in the sense that debates about migration revolved around the effort to render transatlantic migration culturally intelligible and to determine the effects that migration could have on national history and interests. It became a political problem in the sense that Greek migrants were gradually seen as the interlocutors between the Greek nation and the developed world. In any case, migration was not treated domestically as a project in social engineering. As we have seen, in the United States migrant subjectivity became the object of major political and disciplinary projects that envisioned ways of managing cultural difference in a civic manner. The culture of migration that developed in twentieth-century Greece was the product of remittances of images of migrant subjectivity that emerged in the context of transatlantic visions of social engineering and management of national, ethnic, racial, and cultural difference globally. As we shall see in the following chapters, migrant communities developed their own expressions of migrant subjectivity and ways of being a subject in migration that were acted out on different levels of diasporic imagination, mnemonic biographical reflection, and intellectual production.

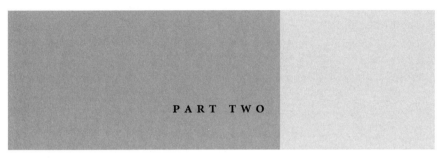

PART TWO

IMAGINATION

THREE

Short Stories of Migration and the
Literary Process in Diaspora

I think the literature of ethnicity writes itself between *ethnos*—a writer writing for her *own* people (whatever that means) without deliberated self-identification as such—and *ethnikos,* the preoperatively defined other reversing the charge, (de)anthropologizing by separating herself into a staged identity. The literature of ethnicity in this sense thus carries, paradoxically, the writer's signature as divided against itself, for the staging of the displacing of the dominant must somehow be indexed there. . . . A woman's relationship to a patriarchical or patriarchalized ethnicity makes her access to this signature even more complex.

—GAYATRI CHAKRAVORTY SPIVAK,
"TEACHING FOR THE TIMES"

Publishing has played an important role in the formation of the public sphere in migrant communities. Despite high percentages of illiteracy, the establishment of numerous publishing companies followed the relocation of South European migrants in various urban centers of the United States. For migrant communities publishing expressed the migrants' claim to public representation, as well as the need for outlets of communication. Publishing companies often undertook this role because of the absence of alternative forms of public representation, institutional forms of public communication, or networks of collective interaction.[1] In this context, the migrant press provided the main literary means for the mediation of migrant experience on a supra-regional and transnational level. Producing and communicating information about the migrant is a central part in the process of formation and expression of subjectivity. As we have seen in previous chapters, during the first decades of the century information about the migrants was systematically produced and communicated on the level of policymaking and public and official discourses on both sides of the Atlantic. However, it was within the migrant communities themselves that information about the experience and conditions of migrancy was produced and disseminated culturally. In this chapter I propose that the literary process (a process that involved writing, publishing, distributing, and reading) provided the mode of information that configured the communication of images and representations of migrancy in the diasporic context. In this sense, the literary process provided the network for the formation of new languages of social relations and the subjects that they constituted.[2]

The intensity of the literary process was impressive in the case of Greek communities in the United States.[3] The beginning of the twentieth century saw the growth of a considerable volume of literary production written in the Greek language.[4] The price catalogues published and distributed by the two major Greek publishing companies, *Atlantís* and *Ethnikós Kýrix,* reveal a great deal about this production.[5] As the catalogues show, literary production consisted mainly of novels, poetry, theatrical plays, chronologies, and histories, as well as almanacs, etiquette books (cookbooks, social behavior guides, letter-writing guides), Americanization guides and citizenship manuals, maps, dictionaries, methods for learning English as a foreign language, and course-books that were used at the Greek parochial schools established in different cities of the United States.

As often stated in the introductions to the price catalogues, the publishers' primary goal was to keep the migrant readership in touch with contemporary literary production in Greece—in their own words, to preserve the "heavy shadow" of the homeland literary establishment over the Greek migrant literary and literate circles in the United States. This became even more evident during the second decade of the twentieth century, when both *Atlantís* and *Ethnikós Kýrix* initiated the publication of monthly literary journals.[6] The monthly publications had a very particular character, emphasizing cultural and literary concerns. The editors of the special issue that celebrated the first decade of continuous publication of the monthly magazine of *Ethnikós Kýrix* noted that the main purpose of the monthly was to familiarize Greek migrants with Greek national literature. What was the particular importance attached to Greek national literature in the context of migration? As one of the editors put it, "Greek literary production is one of the greatest sources of national unity and national elevation. . . . While politics often strives in vain to cultivate State patriotism, and by doing so it provokes political passions . . . literature is successful in cultivating a broader national patriotism which is rooted in the human subconscious."[7]

Two concepts of nation and nationalism were thereby distinguished: state nationalism and cultural nationalism. State nationalism was based on the idea of the nation as a terrain of social and political conflict over power and control of the state. Cultural nationalism was grounded on a more transcendental idea of nationhood: nationhood as an expression of civilizational "drive." Cultural nationhood was grounded on the assumption that the nation represents a terrain of consensus. As such, nationhood was experienced privately and internally. This internal and private nation—as private as the "human subconscious"—was the nation that the migrants were instructed to endorse at the physical location of their migrancy.[8] This idea of nationhood referred to a subjectively remembered nation that became collective and was shared by means of its transformation into literature and its transportation from the homeland to the "foreign land," the site of expatriated life. The editors of *Ethnikós Kýrix* considered that Greek literary production constituted a narrative expression of the migrants' memory and thus attempted to transform it into a form of cultural capital of the nation in diaspora. "Greek literature does not simply present to the expatriated Greek the beautiful aspects of Greek life. It does not simply educate his soul, but it also gives him injections of national life . . . it gives him back his color that has faded under the new conditions of life. The services that our literary men and our intellectuals provide are sacred. And the *Ethnikós Kýrix*'s great service is that it provides them with the most advanced Greek journalistic means of transfusion of soul and diffusion of the intellect of our national metropolis to its dispersed children all over the Globe."[9]

Although the editors of the monthly *Ethnikós Kýrix* claimed that the main focus of the journal would be Greek national literature and its transfusion to the migrant community, many of the columns were actually devoted to the experience of migration, as well as to issues that concerned the lives and activities of Greek migrants and their associations in the United States as well as in other diasporic locations.[10] The literary process was also a mode of communication of information about the experience of migration; in this regard it must be viewed as a mechanism for the production of migrant subjectivity and its cultural representations. How was migration conceptualized and portrayed in a publication that proclaimed its focus on the canon of national literature and literary culture? One of the first appearances of the issue of migration in these monthly journals was through the publication of short stories. Short stories were one of the standard features of these publications from the 1910s through the 1930s. The experiences of migration provided the main theme for these short stories, which were sometimes published under a pen-name and were typically written by amateur writers and freelance contributors.[11] The genre became so popular that by the late 1920s and through the 1930s, newspapers and literary journals invited the readers to participate in literary contests and gave awards for the "best migration story."

Short stories of migration constituted a minor literary genre within the context of Greek literature of the times.[12] As Gilles Deleuze and Félix Guattari have proposed, a minor literature doesn't come from a minor language; it is rather that which a minority constructs within a major language.[13] The notion of "minor literature" becomes somewhat more complicated in the case of Greek short stories of migration because of the multiplicity of the languages within which these short stories were placed as "minor." Short stories were usually written in a vernacular idiom, while the language used in the magazines was a more purified and archaic version of the Greek language *(katharevousa).* The vernacular was also enriched with linguistic elements from local dialects and idioms, as well as with hellenized English words, which the Greek migrants were constantly incorporating into the Greek language. Short stories were written in a language that was "minor" within more than one major language. The "minor" character of migrant short stories published in Greek-language popular magazines in the United States expressed the relation between nation and the locations of migrancy. Deleuze and Guattari note that "the three characteristics of minor literature are the deterritorialization of language, the connection of the individual to a political immediacy, and the collective assemblage of enunciation."[14] Accordingly, short stories of migration expressed collective experiences and moral positions. They were also supposed to attribute a popular character to the literary, since they were addressed mostly to a lower middle-class or a blue-collar, working-class readership.[15] The popular character of the migrant press in general, and of short stories as a genre, was explicitly stated and discussed in different ways by intellectuals and scholars of the period. Early scholars of migration like Robert Park celebrated the popular character of the foreign-language press as an indication of Americanization. According to Park, the finances of publishing, determined as they were by the social conditions of migrancy, forced the foreign intelligentsia to popularize their "elite national cultures."[16] Park viewed the process of popularization as a step toward the transformation of foreign national cultures into domestic (American) ethnic cultures.[17] The inscription of Old World national literature in the migrant literary production did not take the form of a direct "transfusion." Under the terms of its existence, the migrant text redefined national literature, in the same way that migrant nationalism redefined existing notions of nationhood. Park and other Americanization theorists of the time suggested that migration tended to decodify the European national cultures and recodify them in the context of American public sphere and popular culture.

The conditions of existence of the migrant press were marked by the contradictions that characterized the transnational operations of nationalism on the level of subjective experience of the nation-in-migration. In 1926 the editors of the monthly *Atlantís* confirmed their commitment to publishing stories about— and addressed to—the Greek American public. The editorial that was published in the January 1926 issue (sixteen years after the first publication of the magazine and six years before it ceased publication) announced the turn toward "more popular and lighter" readings.

> When *Atlantis Monthly Illustrated* was first published, it was circulated in all places where strong and lively Hellenism could be found. *Atlantís Monthly Illustrated* used to sell as many issues in Thrace, Asia Minor, Russia, and the Balkan countries as in the whole of America. This period was followed

by the period of wars, blockades, disasters, and great transformations that
hit Hellenism deeply at all the vital points of its strength. Along with all the
other similar publications, *Atlantís* had to adjust to the new circumstances
that were created by the war. It had to become more popular, cheaper, and
simpler, without losing any of the richness of its content and its illustrations,
and that is what it is doing today as it presents itself to its friend in its new
ambiance.[18]

What is most interesting about this proclamation is the way in which the popularization of the journal was related to the overall political circumstances that
concerned the international circulation and readership of the magazine. Political developments of the late 1910s and the early 1920s led to the devastation
of Greek communities outside of Greece, particularly those that were located
in Asia Minor, Russia, the Balkans, and Thrace. These developments narrowed
geographically the circulation of the magazine, since the major part of the readership was now those residing in North America. As the Greek diaspora in the
East was shrinking, the transatlantic migrant communities were becoming the
protagonists in the generation of new forms of diasporic imagination and re-
codification of national literature and culture. In this context, the editorial board
decided to concentrate on the Greek-in-America readership, a turn that required
the popularization of the publication's content and character. Although emphasis would still be on literature and culture, the magazine would attempt to relate
more to the experiences and the lives of Greek migrants in the United States. The
introduction of the short story contests was one of the means of popularization.
Short stories were supposed to draw their inspiration from the resources of the
migrants' experience, and they were thus considered to be more appropriate for
a migrant readership. The magazine was supposed to contribute to the formation of such a readership as well as authorship. The editors' objective was to
render the magazine a medium for the development of an indigenous Greek-in-
America literary/literate community.[19] Thus, the magazine undertook a twofold
task. On the one hand, it would function as a medium of interaction between the
international, and more particularly the American, and the Greek national literary production. On the other hand, it would encourage the literary expression of
Greek migrants in the United States. In both cases, the purpose was to cultivate
a literate and literary migrant subject, who would read and sometimes write and
publish. This cultivation involved a process of literary and cultural training of
the migrants' imagination.

Editors and publishers often recognized that short stories of migration did not
exactly meet the requirements of proper literature. As the editor of *Protoporos*
[Pioneer], a socialist journal published monthly by the Greek Workers Educational Federation of America, noted:

> We have to confess that there is not, and never has been, worthy literary
> activity within the Hellenism of America. The few exceptions that do exist
> are not enough to prove this judgment mistaken. . . . We think that it is a
> good strategy for *Protoporos* to encourage the writing of pieces on life, stories,
> descriptions, opinions. Something that is not literature, does not claim to be
> Art, but has its own value since it expresses the thought and the feelings of
> people who, although they are not authors, have a heart full of feelings and
> want to talk and have something to say. . . . [We have] the desire to present
> some events that are interesting for Hellenism, and to present them in the
> way that they understand themselves, in a way new for the majority.[20]

The publishers' interest in life stories derived from their belief in the political
value of the retrieval of experience as a means of raising political and social consciousness. Viewing itself as a means of political intervention, the journal sought
to encourage the expression and communication of lived experience. The interest in subjective versions of Greek nationhood indicated the socialists' persistent desire to articulate alternatives that would be antagonistic to the hegemonic
bourgeois discourses of the nation. From this point of view, the journal considered the literary/literate public of Greek migrants as an already constituted
subject that possessed resources of subjective experience and a consciousness
that had only to be retrieved. At the same time, the journal served as a socialist
educational mechanism aimed at the cultivation and the political training of the
migrants as political subjects; it thus aspired to become a mechanism of subject
formation as such. The publication of short stories about life in migration was
accompanied by responses, comments, and advice to the contributors. As these
responses indicated, not all the stories that were submitted were actually published. The journal was interested in stories "with a purpose." The editors would
comment on the narrative form and use some of the published stories as examples of narrativization of experience and memory. By means of its educational
and political intervention, *Protoporos* was a force of subject formation since the
publication had a pedagogical role in educating both readers and contributors
in the "proper" ways of narrating one's personal migrant, proletarian experience. In more mainstream journals the educational and pedagogical function of
the press was also very evident, although this usually went unstated. During the
1920s most journals acquired a more popular character, and their pedagogical
role was expressed through the organization of literary contests that invited readers to contribute short stories related to their experiences in the United States.[21]

    During the early twentieth century the short story and the chronicle became
the most appropriate genres for narrating experiences of migration, dreams of
repatriation, and memories of the homeland. Short stories were collective in the
sense that they represented types of people easily identifiable by the readers; the

purpose of the short story was not to build an individual character, but to present a particular incident in the lives of people to whom readers could relate, though in different ways and for different reasons. The protagonists had to be recognizable already at the beginning of the story; the end was expected to justify and satisfy what was already known in advance. Through reading these short stories published in monthly journals over a period of approximately three decades, from 1910 to 1940, one recognizes the recurrence, circulation, and adaptation of particular stories and themes. The recurrence of particular stories, themes, plots, characters, topics, and territorial references sketches out the process of formation of a corpus of narrative material (devices and elements) that were used in the representation of migrant experience in the sphere of literary/literate mediation. As we shall see in the following chapters, many of these recurrent elements can be traced also in narratives of subjectivity that were articulated in different spheres of cultural production and mediation (theater, music, autobiographies). Furthermore, some of the recurrent themes were further used by the postwar literary and historiographical production on Greek migration in the United States: the hardships of labor, the successful migrant who becomes rich, the admiration of America, stories of repatriation to Greece, the dangers of disease and the fear of death in the foreign land. However, this does not mean that the stories remained the same over this period. Certain elements and themes were present consistently, while others were modified according to different historical circumstances and the social antagonisms within which cultural production was inscribed at a given historical moment. However, popular fiction of this early period constituted one of the formative moments of many of the "stories" that later became dominant versions of the migration narrative both in the American and the Greek public sphere.

Short stories of migration were collective in character, while their content consisted of personal and subjective stories. As the writers of the stories often pointed out, the subjective experiences of migration were adding up to a collective experience and constituted the basis for a communitarian conceptualization of migrancy. The intertwining of the collective with the subjective level of representation became apparent in the cases when the publication of a particular story would initiate a dialogue between readers and writers. The publication of certain stories often provoked particular readers who recognized themselves in some of the realistic stories to respond by writing to the editor or directly to the writer. In some cases readers would disagree with the ways in which the facts were fictionalized and "distorted" in short stories and would offer different versions that in their minds were more faithful to what had actually happened.

Short stories published in journals constituted a way of conducting a public dialogue on the content and principles of migrant subjectivity in its formation. Although the characters were fictional, the storytellers usually made remarks that indicated the close relation between fiction and reality. As writers often put it, the short stories should be seen as narration and dramatization of facts. As a result, readers were often compelled to debate and respond publicly to the ways of representation of their lives within the context of fictional narration. As these interventions and responses often indicated, although the short stories had collective character, they were not inclusively representative of the diverse experiences of Greek migrants. These narratives were collective in the sense that they claimed, by means of literary narrativization of experiences of migration, to represent an emergent Greek migrant subject. In the first stages of the development of migrant popular literature, we witness the making of hegemonic forms of migrant subjectivity as new inclusions and new exclusions of notions of Greekness were produced or exposed through the experience of migration. Short stories reflected the process of production and mediation of a literary and literate migrant subject. Given the particular circumstances of migrant life, this mediation propagated popularized versions of national culture, as well as notions of subjectively experienced nationhood that were often distinct from the political ideology and the practices of the nation-state. How was the experience of migration registered in writing and publishing, and in the reading of and responses to publications? And how were the conceptual mechanics of the nation altered, modified, or reinscribed within popular narratives of the experience of migration?

Homeland and America

Although the actual plots of migration stories varied considerably, the themes, elements, and issues were continuously revised, recirculated within different scenarios, retold many times, and finally consolidated as the constitutive elements of migrant subjecthood. One of the main features of the stories was the persistent preoccupation with location. The narrated events took place in a space that in most cases included both America and homeland, although in migration stories both these terms referred rather to specific locations of migration than to Greece and the United States as political entities. The Greek term *Ameriki* [America] did not refer to the United States in general, but to a particular town in the American Midwest, or to a workplace, to a specific period in the life of an individual, or even to a particular emotional situation. In a similar way, the term *homeland* did not refer necessarily to Greece in general but to a village, a province, a locality, and also to personal relationships, bonds, and social relations. Migration stories transformed national names into signifiers whose signification was continuously deferred. The two concepts of Ameriki and homeland were intertwined through the event of migration, and migration stories constituted the narrativization of this intertwining. The entanglement of notions of homeland and Ameriki in migrant popular fiction challenges the idea of "America" as a unified, singular cultural concept. This unified idea of America is often present in anthropological, historical, and sociological studies of transatlantic migration in general, as well as in studies of particular ethnic groups. By assuming the commonality of causes and conditions of transatlantic migrations at the beginning of the twentieth century, many scholars also assumed the homogeneity of cultural representations of the United States as America in all the different contexts and cultural milieus. Totalizing approaches to the notion of America indicate the nationalist predicaments of migration studies—especially when the migrants' America is conflated with ethnocentric conceptualizations of America as the United States—but they do not offer any insight into the ways in which the very experience of migration gave rise to historically particular structures of being in the United States as a migrant.

Short stories of migration took place in the space defined by Ameriki and homeland. Although migration narratives did not always concern directly the theme of migration, but diverse aspects of everyday life and social experience, the location of migrant social experience in these short stories was still represented in a dualistic manner: Ameriki/homeland. Even in variations where the whole story took place within the geographical territory of homeland, the concept of Ameriki, which necessarily referred to the conditions of migration, was always present in the description of everyday experiences, interactions, and memories. Migrant stories can be divided into two main categories according to their spatial reference: stories where emphasis was on Ameriki and thus homeland appeared only in the background; and stories where the emphasis was put on homeland and Ameriki was referred to only as an illustration.

The recurrence of themes makes possible an overview of the plots and variations included in each of these two categories. The first category (emphasis on Ameriki) includes stories that concern the Greek migrants' first years in the United States. Emphasis here was put on the geography and major elements of migrant life: social spaces inside and outside the Greek community, interactions with other migrants and racial groups, male friendships and bonds created through the experience of migration, and the description of social types and characters. Such types and characters included the *bossis* (boss), the policeman, the *sportis* (sporty guy who dresses up, speaks English, goes out with women, has some money), the consumptive (the migrant who suffers from tuberculosis, usually because of bad conditions of life and hard work), the peddler, the young boy working at a shoe-shining store (*sainadiko*), women migrants, the young picture-bride, the faithful wife, the unfaithful wife who ran away with a younger man. Most of the stories in this category concern the "first years" of migration and convey the message that those years are gone forever. Stories of the "first years" formed a version of migrant mythology, and the remembrance of this mythology of origins reinforced the idea that the migrants had really advanced socially and culturally since those early days, when they first arrived in the "new" country.

Other stories referred to the migrants' everyday life in Ameriki. Here the topics concerned celebrations and rituals. Very common were the stories that concerned loss and death: the death of a beloved person in the homeland, fear of death in Ameriki, fear of death outside the Greek community. Many of the stories of everyday life referred to the continuous physical movement of people from Ameriki to homeland and vice versa. Migration did not appear as a once-and-for-all relocation. On the contrary, it appeared as a continuous flow that connected different places and homelands; the decision was never finalized; the movement was never completed. Other common variations of this theme concerned unexpected encounters with compatriots, usually people coming from the very same locality in the homeland, like the same village, but also people who met for the first under the adverse circumstances of the first years in Ameriki. The recollection of these first years involved a narration of incidents that described the first years that migrants had spent in the United States. The group of stories that took their themes from the migrants' everyday life in Ameriki also involved narrations of visits to American institutions, such as mental asylums, workers' unions and federations, and courtrooms.

A third group includes the "deviation stories." These stories portrayed the type of Greek migrant who, for different reasons, lived in Ameriki but outside the Greek community. There were many variations on this theme. The most common variation concerned migrants who were blameworthy or queer according to a presumed consensus of etiquette of social behavior, such as the woman who came to Ameriki as a picture-bride, but finally abandoned her husband and the community; the man who participated in unionism and later joined the Salvation Army; the couple who divorced; or artists. In this group of stories we encounter a theme that was quite common in different ethnic literatures in the United States: stories about racial "passing." In the case of Greek migrants, these stories concerned migrants pretending to be Anglo-Americans and concealing their migrant backgrounds. Another variation of deviation stories portrayed migrants who forgot their duties and obligations toward the families they had left behind in their homeland. These stories were very important, since they demonstrate how Ameriki represents a particular structure of feeling: the fear of oblivion, which in this case meant forgetting one's own background and thus being forgotten.

As noted above, the other broad category includes the stories that refer mainly to the homeland (as seen from Ameriki). These stories follow the narrative and stylistic form of recollection and revery. They are dreamy and hazy to the extent that it is sometimes difficult to follow the plot in its logical sequence. One of the main variations in this group consists of stories that present recollections of the homeland.[22] Elements include the physical place of origin (the village, the mountain, the field, the garden), people (family, lovers left behind, lovers who betrayed or renounced love and commitment, friends, social circle, the teacher, the priest, the local authorities), conditions of life (poverty, carefree lifestyle, and emotional, social, or sexual oppression and dependency), more general political events (mainly the Balkan Wars of 1912–13, the expulsion from Asia Minor and eastern Thrace in the period 1910–22, the exchange of populations between Greece and Turkey), and the increase of migration as a massive movement out of villages and provincial towns.

Similar, although different in emphasis, are the stories focusing on the reasons that forced the subjects to migrate. These stories always referred to the general political, social, cultural, and economic conditions in the homeland. This discussion was conducted through the narration of personal stories and experiences (many variations of troubled love stories, financial debts and family problems, compulsory army service and war). The stories offer an insight into the ways in which collective and official history was reinscribed in stories of subjective experience and personal lives. History was recalled through the invocation of personal feelings and sentiments, such as anger at the forced separation, longing for the loved one, and bodily desire for the one left behind, but also through expressions of relief, of feelings of liberation and pride for those who managed to escape the social, political, and economic determinants of their homeland lives. These stories are particularly important for the study of Greek migrant conceptualizations of nation and nationhood in the location of Ameriki. Narrative conceptualizations of the nation referred to the intertwining between homeland and Ameriki. This migrant nation was imagined in relation to specific structures of feeling that the migrants developed under their conditions of life in migrancy. Memory of the homeland became a presently lived experience and not just a quaint recollection.

Ameriki Time and Again

The subjective character of conceptualizations of the topoi of homeland can be illustrated by underlining the connections between location and temporality. Representations of time can be traced in the intersection of homeland and Ameriki in the different plots of the stories. A common characteristic of stories was the inscription of migrancy in a *circular temporality.* Descriptions of the migrants' everyday lives in Ameriki exuded a feeling of continuous repetition and circularity of experience. A recurrent element in the stories was the emphatic reference to the number of years that the characters had already spent in Ameriki.

> "How many years have you been in America, Old Panayi?" asked a lady from the company.
>
> Old Panayi raised his snow-white head, his eyes sparkled for a moment, and then he said with a short laugh:
>
> "I have served a long time, my child! Thirty-five years! I bought the first issue of *Atlantis* and I have read it—let's say—a thousand times!"[23]

This introduction to a story that concerned the old man's life had a double function. It located the story within circular time (thirty-five years in America), while the use of the army metaphor ("I have served") put emphasis on the repetitive nature of the time period. The repetitive and homogeneous character of the years spent in Ameriki is also invoked by the image of the old man reading the same issue of the Greek newspaper "a thousand times." The particular incident that constitutes the theme of the short story was often introduced by reference to the number of years that the migrant had spent in Ameriki, followed by phrases such as "many years went by, until one day . . ." In this way, the narration of a particular experience was introduced by reference to a homogeneous, repetitive, and undifferentiated time that started with one's departure from the homeland. This time was usually interrupted by an event that reconnected the person with the life he had left behind (a death in the family, an unexpected encounter with a compatriot, repatriation).[24] The notion of homogeneous time was usually employed in order to describe migrant labor in Ameriki: "As time was passing by and through his consistent work Yioryis managed after lots of labor . . . to gain his independence enjoying the good things of life with moderation."[25]

The reference to "regular work" pointed out the repetitiveness of time, while the idea that long labor and hardship led to success bore a striking similarity to the army metaphor used by "Old Panayi," and was definitely tinged with a promise that hard work can lead to "redemption" and salvation from poverty.[26] Homogeneous time erased from memory events, people, and a whole part of one's own life that, through the intervention of this block of still time, became alien:

> In the beginning and for some years I was writing to my old folks frequently and later gradually I stopped writing to the guys and stopped writing to the old people, because I was thinking that it was enough for them to get my news from the others.
>
> You see, all of us, the migrants, we leave our villages and our people with the idea that it is not going to take a long time, but then all of us put it off year after year, and in this way, the one delay after the other, I ended up forgetting how many years I was gone.

> When the time came at last and I started feeling the time weighing heavy on
> me and I could not even recognize my face in the mirror anymore, when I
> was comparing it to pictures of me when I was younger, I remembered the
> village and my old people and I did not know if they were alive or not.[27]

The passing of time was often related to forgetfulness in different forms of popular narration, such as fairy tales, folklore, and everyday talk. In migrant stories,
however, it had special importance, since it was related to a very particular notion of time. In these stories the repetition of circular time spent in Ameriki was
interrupted almost exclusively by events related to life in the homeland. These
interruptive events were the most common theme of short stories. Most stories narrated exactly the moment when, and the circumstances under which, the
repetitive time of life in Ameriki was interrupted by an event that reconnected
the protagonist with his previous life in the homeland. In the passage quoted
above, the writer used the motif of forgetting his previous life and commitments
as an introduction to his story of returning to his homeland, where he discovered
that his parents had died, his siblings were also lost somewhere in Ameriki, and
the people of his village did not recognize him, but instead remembered him
as a disgraceful son. The reference to the function of time thus operated as an
introduction to representations of life in the homeland: images of a deserted and
abandoned territory ruled by death, loss, and inertia.

Conceptualizations of time in relation to labor were central for the understanding of migrant images of Ameriki. The short stories published in the socialist journal *Protoporos* represented a particular variation on this theme. In
socialist stories of migrant life, circular temporality concerned predominantly
the relation between industrial labor and the daily organization of time under
capitalism. Most of the stories published in this journal concerned incidents in
the daily life of workers. The routine and alienation of everyday life were recurrent themes of these stories, which were inscribed in the broader project of
critique of capitalism and industrial conditions of life. Typical stories of this kind
described details of the workers' labor: the nature of the work, the line of production, the unchanging pace of work in the factories, the unchanging conditions
of exploitation. The notion of time in these stories was not progressive, in the
sense that the subjects (immigrant workers) were represented as ensnared in the
system of capitalist exploitation. The promise of salvation and improvement of
the conditions of life through hard labor was explicitly rejected as a possibility.
On the contrary, the protagonists in the stories (immigrant workers) appeared to
be conscious of their entrapment in the mechanism of capitalist exploitation and
of the fact that the only "gain" of their labor was their mere survival. Here, the
interruption of repetitive time was not effected by memories of homeland, but by
consciousness of exploitation and development of a vision of social change and

resistance. For example, one story tells of the worker who on his way back home after a hard day in the tin factory reflected with horror on the uninterrupted repetitiveness of his daily life:

> I was looking for isolation so that I could put my thoughts in order and feel calmness in my soul that was upset.
>
> The thought that tomorrow it would be as hot as today and the "stuff" even hotter was torturing more than the thought of hell used to torture me when I was a kid. And the suffering that I went through today would be continued tomorrow and the day after tomorrow and . . . god, god . . . I pressed my head between my hands. Innumerable piles are waiting for us tomorrow to pull them off.[28]

The belief in labor as a means of salvation, progress, and betterment was rejected in this type of story. The promissory stories of migration and hard labor were negated by emphasis on the unchanging status of the migrant who labored just for his physical survival. Migrant dreams of success were mocked and deromanticized:

> Makis, one of my two partners, is a huge man but he does not stand the work . . . Whenever he gets his salary and he pays off his debts, he gambles with the rest of the money. And the next day he comes to work with his head turned down to the floor. "What do you want," he tells me, "you are not going to be saved by the stupid little money that you have left. So you play with it and either you win more, or you are right at the beginning again . . ." Next to us is Thomas, a strong and vigorous boy from Dodecanese. His dream is to save some little money and open a fish-shop. . . . His compatriots say that Thomas has been dreaming of the fish-shop since he set foot in America, eighteen years ago.[29]

The socialist journals often criticized the mainstream migrant dream of progress and upward class mobility through hard labor. They supported the idea that the only alternative to the migrants' suffering was political organization and collective struggle. The emphasis on labor, together with the belief in socialist internationalism, led to a refusal to distinguish between the life of native workers and that of the immigrant workers.[30] On the contrary, in more mainstream stories that referred to everyday life in Ameriki, the organization and sense of time of the migrant's life was distinct and separate from the organization and sense of time of the native society. The circular and repetitive time of migrant life was inscribed within the temporality of the recipient society in its dominant forms and manifestations, but remained separate. This became more apparent in stories that illustrated the gap between the migrants' private and public lives. The separation between the private and the public sphere was an element of many representations of migrant life. This separation offers an insight into the parallel operation of two different forms of temporality and the importance of this dual temporality for the analysis of migrant short stories.

The distinction between public and private was closely related to the distinction between the domestic and the social. Because of the frequent separation of families, economic migration often ruptured the connection between private and public lives. Thus, the themes of migrant family and nuclear domesticity were almost absent from the early stages of Greek popular fiction in the United States. Most of the stories narrated incidents that had taken place among male companies of Greek migrants. It was *their* lives and experiences that constituted the main theme of the short stories published in popular magazines in this period. In this case, the term *private life* referred mostly to life within the community of Greek migrants, and it defined the difference between this sphere of social interaction and the public sphere outside the community.[31] Around the end of the 1930s the issue of separation between the private and the public spheres of migrant life had begun to feature in debates over the future of Hellenism in the United States.[32] The separation would lead to the Americanization of the public sphere, mainly the business and enterprise world, and the preservation of the "Greekness" of the domestic sphere, mainly by means of control over female sexuality and family.[33] Stories of migration referred to the idea of separation as a necessary condition for success, although the ultimate impossibility of this separation was also invoked. The separation of the private and the public could not be sustained at particular moments when the migrant's temporality was incompatible with the mainstream time of the recipient country. Religious celebrations constituted the moments when the circularity of migrant life was exposed and reinforced. Religious celebrations referred to the symbolic order of the homeland. The reinscription of this order—this Old World regulation of collective time—at the site of Ameriki exposed the impossibilities of migrant life and the incompatibility between mainstream temporality (nonmigrant America) and the temporality that characterized migrant life as such. The short stories were concerned with these moments of exposure, because these moments encapsulated the experience of migrancy.

The centrality of religious celebrations in narratives of everyday migrant life indicated the important role of labor in subjective conceptualizations of the process of migration. Religious celebrations were associated with the interruption of labor and with collective forms of entertainment. Through the separation of public and private life, collective entertainment became one of the main instances of the migrants' self-realization as a minoritarian collectivity. One common theme in the short stories concerned the difficulties that Greek migrants faced in the observance of their national and religious celebrations.[34] The division between laboring time and celebration time, and the manifestation of this division in different cultural forms, constituted one of the primary means by which Greek migrants in the United States conceptualized themselves as a distinct part of the Greek nation. The nation-in-migration was primarily conceptualized by means of cultural practices of division between time of labor and time of entertainment. It could be argued that the nation-in-migration was *culturally* defined mainly as the *laboring nation*.

The Nation in Labor

How was the laboring nation of migrants imagined in migrant popular literature? Disease and physical deterioration were common references in stories about the migrants' work life, and tuberculosis was often presented as one of its typical characteristics. Stories of repatriation reflected the notion that migration actually led to the degradation of the physical condition of the migrants. In these representations migration was experienced bodily as devastation. Frequent references were made to the superior physique of newly arrived migrants and the rapid deterioration of their bodies as a result of the living and working conditions. The story of the laboring-nation-in-migration was not a story about the achievements and the glory of Greeks in diaspora, but one that reflected the horror of physical elimination. The discourse on the body that developed in socialist stories of migration did not reproduce the mainstream stereotypical rhetoric of migrant pathos and hardships. The difference between discourses of the body and the rhetoric of hardship was that the former, unlike the latter, assumed that sacrifice was necessary for eventual achievement, or that the fittest and the most industrious would prevail and achieve success. The conditions that caused the physical degradation of migrant bodies were considered to be beyond the individual's control, as they were inherent characteristics of modes of production and exploitation in migrancy. The narrative representation of industrial labor was often tightly intertwined with representations of the body in pain.

The factory as the site of labor also represented the location where the body became alienated. Migrant narratives often made reference to this site in order to describe the transformations of the conditions of life that resulted from migration. The factory became a symbol of Ameriki. As such, it was often presented as the site of evaluation of the male migrant body in terms of its productive (profit-making) ability. In many stories, we encounter descriptions of the process of physical examination that prospective workers had to undergo in order to be employed at the factories. Physical examination was described through references to the embarrassment that derived from nudity, the anxiety felt during the comparison with the physique of migrants of a different national origin, the frustration that accompanied the experience of commodification of one's physical condition as a factor of production, and subsequently the commodification of national physical characteristics within the transnational context of the capitalist market of working bodies.

The centrality of discourses on the body was related to the conditions and practices of the movement of migration. Within this movement, the migrant had to undergo several stages of evaluation of his physique (as well as of his intelligence) in terms of the productive ability of his body. These stages included physical examinations at European ports of departure, inside the steamboats before disembarkation at the different ports of the United States, and at employment agencies and factories. Stories of the migrants' experience at Ellis Island indicate the importance of this experience. Another aspect of this issue was presented in stories of the physical degradation that resulted from the conditions of life in migrancy. The hospital, the sanitarium for consumptives, the asylum often served as the location for migrant stories. These stories often represented the experience of the migrants in their first encounters with American institutions.

> The county hospital for consumptives was located outside the town, a narrow and long slum, about a hundred feet long and twenty feet wide.
>
> There were about thirty little beds on both sides of the room, and all of them were full. There was no furniture, nor any decoration. Five or six chairs only. There was one woman taking care of everybody. . . . Some of the patients were up . . . the others who were in the beds were half uncovered and naked because it was so hot. The image was such that we just stood there for a few minutes, unable to talk and trying to overcome the cold feeling of fear and disgust that was pushing us to fly away from this shadow of death and to jump into the shiny sunlight which was making every stone, every little leaf of the grass, every insect sparkle.
>
> An old man was lying across from the door where we entered. He looked like a skeleton with a black and yellow, thin layer of flesh hanging loosely over him. He was breathing with anguish . . . there was a knot as big as a chestnut hanging behind his shinbone, his calf.
>
> Another one was lying down and his thorax was sticking out, but at the end of his sternum, instead of a stomach, there was just skin hanging down, as much as a foot deep. He must have been a giant once upon a time.[35]

The systematic recurrence of the asylum and the sanitarium in migrant popular literature reveals the central role that those images of physical and mental deterioration played in the making of the migrant imagination. Quite differently, in stories that took place in the homeland, the impoverished, repatriated migrant body stood out as social miasma and a source of national humiliation. Stories of repatriation often stressed the horror, embarrassment, and anxiety that followed the return of the sick migrant to his homeland. The migrant who returned to his homeland to die represented the horrific aspect of the migration narrative.[36] In mainstream narratives, we notice an attempt to conceal the presence of the consumptive repatriate. In these narratives, emphasis was put on the marginality of the phenomenon, whereas in socialist stories the emphasis was definitely on the centrality of the experience of physical deterioration. The difference was that socialist narratives expressed a critique of the material conditions of life in the context of migrancy, while mainstream narratives resonated with the migrants' investment in the hope for general improvement and material betterment through migration and sacrifice.

Representations of the nation-in-migration as a laboring nation had very strong gender connotations. Within the patriarchal representational order, labor was a gender-specific concept. The relation between labor and nation in narratives of migration was related to very particular representations of manhood, and economic migration was represented as a male deed. However, the male doer was not represented as a heroic subject, but rather as a disempowered figure caught in and ruled by powers and structures beyond his own control. Similar representations of migrant subjectivity underlined contemporary references to migration as a *massive* movement, characterized by powerful *flows* and *waves* that *swept* the actors along to Ameriki. Migration in this period was never represented as an individual movement and it was never the result of individual motivation and causes. There were no action heroes in migration stories. At best we encounter eventually justified figures. The male migrant subjects were making history while being caught in historical developments beyond their control.

Masculine and feminine representations of the subject-in-migration (including representations of women and men either in the homeland or in Ameriki) corresponded generally although not precisely. The male figure, who was forced to migrate mainly by poverty and by his responsibilities as the head and protector of his family, often corresponded to the female figure who was left behind in the homeland. This figure was usually a mother or a wife, although quite often she was referred to not individually but collectively as "women in the homeland." For instance, reference was made to whole villages populated exclusively by women, since all the men had migrated. The women left behind were presented as necessarily "lifeless." Stories about the death of the mother, the wife, or the betrayed lover were very popular and frequent. Equally common were the stories of women's lives revolving exclusively around the expectation of the migrant's return or his letters. The waiting woman was elevated to the status of a heroic figure, which reminds us of popular representations of women as mothers of the nation. In popular fiction of migration, women entered the symbolic order of the homeland through the narrativization of their unconditional and eternal commitment to the male migrant and their own eventual sacrifice. This representation transformed the female figure into an embodiment of the male migrant's eternal and indissoluble bond with his homeland; it thus made possible the continuous return to a notion of origin and roots guaranteed by the female body's pain and longing. Male authority and the migrant's inalienable imagining of a female body safeguarded his right to his native origin that desired to be controlled and owned. Stories about the repatriation of migrants always made reference to the women whose main desire was to marry a returning migrant. These figures of longing women usually constituted the background that staged the imagined scenes of the migrant's return to the homeland.

According to the different plots used in short stories, men and women were differently disposed toward Ameriki. Male figures were presented as desiring their flight to Ameriki as a way of magical dissolution of the impossibilities of their lives. Male repatriates expressed an admiration for Ameriki. Male attitudes toward Ameriki took the form of emotional investments and aspirations. On the contrary, female characters that appeared in the stories did not have any similar aspirations. They often felt migration to Ameriki as a form of separation similar to that effected by physical death. The articulation of masculine as well as feminine representations of migrant subjectivity served to reconcile the insurmountable contradictions that marked the ways in which migration was registered in the consciousness of the migrants during this early period. These contradictions concerned the experience of migration as simultaneously the fulfillment of aspirations and metaphorical death, empowerment and oblivion, gain as well as irretrievable loss.

Similar correspondences can be found between male and female figures that were located in Ameriki. In stories of the migrants' early years in Ameriki, we often encounter the theme of male friendship and companionship uninterrupted by the presence of women.[37] Male friendship and companionship were grounded on the absence of women. Men were forced by the conditions of migrancy to live together and to take care of their own and each other's everyday personal needs. Homosocial friendships are created and become stronger in circumstances that impose proximity and intimacy between men.[38] In the passage quoted above, the reference to male homosociality was preceded by a reference to the men's work in the factory. The reference to labor operated as a guarantee of manhood and thus made safer the reference to an idealized form of male homosociality. References to male companionship represented the demographic consistency of the Greek communities during the early period of Greek migration to the United States. In stories about this early period female figures appeared exclusively in the background and their presence was secondary. The representation of numerically male-dominated communities reinforced the patriarchal understanding of migration as a primarily male process. The maleness of the early Greek communities in the United States later supported the powerful image of migration as an exclusively male affair.

The appearance of the first Greek women in Ameriki was represented as a celebrated event, since it transformed the male communities from playful companies of young boys to family-oriented communities. References to the first Greek women in the United States were very diverse and often contradictory, even in the same story. On the one hand, the female presence was praised as a fortunate event, because it was so rare.[39] On the other hand, it was blamed as overvalued and sometimes oppressive.

> In that period, when we used to be about seventy Greeks in Chicopee, another guy from Patras came, with his wife. She was the first Greek woman who came to our village and we were all waiting to see her, as if she were a princess from a fairy tale.
>
> A Greek woman in that wasteland! . . . I thought I was seeing the Virgin Mary herself in front of me. For the first time, after a year and a half of living miserably as a bachelor, I ate nicely cooked food at a table with a tablecloth. And the kind of food I ate! Meatballs with tomato salad and Turkish coffee![40]

The feminine figures operated as representations of an idealized Greek private family life. These representations were at the antipode of idealized representations of male homosociality. Although the female presence was praised, since it represented the genuine Greek way of everyday life, it was also despised, since it was thought to be oppressive to the independent homosocial male life of the migrants. Gender-specific representations of Greekness served to reconcile the contradictions through which men conceived themselves as subjects. Feminine representations embodied an extreme and almost neurotic Greekness, a Greekness that was implicitly despised by the male subjects. In the following passage, the disagreement between the two friends, when one takes the side of the woman and the other opposes her, illustrates this double face of migrant male subjectivity:

> But what made her seem very weird was her unbearable cleanness.
>
> —Brother, we are going to become hypochondriacs in here with all her Greek stuff. . . . Tell me, do you like this kind of life?
>
> —Of course I like it, because we are better off than living like bachelors.
>
> —For God's sake! Do you call that life, going around in the kitchen with an ashtray in our hands so that we do not drop ashes on the floor . . . ?
>
> —Poor Kazamia, compromise a bit, now that we live somewhat like human beings. In any case, a little cleanness is not going to harm us.
>
> —Does it harm us? It harms me, my friend, and it gets on my nerves if somebody else is imposing it on me. . . . I am a Cretan, my friend, and neither my neck nor my feet can stand the yoke. I will leave, and you stay if

you like slavery. . . . Let her go to hell, herself and her cleanness. My feet are mine and I will wash them whenever I want and not whenever she wants. Did I ever tell her when she should wash her feet? She can let them rot, if she wants to. If I do not care about hers, why should she care about mine?[41]

Proximity and intimate interaction with women—which in this case was represented through the depiction of a specific form of genuine Greek home life—undermined male independence and selfhood. One of the two friends was ready to sacrifice independence for propriety, while the other rebelled against the conventions of proper Greek family life and finally fled to New York City. In idealized representations of the early years of Greek migration, we can trace a sense of nostalgia for a male homosocial life independent from family requirements. In some stories that early period was represented through the narration of incidents that concerned the migrants' free sexual behavior in Ameriki and the flirtatiousness of their casual interactions with women of different nationalities. Representations of flirtatious young men were often counterbalanced by the figure of the older Greek man who patronized the young migrants and reminded them of their duty to families and lovers whom they had left behind in their homeland. The positive manly image of the young Greek migrants who interacted with foreign women was also counterbalanced by other stories that narrated the pitfalls of marriage with foreign women.

Contradictory representations of manhood in relation to migration and national character illustrated the diversity and multiplicity of the ways in which conceptualizations of manhood, nationhood, and migration were related in the context of everyday life in migrancy. National character was conceptualized through the totalization of different narratives of sexuality and gender (narratives of flirtatious manhood, patriarchal responsibilities and duties, independent male homosocial life, desired masculinity, laboring masculinity) around the conceptual kernel of Greekness. The study of this process of totalization in the context of migration shows that neither the narratives of the nation nor those of sexuality and gender were static or fixed, but always a matter of negotiation in the context of everyday interactions. Another example of this type of exposure occurs in stories where male migrants' contradictory disposition toward the private and homely aspects of proper Greek life was expressed through descriptions of women characterized by physical ugliness, mental simplicity, and rough manners. In these stories Greek women's ugliness and stupidity were measured by degrees of proximity to Americanness. The ugliness and stupidity of Greek women often embarrassed—and were always mocked by—the males who had become more accustomed to the American social and cultural rules. Descriptions such as the following were very frequent: "No matter how ugly or simple-minded [the women] were, the nostalgic migrants were looking at them

as if they were celestial creatures, just because they were Greek, and for this reason they were getting the best men. . . . [The Greek woman] was sun-burned,
clumsily dressed, illiterate and sullen."[42]

The "clumsiness" and "roughness" of Greek women were common points
of reference also in different types of popular entertainment enjoyed by Greek
migrants in that period, mainly theatrical plays and comedies. Popular magazines of the same period showed a fascination with depictions of womanhood.
Monthly magazines such as *Ethnikós Kýrix* and *Atlantís* repeatedly published
numerous pictures representing different types of women, especially Greek and
Anglo-American women.[43] Greek women were usually photographed in traditional costume. One of the most commonly published pictures was that of
an old, wrinkled Greek woman riding her donkey through the village streets.
Pictures of Anglo-American women, in contrast, depicted fashionable, artistic,
seemingly intelligent women. The subtitles of these pictures referred to the gai-
ety and cheerfulness of the modern American woman, who could claim a more
equal position in the male-dominated world by virtue of race and class. After
all, the Greek American press of that time was very favorable toward the American feminist movement. The movement was celebrated by Greek journalists and
writers as an indication of the liberalism and progressivism of Anglo-Saxon societies. On the contrary, the emergence of a feminist movement in Greece was often mocked and unquestionably condemned.[44] In 1921 the Greek government's
support of a bill that would give Greek women the right to vote was judged in
the following way: "We do not know the reasons why the Greek government is
supporting the bill on women's voting rights . . . to the surprise of the Greeks of
America. . . . It is not even possible to compare the intellectual development of
women in America with that of women in Greece, whose . . . exclusive preoccupation is how to become good mothers."[45]

We can only understand representations of the first generation of Greek
women in Ameriki in the context of the distinction between Anglo-American
and Greek womanhood as portrayed by mainly male authors and journalists
writing popular fiction in that period. This distinction, however, was inscribed in
the broader distinction between Greekness and Anglo-Americanness. In stories
of migration, Greek women characters were often unable to adjust to the more
advanced ways of life in Ameriki. They adhered to their peasant origins and were
unable to accustom themselves to the necessities and particularities of urban life
in an advanced industrial society. They were also often unable to conceal their
inability to adjust. Representations of Greek women who were unable to adjust
opened a narrative space for representations of adjustable Greek men. Binary
representations of Greekness in Ameriki resonated with anxious negotiations
over issues of nationhood, citizenship, nationality, race, and ethnicity that were
taking place in the same period within Greek communities in the United States.
In popular fiction, the split between the private-communal and the public-civil

sphere resolved this anxiety. The study of female figures as they appeared in popular fiction offers an insight into the gender-specific character of this split. The narrative configuration of femininity in the short stories appeared as a constellation of the unassimilated components of Greek migrant subjectivity. The distinction between male and female versions of Greekness offered a narrative resolution to the impossibilities that characterized the male migrant's life as a minoritarian national group within an assumed racially superior majoritarian regime. "Woman" thus became the symptom of the ever postponed and concealed inability to become majoritarian. However, these narrative resolutions were neither compact nor solid. To the extent that popular fiction resonated with everyday life experience, narrative resolutions of this type were always open-ended and gave rise to contradictory representations. At the opposite extreme of the character of the backward Greek woman, we find the woman who was so accepting of modern life that she uncritically endorsed the "American way of life" and eventually subverted the principles and conventions of proper Greek life. The juxtaposition of images of madonnas and whores is generally very common in patriarchal representations of femininity. The particularity of this binary system of representation in the case of stories of migrant life was that the principle according to which the two poles (madonna/whore) were perceived as such was the ability, or inability, to keep a balance in the process of Americanization.[46]

This representational order was interrupted by women migrant authors who gradually gained access to popular fiction during the mid-1920s.[47] The work of Theano Papazoglou is an example of this kind of interruption. Papazoglou started publishing in the journal *Protoporos* during the late 1930s. Her first contributions were not literary; she published articles on the status of women under the communist regime, where she saluted the beginning of the era of women's emancipation in the Soviet Union.[48] Her first short stories were also published in *Protoporos* in the column "Life Stories."[49] Her writing constituted a chronicle of Greek migrant presence in Ameriki; it was thus inscribed in the representational order of early popular fiction, the early signature of the ethnic writer. Papazoglou's chronicle, however, was definitely focused on Greek women migrants as the protagonists in the narrative of migration. She never claimed that she narrated "women's stories," and she always presented her stories as stories of Greek migrant life in the United States. Men were always present in her stories. Yet the focus was on women. The figures that appeared in the stories were both female and male, and their interactions within the context of migrant Ameriki were often teased out in narrative representations of everyday life and experience. Yet the focus remained on women's experiences of migration.

Papazoglou's work was not recognized as exemplary Greek migrant fiction until the 1960s. In its spring 1963 issue, the Greek American literary journal *Athene* published a review of Papazoglou's collection of short stories, *The Chronicle of Halsted-Street,* which had been published the year before.[50] The stories were written in Greek. In 1963 the collection won the first prize of the Athens Academy literary contest in Greece. This was the first time that a Greek American author was awarded this prestigious national prize.[51] The award can be seen as an official acknowledgment of migrant literature in the register of national literature.[52] The *Athene* reviewer presented Papazoglou's work as a chronicle of Americanization, since this would safeguard the ethnic sensitivities of the 1960s in the United States. Thus, the chronicle of migrant lives in Chicago was appropriated as a linear chronicle of adjustment and assimilation, and Papazoglou was recognized as probably the "best Greek-American author." Yet two points were still problematic, according to the reviewer: her insistence on the use of the Greek language, and her insistence on narrating the stories of Greek migrant women. Papazoglou's fiction was not easily acknowledged as part of the narrative tradition that was its actual origin—namely, the early stages of popular fiction of Greek migration. Its inscription in the corpus of Greek literature written in the United States had to be postponed for almost three decades and was possible only after the "signature" of this literature had itself been modified: from Greek migrant literature to Greek American "ethnic" literature. The woman writer's access to this signature had to be preceded by the modification of the conditions that led to the emergence of a patriarchal or patriarchalized ethnicity.[53]

The Nation Remembered

Memory of the homeland and temporality play an important role in the formation of imagination in migrant popular fiction. Migrant imagination was organized around notions of temporality that derived from processes of recollection. Early migrant popular fiction represented the migrants' recollections of their homelands. These recollections often referred to a variety of events, including war, military mobilizations, political instability, and economic recession. The similarity of these types of experience lies in their representation as almost natural catastrophes caused by powers beyond local control. The subjects were caught within the swirl of developments. Migration and war alike seemed to represent the moments when larger history caught up with people' s own lives, the moments when national history imposed itself forcefully on subjective life. The narration of migration by means of reference to themes that linked life history with the history of the nation (religious celebrations, military mobilization, wars) was underlined by a conceptualization of time structured as memory. The conceptualization of migrant time, as it was represented in the short stories of migration, corresponded to a temporality of remembering. This became more apparent in the cases where the story took up the plot of a dream. Remembering the homeland was often narrated as a dream.[54] The temporality of these dream-memories was deprived of depth and duration. Dream-time was a *flat* or, in Freudian terminology, *compressed* time.[55]

In migrants' popular fiction, homeland was represented through a temporality in which the time sequence was not necessarily progressive or unidirectional. The narration of a single event in the life of a migrant could be illustrated by images of homeland (landscape, history, politics) that were retrieved without following a chronological sequence. Such images were often presented in the form of the dream. According to Freud's formulation of dream temporality, "in the first place, dreams take into account in a general way the connection which undeniably exists between all the portions of the dream-thoughts by combining the whole material into a single situation or event. They reproduce *logical connection* by *simultaneity of time.* Here they are acting like the painter who, in a picture of the School of Athens or of Parnassus, represents in one group all the philosophers or all the poets. It is true that they were never in fact assembled in a single hall or on a single mountain-top; *but they certainly form a group in the conceptual sense.*"[56]

To use the Freudian formulation, these images of the homeland in migrant popular fiction constituted a "group in the conceptual sense." A representation of temporality in the form of a diagram may help our analysis. If we think of the individual life course as a horizontal axis of time (a line), then *simultaneity of time* should be represented as a point on the line, in the sense that simultaneous time does not operate as a continuum: it is static and momentary.

SIMULTANEITY OF TIME

The time of recollection started at the moment of departure. Before the departure the homeland was not recollected, it was rather lived daily. On the axis of the life course, the moment of simultaneity of time coincided with the moment of migration that divided the axis into two parts: life located in the homeland, and life located in Ameriki. The stories indicated this coincidence. Recollections of the homeland almost always included memories of the very last things that had happened before the departure (the mother's words and wishes, the lover's clothes, the weather conditions). The conception of past time as simultaneous was established at the moment of migration and exactly because of the act of migrating.

LIFE IN HOMELAND   MOMENT OF MIGRATION   LIFE IN AMERICA

(SIMULTANEITY OF TIME)

The memory of homeland was formed through and by means of recollections of one's own experiences. However, all the terms and the rhetoric employed in the short stories did not refer exclusively to the individual, but also to collective experiences. The stories of homeland recollection narrated, though in an indirect way, the processes of nationalization of the peasants before migration. They referred to the contacts that peasants had had with the state mechanism and the ways in which developments in national politics had influenced their lives at the local level. War and military mobilization were the main aspects of nationalization that can be traced in memories of homeland—aspects that were in all cases recollected as painful and unsettling experiences. The history of the individual or the village communities was inscribed in the broader context of the national history through references to events such as wars and experiences such as the military mobilization of the peasants. The migrant short stories offer an insight into the ways in which the experience of migration led to conceptualizations of homeland as a subjectively remembered nation: the nation conceptualized through the subjective remembering of particular lives. Through migration the nation as a subjective experience became a truly personal matter. Ideas of nationhood were traced within everyday life and everyday remembrance of one's own past. The personal and subjective character of nationhood in Ameriki was intensified by the physical and political remoteness from the Greek nation-state, and by the fact that many migrants originated from areas outside the national territories of the Greek state.[57]

It could be argued that a notion of *self* and of *nation* recalled within a simultaneous time was necessarily a fixed and unchangeable, even transcendental notion. The simultaneity of time erased historical change, transformation, and plasticity. The nation imagined from the location of Ameriki was a nation whose characteristics were not necessarily the effects of historical conditions; the nation could be traced in the continuum of time transmitted and inherited according to quasi-genetic rules and principles.[58] In the stories of repatriation we also find representations of a fixed and unchangeable nation. Emphasis on the description of nature and rural scenery was a common characteristic whose recurrence was certainly related to the rural origin of the vast majority of Greeks in the United States. The sense of stability and fixity that was projected by images of nature was made even more intense by comments such as this: "I looked around in my home, and I saw that they had changed nothing in the interior. I thought I was seeing things as they used to be. Everything was in the same position, the way I had left them, and only the people had changed, all of them. Among them, some kids had become brides, others from youngsters had become elders, others had been born, and others, unfortunately, were gone forever!"[59]

Here, domestic arrangements had remained the same. Even changes that people had undergone followed the unchangeable and eternal stages of the "natural" life course: birth, growth, marriage, reproduction, and death. References to events such as wars, revolutions, and political instability presented these events as features of the background scenery or as periodic "natural" disasters. None of the characteristics attributed to the homeland was ever presented in its newness. Furthermore, one should note the emphasis on repetition, fixity, and the "always-already" oldness in rare representations of urban centers of Greece, descriptions of which seldom occurred in migrant popular fiction. One such representation describes the city of Athens:

> For the Greeks who were living in Thodoris's village, and the same was true for all those who were living in other places all over Turkey, Athens was an ideal place. Memories and past glory that they used to read in history books, and the stories that were told by those who had been in Athens, were creating in the people's heads something sublime, something that only through imagination could be conceived and represented . . . something that was unspeakable, it did not have a periphery, it was beyond territory, time, life, matter . . . with these ideas in his head Thodoris arrived in the Greek land. He laid his eyes on Lycabetus, the Akropolis, the antiquities, the greengrocer, the drudge, the boatman.[60]

In this story the migrant left his village somewhere in Asia Minor and came to Athens in order to leave then for Ameriki. Thus, Athens was not presented as a homeland but as a place of migration.[61] Yet, although Athens was presented in the story as a developing urban center, the emphasis of the description was on the *oldness* and the *classic* character rather than on modernization and change. Athens was not represented as a modernizing urban center, but as an *ideal space* that condensed memories of the national past.

Both scholarship and popular perceptions of migrant culture stress that migrants suffer from a time lag, since their relation to their homelands is shaped by memories of the time when they left it, memories that remain unchanged for decades. The emphasis that migrant notions of nationhood put on the fixity of the nation is often attributed to psychological phenomena of nostalgia or explained by means of class-specific arguments concerning the migrants' peasant background. However, if we avoid reducing the analysis of migrant images of their homeland to ahistorical psychological arguments, we need to relate migrant imagination to the conditions of migrancy in the particular context of the United States in the early twentieth century. Fixed identification of national origin was an essential condition for the socialization of migrants in the recipient society. This requirement was manifested in institutional practices of socialization (registration and naturalization practices and migration restriction policies were based on national origins and quotas) and in economic structures and mechanisms that forced the new migrants to rely on national-ethnic community networks for employment and basic social welfare.[62] It was also revealed in cultural and ideological legacies according to which social recognition was possible only through the incorporation of the migrant on the scale of contemporary racial hierarchies, and in institutional practices of Americanization, where emphasis was put on the preservation of ethnic cultures in the form of folklore, while the civil aspects of life would be homogenized according to models of Anglo-American statehood and citizenship.

However, analysis of the mechanics of remembering the homeland and experiencing life in Ameriki, as these were illustrated in literary representations of the laboring nation, indicates that the emergence of the notion of the *unchangeable nation* was related to the split temporality through which migrants were experiencing everyday life in Ameriki. We could complicate the diagram of time used earlier by representing the two distinct types of temporality that characterized migrant life in Ameriki (the private or circular/repetitive, and the public or linear/progressive). Circular temporality is represented by circles that correspond to each year of life in Ameriki, whose tangent point is the moment of migration (since the years in Ameriki are naturally measured by reference to the time of arrival). On the line of progressive time (public time) this point also represents the simultaneity of time, that is, the observation post from which homeland is remembered.

LIFE IN HOMELAND   MOMENT OF MIGRATION   LIFE IN AMERICA

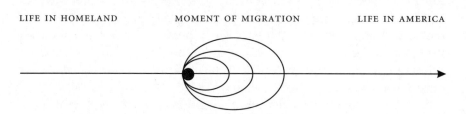

This diagrammatic representation helps us comprehend the ways in which popular fiction registered the process of Americanization and the development of double national loyalties (that is, American and ethnic nationalisms). Traces of this process can be detected in stories that describe how migrants experienced their everyday life through a split temporality: private (domestic, circular, repetitive, religious, "ethnic") time and public (civil, linear, progressive, "national") time. It could be argued that the creation of ethnic enclaves in the United States at the beginning of the century and the cultural, political, and geographical preservation of these enclaves throughout the years of supposed Americanization and assimilation were made possible through the separation of the two spheres in popular imagination and in everyday life.

Fiction, Imagination, Subjectivity

Popular migrant fiction of the early twentieth century reveals a plurality of struggles for the constitution and representation of subjectivity in the context of migrancy. Short stories were an early form of reflection on the experience of migration and thus played an important role in the process of producing, imagining, communicating, debating, and culturally circulating the constitutive and representative elements of migrant subjectivity. As migrants attempted to make sense of changing conditions of life and shifting frameworks of cultural reference, they employed literature as an already familiar tool of cultural intelligibility within the context of their national imagination. However, the grammar of national imagination had to undergo fundamental changes to accommodate the spatial as well temporal references of migrant everyday experience. For one, the particularity of migrant conceptualizations of nationhood lay in how they were determined by references to a different dominant nationalism, in this case Anglo-American nationalism. By this I do not mean to suggest that nonmigrant nationalisms in general develop in isolation and not through their interactions. On the contrary, homeland conceptualizations of nationhood also make reference to other nationalisms; in a sense, local conceptualizations of nationhood always reflect global political, social, and cultural hierarchical structures of nationhood.[63] However, on the level of discursive enunciation, homeland nationalisms tend to erase or hide the transnational aspect of their formation. Homeland nationalisms propagate the nation's uniqueness, particularity, and exclusiveness. Quite differently, migrant conceptualizations of nationhood bring to the foreground and expose their transnational and transethnic character. As our analysis of migration stories has shown, migrant conceptualizations of self and nation engaged with discussions over the conditions of life in the recipient country, adjustment to these conditions, and the cultural values of the supposedly superior native culture. Migrant conceptualizations of nationhood were explicitly extrovert, since they were determined by their reference to the economy of a majoritarian nationalism within which they were inscribed.

Migrant subjectivity emerged at the intersection of different circuits of subjectivation. Popular fiction brings the mechanics of this intersection into the foreground. The reading of short stories, as a minor literary production within a minor literature, offers an insight into the intersection between circuits of subjectivation, particularly between two different models of *being the nation:* as being the national subject (homeland nationalism), and as being a national ethnic subject (nationalism in the United States). In our reading of popular fiction, we saw the ways in which this intersection can be traced in notions of split temporality, gendered representations of subjectivity, and representations of the laboring nation. The intersection between these two orders of nationalism is a central point for understanding the emergence of migrant subjectivity, on the one hand, and, more generally, the operation of nationalism as a political ideology, on the other. If nationalist ideology operates as a totalization of already existing ideological elements around the kernel-notion of the *nation,* as a metanarrative that polices and defines other narratives of social identification, then we can argue that there is nothing contradictory in a nationalism that totalizes simultaneously around two notions: homeland and Ameriki. Both these notions are inscribed in a broader cultural milieu of the "trans-nation." In this sense, Greek migrant nationalism totalized ideological elements that concerned both the homeland (as it was remembered or discovered by the migrants after their migration) and Ameriki (the United States as experienced and learned by the migrants through the experience of migration). This conflation certainly was not always a smooth process. Especially for the first generation of migrants, it entailed contradictions that were felt on the level of everyday life. The short stories reveal some of the ways in which these contradictions were dealt with: separation between private and public life, split notions of temporality, and formation of a dominant, gender-specific representational order.

Finally, one should acknowledge that the popular fiction that was produced by, circulated among, and consumed by the Greek migrant communities in the United States does not offer a complete depiction of the experiences of migrancy, although it does illustrate some of its central symptoms. Inside and outside the text of popular fiction, and, most of all, at its margins, there lay a space of experience that resisted, or did not enter the process of, literary identification. After all, the literary process played an important role in the formation of imagination in diaspora, but still remained one of the numerous cultural circuits where migrant subjectivity was constituted and performed.

FOUR

The Exhibition of Subjectivity: Migrant
Performances and Parody Acts

Practices of performance played a central role in migrant culture, as they contributed to the popularization of self-representations and generated a sense of community. Many aspects of migrant culture were actively performative, extrovert, and marked by the migrants' tendency to present themselves to an external public. In the 1920s and 1930s, the debates that took place within the Greek communities over the character and content of American Hellenism persistently focused on how Greek migrants were perceived by mainstream America. The importance that the community attributed to its public image gave rise to extrovert and performative modes of identification, as in the case of the participation of the Greek communities in parades organized as part of the Fourth of July Independence Day celebrations. The Greek newspapers would publish many pictures of the communities' participation in these parades, whose importance for the migrants increased particularly during and after World War I. As the rise of American nationalism in the context of war politics resulted in the dissemination of strongly antimigrant nativist politics, the migrants' loyalty to the United States and its politics was often doubted by native-born Americans. In a retroactive way, migrant communities were eager to manifest their loyalty, mainly by capitalizing on their native country's alliance with the United States during the war. The blossoming of ethnic nationalisms in the United States in that period was closely connected with the war politics and its impact on the American domestic political scene.

A fundamental stage in the articulation of ethnic nationalisms was the tendency to manifest, publicize, exhibit, and perform the communities' loyalty to their "foster" motherland. The communities' participation in the celebrations of the Fourth of July played an instrumental role in this process of spectacularization of the migrants' loyalty to the United States. Local communities had to submit to local authorities an official request explaining why they wanted to participate in the celebrations. Their request had to be approved by the president of the United States and the local authorities. In July 1918 the mayor of New York City, John Hylan, responded positively to the request that had been submitted to him by the Greek community, and he added: "In response to the application that was submitted by one million foreign born citizens of the United States of

America, the president approved their plan to manifest their loyalty to the nation by means of celebrating the Independence Day."[1]

The parades were widely publicized within the Greek migrant communities. Newspapers and magazines gave extensive coverage to the events, both before and after. Reports on the parades obsessively stressed that the purpose of the Greek participation was to make widely and publicly visible the quality and cultural worth of the Greek "stock" as well as their loyalty to the United States. The spectacularization of migrant identity was accomplished by the publication of numerous pictures that proved the success of the parade. A reporter described the effect of the July 1918 Greek parade in Washington, D.C.: "The Americans were stunned in front of the grandiose spectacle that was presented by the Greek section during the celebrations of the Fourth of July. . . . Only those who saw it themselves can understand the size of the success, while the beauty of the spectacle can be represented only by the lenses of the camera and by cinema."[2]

By 1918 photography had become a source of fascination within the Greek migrant public sphere, as newspapers and magazines had been publishing pictures from European battlefields throughout World War I. Parades attracted the migrants' imagination and fantasy since they combined two strong poles of excitement: spectacularization of public life and national sentiment. The fascination with the spectacular character of parades was often manifested by the publication of a picture of the photographer himself in the reports on the event of the parade.

The Greek participation in parades was marked by high and intense symbolism. The pictures and reports published in the press conveyed a twofold message: first, the Greek migrants' loyalty to the United States; second, the cultural value of the Greek nation. The cultural capital of the Greek nation was demonstrated through references to events and periods in Greek national history that reflected glory and heroism: classical antiquity, the War of Independence, the Balkan Wars, and World War I. The means of representation that were used in parades were spectacular. Historical periods and events were reenacted by participants dressed in ancient, nineteenth-century, or contemporary folk costumes. The performers would either march or ride on chariots that usually represented ancient Greek temples. As indicated by journalistic reports at the time, the purpose of these public performative enactments of important moments of Greek history was to manifest through historical references the cultural worthiness of the Greeks. Representations of historical events in this case not only evoked the glory of the Greek nation, but also served as a strong credential of the cultural and civilizational value inherent in Greek descent. In the context of migrant parades Greek history was denationalized and ethnicized. Historical representations—unlike national celebrations taking place in Greece—did not operate as symbolic representations of national existence and sovereignty, but rather served as symbolic representations of high cultural and ideological traits that were supposedly inherently embodied by Greek migrants.

The performative ethnicization of Greek national history became more explicit in representations of the migrants' loyalty to the United States. This loyalty was symbolically represented and publicly performed by the waving of American flags alongside the Greek banners and the parading of Greeks dressed as Uncle Sam, or as American soldiers of the revolutionary era alongside ancient philosophers, Olympian deities, and Greek War of Independence guerrillas.[3] The coherence of the performance was achieved mainly through emphasis on contemporary international politics. The organizers of these parades were very keen on stressing the alliance between the United States, England, and France during World War I—and, of course, Greece's support to the Allies. The denationalization of historical references was made explicit in the reports on parades, as in the case of Pittsburgh in July 1918: "The Greeks of Pittsburgh demonstrated with their enthusiasm, their artistry, and their patriotism that undoubtedly the modern Greek psyche never ceased cherishing the ancient Greek ideals which are embodied and graced by the great North American Federation. As far as ideology is concerned, Greece and America are one and the same thing in the minds of all the Greek people."[4]

At the end of the 1918 parade in Washington, the representatives of the Greek section offered white and blue flowers to President Wilson and the first lady. On the ribbon that was tied around the flowers was written: "The colors of these flowers represent the national colors of the Greek people. But we are ready to add the red color of our blood in order to produce the tri-color of the glorious flag of our foster fatherland, which is fighting now in order to save the world and establish democracy."[5] The Greek national colors were thus denationalized, since they represented Greek people, but not national political subjecthood. Renationalization took place at the moment when the tricolor of the U.S. flag became representative of contemporary political devotion, commitment, and thus political subjecthood. This renationalization, however, was based on the assumption that the American nation did not "accommodate" just the United States of America, but the world and global civilization. Migrant investments in Americanness were based on the condition that America could accommodate transnational forms of identification, and thus migrant forms of identification often collided with notions of transnationalism.

In the public sphere the transition through different stages of denationalization, ethnicization, and renationalization of migrant political and social subjectivity was marked by performativity and cultural exhibitionism. The migrant form of subjectivity that emerged in the field of social, political, and cultural exchanges was marked by the migrants' desire to present a certain image of themselves to mainstream American society and to be acknowledged by it in specific ways. Migrant self-representations were often characterized by a form of cultural exhibitionism. In psychoanalytic terms the desire to see and to be seen *(Schaulust)* constitutes one of the fundamental drives. As Lacan's elaboration of Freud's archaeological expedition in the realm of drives suggested, "in exhibitionism what is intended by the subject is what is realized in the other. The true aim of desire is the other, as constrained, beyond his involvement in the scene. It is not only the victim who is concerned in exhibitionism, it is the victim as referred to some other who is looking at him."[6] Exhibitionism as a manifestation of the partial scopic drive was presented by Lacan as a form of autoeroticism. The exhibitionist's desire is directed to the object (the "victim"), but it does not stop there. Following the form of an open circuit, the fulfillment of the drive is achieved only through the emergence of an other who is looking at the scene without being involved. In the process of drives coming into play, *a new subject* appears.[7] In his lectures on the partial drive and its circuit, Lacan argued that Freud in his own analysis of *Schaulust* wished to present a radical structure in which the subject is not yet placed.[8]

This form of radical structure can be very instructive for an understanding of the complexity of the processes of formation of migrant subjectivity in the context of performative practices. In the case of parades, the migrant participants shared a desire to be seen by mainstream fellow U.S. citizens and thus to prove their loyalty to the principles of American nationalism. This desire and its cultural manifestations have often been interpreted by historians as well as by social scientists as early signs of Americanization and assimilation to the mainstream American culture. Yet if we view this desire as a radical structure in which the subject—the migrant—is not yet placed, we are allowed to approach "assimilation" and "Americanization" as questions rather than as *a priori* conclusions. The migrants' desire to be seen by fellow Americans and their eagerness to exhibit the riches of their folk culture, the treasures of their history, and the physical beauty of their people could only approximate the curve of fulfillment on the condition that the object of desire—the fellow U.S. citizens—are looked at by an other *(new subject)* while they themselves are looking at the parade. In the reports on the parades the photographer, the journalist, and the migrant public of parades appear to be the emerging new subjects/viewers of the spectacle. The American gaze did not thus trap the migrant subject; the subject was not assimilated, since there was already another gaze fixed on the viewer. Those who looked at Americans looking at the migrant performances and parades shared a form of subjectivity that emerged through the cultural practice of the parade—a new subject. Thus migrant participation in national parades did not constitute an expression of passive assimilation into the principles of Americanism. From a psychoanalytic point of view, parades constituted forms of cultural exhibitionism and national autoeroticism. Migrant parades in particular were a means of consolidation of a certain form of social agency on the part of migrants in the process of the cultural and social engineering of migrant subjectivity.

Migrant Parody and Entertainment

The issue of language was central in performative modes of identification and self-representation, as migrants often expressed their views on the shifting conditions of their lives in migrancy by focusing on the impact that their everyday interactions with the native society had on the language they spoke. For example, during the early 1920s articles on the psychological impact of ethnic names on migrants became quite popular in the migrant press. The practice of obligatory change of Greek names into American short forms was often a point of reference in accounts of negative experiences that marked the early years of migration for many Greeks. Most of the migrants had their names changed by immigration officers at Ellis Island. Many of them kept their attributed American names in order to avoid being identified by Americans as Greeks.

The practice of the change of names was a recurrent theme in many types of migrant performative narratives, especially in theatrical plays. In the theatrical play *Οι Φωστήρες* [Leading lights], a comedy written in 1925 by a Greek American and performed mostly by amateur actors in different Greek communities across the United States, Lemonia, a young Greek woman who has just come from Greece to the United States expresses her uneasiness in relation to the Americanization of her name. The following dialogue takes place between Lemonia and her brother as he gives her some English-language lessons:

> LEMONIA: And what is my name in English?
>
> JIMMY: Your name is *woma*.
>
> L.: What did you say? *Goumeno?*[9]
>
> J.: No, I would not call you an archbishop. . . . *Woma,* I said, my girl, but when you are young they call you *gierl!*
>
> L.: Leave me alone, brother, you are not going to change my name from Lemonia to *woma* or *gierl!* I do not like these strange names, I want you to call me by my name.
>
> J.: All right! Since that is the way you want it, I will call you Lemonia, but bear that in your mind: your name in English is *gierl!*[10]

The change of name resulted in a crisis of self-representation, since the new name did not represent the subject's personal history, while the old name could not represent the current experience and was not intelligible in the American context. Furthermore, the crisis was manifested by the definite and unavoidable nature of the change: "I will call you Lemonia, since that is what you want, but bear that in your mind: your name in English is *gierl!*" In the case of the woman migrant the change also implied the erasure of subjectivity and the imposition of generic gender identification.

The centrality of language as a means of self-representation can also be traced in numerous articles published in the migrant press of this period that stressed the importance of language for individual integrity and success in modern life. These articles clearly revealed an anxiety around the issue of language. An advertisement for an English-Greek/Greek-English dictionary that was published for many years in the pages of *Ethnikós Kýrix Monthly Illustrated* revealed this anxiety and propagated the idea that English represented cultural and civilizational superiority:

HUMANITY AS ONE FAMILY—THE WEAPONS OF PROGRESS IN
CONTEMPORARY CIVILIZATION—THE ANGLO-SAXONS WILL BECOME
THE ULTIMATE DOMINATORS OF THE WORLD—THOSE WHO KNOW TWO
LANGUAGES ACT WITH TWO BRAINS AND BECOME CONQUERORS

The progress of science, the annihilation of distances, the conquest of the air, the radio and all the fabulous inventions, and the establishment of the League of Nations and in general the new ideas toward a global fraternization tend to make humanity one family. A day will come when one and only one language will become dominant as the common tool used by all the peoples on the globe. And this language will undoubtedly be the language of the Anglo-Saxon people which is nowadays spoken by two thirds of the world population . . .

English is the language of 110 million people in the Unites States. And the British Empire has disseminated English to the ends of the Earth . . .

A great author once thundered out the truth that those who know two languages act with two brains, double their intellectual abilities and their overall aims, and achieve twice as fast their goals toward progress and happiness.

Look at America, the land of opportunity. Those of our compatriots who learn the English language progressed and prevailed. They learned the ways of thinking and the methods used by Americans and asserted themselves. Without knowledge of the language of this country, they would be doomed to act within constraints and to remain silent.[11]

The anxiety over language indicated a more general crisis of migrants' native languages as means of representation of the experience of migration. The dominance of English and the gradually dominant idea that English was related to modernization, progress, success, and happiness resulted in a crisis of Greek language as a means of representation of everyday experience. The introduction of English words into the Greek language was an attempt to manage this crisis. However, the process of emergence of Gringlish (Greek/English) was not unhindered or automatic; it was a long-term process that in some cases created new crises of representation and led to internal divisions within the migrant communities between the more educated elites who mastered both English and Greek and the "commoners" who mastered neither and used hybrid forms of language.[12]

The gradual emergence of performative means of cultural signification accompanied the hybridization of national language as a means of representation of migrant experience. Popular cultural forms such as music and theater often used commodities as a powerful means of representation. Commodities and the imagery that rendered them culturally significant complemented linguistic forms of expression of migrant experience. Let us take the example of the music scene that emerged in the early twentieth century in the communities of Greek America. The music industry in general played a crucial role in the process of commercialization of entertainment and development of mass culture in the interwar period. Most of the largest recording companies in the United States in this period, including Columbia and RCA Victor, had ethnic sections. The companies' Greek sections used to record songs performed by Greek or Greek American performers.[13] Most of the popular singers of this period originated from Greece and Asia Minor, and pursued their careers between Greece and the United States. Transnational movements of people, records, tunes, and capital marked the music industry across the Atlantic. Many songs were originally recorded in Athens, Istanbul, and Smyrna, and then rereleased in the United States. Other songs were originally recorded in Athens at American studios for the American market. Returning or visiting migrants later brought many of these records back to Greece. Many Greek performers would record songs while on tour in the United States. Greek recording companies like Panhellenion Record Company, the Greek Record Company, and Pharos appeared mainly after World War I. Performers themselves and their sponsors often founded these companies. During the interwar period most of the Greek singers who lived and worked in the United States were creating their fame through live appearances in Greek coffeeshops, known as *café aman. Café aman* were created in Greek migrant communities during the years of Prohibition and operated as speakeasies. The clientele of *café aman* were of mixed national origin and included Greeks, Turks, Armenians, Syrians, and Arabs.[14]

Greek songs were performed in the *café aman*. The music industry also made it possible for the migrants to enjoy these songs privately in their homes, and records were often sent back to Greece as presents. The lyrics of these songs most often referred to different aspects of the process of migration (life before and after migrating, changes, individual incidents and practices of Greek migrants such as gambling, visiting the *café aman*, getting married, returning to Greece). Other songs described, usually in satirical ways, particular types of Greeks in America. The lyrics often included references to objects and commodities in order to describe the realities of everyday migrant life and the qualities and traits that defined migrant subjectivity. Most of the objects mentioned in lyrics were everyday commodities. Lyrics often used Greek American vernacular. References of this type were fundamental for the operation of the signifying order of lyrical representations. Gringlish references to commodities often attributed to the song its particular character as a song about migration. Omission of words such as *karo* (car), *krema* (cream), *mpoxi* (box), *pouskart* (pushcart), *fritzi* (freezer), or *klampi* (club) would result in a crisis of signification, since in most cases it would be impossible to understand that the song referred specifically to the experiences of Greek migrants in the United States.

The use of commodities as means of representation of the migrant experience was deeply gendered. Although references to objects in general were used to signify a wide range of activities and practices, commodities and consumer goods referred mostly to Greek women migrants. The purpose in these references was to satirically represent and castigate specific female behaviors that were supposedly related to the impact of migration on Greek womanhood. Consumption was often associated with superficiality and frivolity, characteristics that were usually attributed to Greek migrant women as a criticism of women's emancipation in the United States. In the following song, smoking was related to a particular form of Americanization of Greek women.

> —This year I started smoking, and I smoke all day and all night like a crazy woman.
> —I find it so sweet and it makes me drunk more than a kiss.
> —I always hold my cigarette-case and I pull out a cigarette and I smoke it and everybody is looking at me smoking it cutely.
> —In the restaurants I sit separately and when I finish eating I pull out my cigarette.
> —And I pretend I do not see people looking and laughing at me.
> —And when a young handsome man offers me a cigarette we hold it together and we smoke it sweetly.
> —I asked my husband to get me a pipe and cigars
> —and the poor man always cries and tells me that cigars do not suit a good housewife.[15]

Smoking cigarettes was associated with a particular representation of migrant womanhood as prone to frivolity, promiscuous, flirtatious, childish, excessive, and unable to lead a moderate life. The female pleasure in smoking and modern ways of life provoked ridicule and laughter, while at the same time it called for punishment. The song implied that this type of female pleasure was abnormal and suspicious. The song ended with reference to a stereotype that we have already encountered in different types of representation: the consuming woman was oppressive; she tyrannized her husband ("the poor man always cries") and thus threatened and diminished manhood and male sovereignty.

Historians and social scientists have argued that the migrants' encounter with commercialization and practices of mass consumption led to a crisis of community bonds and resulted in processes of cultural assimilation and homogenization. However, the analysis of representations of consumerism and commodification in migrant self-representations that emerged in the context of entertainment offers ground for a critique of notions of cultural assimilation and homogenization. The migrants' encounter with the forces of consumerism and commercialization of popular culture and everyday life certainly created turbulence in already existing forms of identification related to community life and bonds. Yet on the symbolic level this crisis was contained by the introduction of internal differentiations. The threatening aspects of consumerism were related to certain versions of Greek womanhood, while others were related to class mobility and social success. On the symbolic level, diversification helped to contain, exorcise, and habituate the turbulence that was introduced into community life and dominant forms of identification by social change and the transformation of conditions of life. On the level of representation, images of Greek womanhood did not contradict or unsettle images of mainstream (male) Greek subjectivity; rather, the former represented different aspects and varieties of the latter. Symbolic forms of representation of objects and commodities in migrant self-representations played a catalytic role in the process of emergence of this type of diversified subjectivity. The introduction of representations of commodities in popular forms of migrant self-representation was instrumental for the maintenance of cultural intelligibility and relevance of these representations. Through the intervention of commodities as means of representation of specific cultural traits and social relations, the emerging forms of migrant subjectivity achieved contemporary cultural reference and avoided parochialism and social alienation.

These aspects of the process of cultural engineering of migrant subjectivity were illustrated in the amateur theater that blossomed in the United States during the first three decades of the twentieth century.[16] During this period professional theatrical companies from Greece would seldom visit the United States, and when they did, they would restrict their visit to New York and a few other major cities. The authors of migrant theatrical plays were often amateurs and community intellectuals. Most of the plays that were performed described either in a satirical or in a dramatic tone different modes of behavior that characterized Greek migrants and different types of people who embodied these behaviors.

These plays were usually published by Greek publishing companies and were circulated in local Greek communities. The performances were organized by local migrant associations and would usually take place in coffeeshops or in the offices of the association, whenever these were available.[17]

Only a small number of printed scripts of theatrical plays and pictures of performances preserved in libraries and private collections survive to form the contemporary archive of Greek American popular amateur theater. Migrant theatrical plays covered a wide range of topics inspired by the migrants' everyday activities and problems in the United States. Some of the most popular themes included repatriation, hardships during the early years in the United States, interaction between Greek migrants and white Americans, unfortunate love affairs between Greek migrants and white American women, migrant youth delinquency, corruption within the Greek communities, and gender relations.[18] Although entertainment was the basic aim of these plays, they often had a didactic character. As was often stated in the introductions to the printed copies of the scripts, the role of the plays was to point out certain modes of behavior in order to make the public aware of the dangers and problems that the Greek communities were facing in the United States. In the introduction to the play *Ο Κακός Δρόμος* [Going astray], a contemporary commentator characterized it as "a psychological study of contemporary Greek youth in the United States," a study that warned the public against "the deterioration of family bonds, the young people's disregard of parental advice nowadays, the moral decline that follows this disregard, and the youths' inclination to crime, phenomena about which we have already been informed by sociologists and priests."[19] In another case, theater was considered to offer "an exact depiction of our course in the United States, the lethargy of Hellenism in America, which is preparing us for the total annihilation of our principles and is going to erase those principles from the soul and spirit of the young generation and those to follow."[20]

Most of the theatrical plays of this period pointed out certain changes in the Greek migrants' lives and warned the public about the dangerous impact that these changes could have on Greek culture, psyche, and principles. Social, cultural, and historical changes were acted out in the theatrical plays and were represented by different types of migrants. It is important to point out that change was represented as an open-ended process. No change was ever final, or irreversible. On the contrary, the characters in migrant theater changed modes of behavior, personality and attitude according to the development of each story. The subject's ability to change character and modes of behavior and to *perform* different identities was a characteristic often attributed to migrants in different types of popular self-representations in this period. *Performability* was presented as a fundamental element of migrant subjectivity.

In the 1950s Angelos Alexopoulos, known also as Angel Alex, published a the-atrical play with the title *To Foustáni tis Ginaíkas mou* [My wife's skirt].[21] This play was a satirical representation of the antagonisms of a Greek couple in the United States. The play was written in the late period of amateur migrant theater. In the 1940s migrant theater gradually declined, as professional Greek theatrical groups were increasingly visiting the United States and giving performances in migrant communities. In addition, new forms of popular mass entertainment were emerging, especially after the end of the war. By this period the Greek public was already familiar with theatrical representations of the characters and behav-iors that were caricatured in the play *My Wife's Skirt*. In fact, the representation of these characters was the result of a process of cultural distillation that had lasted for three decades; they had become stereotypical elements of theatrical representations of migrant life.

In this play, the story took place "somewhere in America." The main charac-ters were a Greek man married to a Greek American woman, the husband's niece, his male friend, his chauffeur, and the chauffeur's girlfriend. The main theme of the play concerned the husband's subjugation to his wife's desires, according to which he was forced to take on all the housework while she was busy enter-taining herself according to the imperatives of modern life in the United States: shopping, cocktail parties, dancing, listening to the radio, and flirting. In the course of the play the husband was driven to excessive degrees of frustration by what he perceived as his effeminization, and so he began planning his rebellion. The husband finally found the courage to gain control over his wife, who was transformed by the end of the play into the "perfect type" of submissive woman.

The theme around which all interactions took place was the transformations that modern conditions of life and migration imposed on the protagonists' char-acter, identity, behavior, attitudes, and moods. For Stathis, the husband, these transformations were effected by his marriage to a Greek American woman, whom he referred to as "the American." In long monologues Stathis described his transformation as a process of gradual effeminization as he had had to take on roles and responsibilities that were traditionally performed by women: doing the housework and submitting to his spouse's will. "She made me put her dress on and we changed like Christine Jorgensen! The male became female, the female became male and so on! If we had a child, it would be certainly neutral! . . . But am I going to become a toad, crawling under the Greek American's feet who is trying to tame me?"[22]

Stathis contrasted his current situation with the status he used to have when he was in Greece, before his migration to the United States and his marriage. He also contrasted his current domestic situation with the high status and re-spect that he enjoyed in the business world. In the scenes where Stathis interacted with his friend Apollon, his behavior was manly and friendly, while in the scenes where he interacted with his wife Lilika, his behavior was docile, submissive, and reserved. In the end, Stathis decided to take control over his life and to reestablish traditional gender roles in his household. Stathis, as the central character in this play, also commented on the transformation that his wife Lilika had undergone from a "proper woman" to an uncontrollable "modern woman." Descriptions of Lilika's behavior included mostly references to commodities and objects related to American popular culture. As Stathis is washing the dishes, he speaks to himself: "It is not my business to wash these oily dishes and the COCKTAIL GLASSES and OXYDOLS and soap. She sits in her armchair admiring the Hollywood stars on TV! She holds her cigarette between her colored nails. Her little puppy is sitting on her lap. . . . Go to hell, you modern, crazed feminist!"[23]

The stage directions described Lilika's appearance at the scene where she was supposed to appear on the stage for the first time: "She wears an evening suit in a light color, she wears a lot of facial makeup, her lips are overwhelmingly red, and she has a little hat on her head. She swings her handbag provocatively as she looks at Stathis furiously."[24]

The representations of Stathis and Lilika implied that both of them were forced by the current circumstances of their lives to perform an identity that was not essentially their own. The change of roles at the end of the play was also presented as a circumstantial adoption of different modes of behavior. In *My Wife's Skirt* the transformative nature of identities constituted the leading thread of the narrative. Most of the characters presented in popular migrant theater were marked by a tendency to transform according to the circumstances of life. The changes that migration and modern conditions imposed on migrants' lives and the ways in which migrants reacted and dealt with these changes became the dominant topics in migrant theater. Thus, theatrical representations of migrant subjectivity consolidated and popularized notions of performed and fluid migrant social identities. Rather than propagating solid images of what women are, the representations of women in migrant theater explored the different modes in which one could be or become a woman under the contemporary social and cultural circumstances.

The emphasis on the performability of migrant identities—the fact that one could perform different identities according to one's own choices or constraints, in the same way that one could use or not use his American or his Greek name according to the circumstances—introduced parody into migrant self-representations. This parody can be traced in the ways in which traditional as well as modern identities were presented as different modalities of social existence and not as the migrant subject's essential traits. I would argue that in the sphere of popular entertainment this mode of representation was more explicit exactly because the notion of performed, flexible, and fluid subjectivity offered comfort and enjoyment to the migrant public who indeed performed in that way in their everyday lives. Parody as a form of self-representation facilitated the migrants' dealing with the social contradictions related to migration. Tracing acts of parody in migrant self-representation can help us find historical examples that illustrate the ways in which the experience of migration generated cultural modes of national, gender, and class identification that were marked by a tendency to undermine notions of solid, fixed, and essential selves although they maintained at the same time their collective and communitarian character.

On the symbolic level, these representations were made possible by narrative, iconographic, and performative reference to objects—mostly but not entirely commodities—and their function in migrant popular culture. In the context of what was often perceived by the migrants themselves as a crisis of language as a means of self-representation, the intervention of visual representations of objects supported the emergence of performed identities and acts of parody.

Consumption, Objects, and Subjectivity

Migration is not merely a movement of people from one place to another; it also involves the movement of objects, goods, and cultural artifacts, as well as images, representations, ideas, customs, and material ways of living. The upheaval of labor migration from Greece to the United States was followed by the gradual increase of commerce between the two countries. The decrease in the number of new migrants after 1924 did not curb the increase of commerce, which continued into the 1950s. As Greek economists of the day argued, the increase of commerce between the United States and Greece reflected the commercial needs of the newly established Greek migrant communities, especially in terms of food and entertainment products, including music recordings and films.[25] Practices related to commerce, trade, and exchange of goods were necessarily supported by migrant networks that facilitated interactions and were grounded on technical infrastructure. These networks accommodated the activity of numerous groups and interests, including trade companies, individual entrepreneurs, travel agents and steamship companies, embassies and state services (such as postal services), importers, trade representatives, distributors, salesmen, and shopkeepers. These networks supported different types of economic and cultural exchange and communication between the homeland and the migrant communities. The vitality of these networks was based on the migrants' need for communication with their places of origin, yet the very existence of these networks cultivated the need for homeland products, as in the case of the entertainment industry.

In the early twentieth century networks and practices of commerce, exchange, and consumption of goods defined a space of cultural and economic activity that generated images and representations of migrant subjectivity within which notions of national, gender, and class identity became objects of constant negotiation. Within the Greek migrant community commerce and trade as types of professional occupation were endowed with special moral and cultural value. Trade was considered an exemplary manifestation of higher forms of Hellenism as well as proper Americanism. With reference to earlier Greek diasporas in the Near East, Egypt, and Central and Southern Europe, the stereotype of the affluent Greek merchant of diaspora was already widespread and familiar in different types of literature that presented exemplary figures of Greek migrant subjectivity. In the case of Greek communities in the United States, early representations of the entrepreneur as an exemplary type of migrant are found in community handbooks and guides.[26] In the context of migration, the sphere of commerce was morally and culturally valued mainly because commerce provided links between the migrant communities and the homeland, on the one hand, and migrant communities and the mainstream host society, on the other.

Greek American commercial activities were not restricted to the exchanges between Greece and the United States. The emergence of mass popular culture in the 1920s and 1930s in the United States was certainly reflected in the patterns of consumption within the Greek migrant community. American products and popular culture (music, movies, garments, cigarettes) were gradually introduced in the Greek migrant communities and were rapidly related to particular modes of behavior, attitudes, and ways of life. The emergence of mass culture in the United States at this time had a great impact on migrant and ethnic communities and defined the ways in which notions of ethnicity were attached to modes of consumption. Historians have often defined this process as a homogenization process and have argued that migrant ethnic communities experienced mass culture as a threat. According to this argument, Hollywood motion pictures, chain stores, standard brands, and the radio challenged existing community values and relationships, and functioned as the most effective means of integration and assimilation into American culture, principles, and ideals.[27] Foregrounding the centrality of subjectivity, some labor historians approach popular culture and consumption from the point of view of subjective experiences and explore how the working classes related to popular and mass culture on the level of everyday life.[28] As Liz Cohen has put it with reference to the 1920s and 1930s in the United States:

> A longer view makes it possible to move beyond the prevailing contemporary assumption that the abundance of these new cultural forms meant that all people responded to them in the same way, and exposes the complex process by which mass culture and consumption entered different people's lives.
> It is my contention that mass culture . . . did not itself challenge working

people's existing values and relationships. Rather, the impact of mass culture depended on the social and economic contexts in which it developed and the manner in which it was experienced, in other words, how mass culture was produced, distributed and consumed.[29]

Historically, the consumption of objects of popular as well as high culture has met the specific psychological and cultural needs of dynamic social groups by providing them with a sense of individual identity, social connection, and community.[30] Considering the importance that consumption of popular culture had for the formation of ethnic communities in the United States annuls any attempt to define migrant consumption in terms of alienation versus consciousness and assimilation versus preservation of ethnic culture. On the contrary, the exploration of migrant popular culture proves that trade, transportation, consumption, collection, preservation, and demonstration of objects and commodities were central in migrant culture and subjectivity.[31] The formation of migrant communities followed the articulation of codes and practices that allowed the migrants to develop relations both inside and outside the community, and with both the native society and their homelands. Objects and the practices related to them constituted an important part of this network of cultural and economic relations. From this point of view, migrant cultural practices resemble subcultural movements, especially as far as concerns the use of objects as symbols of differentiation from, and connection with, dominant mainstream cultures. As Dick Hebdige has observed in relation to subcultural movements:

> The relationship between experience, expression and signification is therefore not a constant in subculture. It can form a unity which is either more or less organic, striving towards some ideal coherence, or more or less ruptural, reflecting the experience of breaks and contradictions. Moreover, individual subcultures can be more or less "conservative" or "progressive," integrated *into* the community, continuous with the values of that community, or extrapolated *from* it, defining themselves *against* the parent culture. Finally, these differences are reflected not only in the objects of subcultural style, but in the signifying practices which represent those objects and render them meaningful.[32]

The frequency of references to objects, goods, and belongings in migrant narratives and other forms of self-representation indicates the importance of objects and the practices related to them for migrant subjectivity. Aspects of subjectivity emerged within the cultural space that developed among objects, images, and texts, as subjects reflected on the ways in which they experienced themselves in relation to practices and rituals that attributed meaning and cultural value to the use of particular objects. We have already discussed the function of objects and commodities in performative expressions of migrant subjectivity. In the field of advertising the symbolic function of objects and commodities in the context of the migrant communities was manifested in the most eloquent way. Advertising operated as an important means of production, proliferation, and manifestation of images within the Greek migrant community. In the 1920s American sociologists like Robert Park had suggested that advertising constituted an effective means of Americanization, since it would initiate migrants into American ways of life.[33] Park advised advertisers to advertise in migrant newspapers and magazines. Advertisements were very common in the Greek migrant press from the first years of its existence. In some cases Greek travel agencies and steamship companies owned publishing companies, and thus advertisements were directly connected with the reason of existence of newspapers and popular magazines. In these cases the publishing company served the commercial interests of the parent company, while at the same time it provided Greek migrants around the United States with information regarding travel, steamships, fares, scheduled arrivals and departures, and accommodations in New York City.[34] By 1910 all the major Greek newspapers and magazines published illustrated advertisements for a wide variety of products and services. In the following years, the numbers of advertisements published in the daily, weekly, and monthly Greek press multiplied, while at the same time the intended commercial public diversified. For example, toward the end of the 1920s most major newspapers and popular magazines devoted columns to women's issues and featured advertisements for women's fashion and beauty products.

Advertising addressed different spheres of migrant life and social interaction both within and outside the migrant community. In the early years of the migrant press, advertising mostly focused on the issue of travel and transportation between Greece and the United States. Among the steamship companies that advertised were Booras Bros., Austro-American Line, French Line, Hamburg-American Line, North German Lloyd, Transatlantic Greek Steamship Company, and Cosulich Line. Over the years the number of travel agents that would guarantee competitive prices, reliability, and safety for their customers increased. Some travel agencies also provided such services as accommodations in New York, luggage storage, and transportation to the port. Throughout the 1910s all advertisements that related to travel insisted on the issues of safety and reliability. Travel agencies provided practical information about migration matters. Since most of the advertised travel agencies were owned by Greeks, the advertisements insistently propagated the idea that migrants would be safer if they conducted businesses within their own community rather than elsewhere. Travel was a shared experience among the migrants and was often represented by the image of a ship cruising through the Atlantic. The image of the ship was very common also in fictional and autobiographical accounts of migration. Migrant writers dedicated many pages to detailed descriptions of the ships that brought migrants to America.[35] Even American commentators on the phenomenon of migration were fascinated by the image of the ship, which they often described as a condensed representation of social relations in modernity.[36] In migrant advertisements, the image of the ship was related to notions of solidarity and fraternity within the migrant community. The ship became a signifier of the interrelation between traveling, survival, and the importance of community networks. This interrelation operated as a constitutive element of conceptualizations of migration as a shared subjective experience.[37] In the course of the 1920s and 1930s advertisements of travel agencies focused more on issues of comfort, luxury, and entertainment. This shift was related to the development of mass tourism in the period. In the late 1920s migrant associations, including the two major associations, AHEPA and GAPA, started organizing and advertising group visits to Greece. These were tourist visits, and as such they were very different from other types of temporary return migration. Tourist visits were short, they included visits to Athens and other major archaeological and historical sites, and they took place during Christmas and summer holidays. As the theme of tourism became more and more dominant in the 1930s, the image of the ship gradually disappeared from travel advertisements, and travel agencies focused on luxury and entertainment instead.[38]

The interrelation between migration, survival, and ethnic networks of interaction was also a major theme in the advertising of banks. The period around World War I was marked by the transformation of the migrants' saving and banking experience in the United States. Until that period, the migrants' main monetary practice had been to save privately and send remittances to relatives in Greece. During the migrants' first years in the United States, remittances were made through postal savings banks.[39] After World War I, however, the migrants were actively prompted by various ethnic and national banking schemes to become more enmeshed in the commercial world of banking and to participate more actively in the economic growth of their host country.[40] From an economic point of view, the migrants' introduction to commercial banking was opposed to the principles of fraternalism and mutuality that had characterized community associations and practices of saving in the first years of establishment in the United States.[41] Advertisement, however, indicates that on the level of symbolism the association between fraternalism and banking persisted during those years of commercialization of banking. This is particularly true in the cases where banking involved remittances sent from Greek migrants to their families in Greece.

Advertisements for different banks are found in abundance in newspapers such as *Atlantís* and *Ethnikós Kýrix* in the interwar period. The banks that advertised most often included the Greek-American Bank, Guarini & Candela Bank, National Bank of Greece, and Bank of Athens Trust Co. In the 1910s and early

1920s bank advertisements stressed mainly the services that each of them offered and informed future customers about the number of branches that the bank had in different locations in New York and other cities in the United States, Greece, Turkey, Egypt, and various North and Central European countries. Toward the end of the 1920s, however, Greek banks launched more aggressive commercial campaigns in the Greek American press. Advertisements of the National Bank of Greece and the Bank of Athens were typical of the imagery that was used to attract migrant customers and to gain their trust. Remittances were the main theme in these campaigns. Illustrated advertisements used visual representations of the physical distance between the American metropolis and Greek villages. Most illustrations depicted a split between the two scenes. Images of New York were juxtaposed with those of a Greek village. And depictions of smartly dressed Greek American men in suits standing in front of a bank were juxtaposed with images of elderly Greek mothers sitting in Greek village houses waiting for invoices from America. These illustrations stressed the multiple ways of representation of the distance that separated the homeland and America. This distance was represented in terms of differences between urban and rural settings, generations (old villagers versus young migrants), dress codes (traditional costumes in the villages versus fashionable suits in America), and gender (women in the villages versus male migrants in America).[42] In some advertisements the banks represented a powerful and institutional link between the two sites. The bank was often iconographically represented as the sun rising over the Atlantic or as a paternal arm stretching from the American cities and reaching out to little villages in Greece. Other illustrations presented images of institutional buildings in Greece where villagers dressed in traditional costumes waited patiently and confidently for their checks. Advertisement of banks stressed the diasporic community's power (represented institutionally by the bank) to overcome physical and cultural distance. Symbolism was thus based also on the interrelation between migration, community, and survival.

Advertising also concerned consumerist goods imported from Greece in order to meet the needs of the newly established or establishing Greek communities in the United States. The nature of these goods varied. Advertised goods and activities included imported food products (cheese, oil, olives, wines); books in Greek published in the United States (American history books, fiction, guides, handbooks, and almanacs); Greek, Arab, and Ottoman musical recordings; Greek films and theatrical performances; postcards; association symbols, such as pins, rings, medallions, pictures, and flags; American and Greek flags; and christening and bridal cloths. Overcoming the cultural and geographical distance between homeland and diaspora was the symbolic aim of advertisements of products imported from Greece. Food packages would often be decorated with pictures of Athens or Piraeus. These decorations did not picture the place of origin of the products but the port or the commercial center through which these products were forwarded to Greek American tradesmen and distributed in the United States in order to cover the needs of Greek America. Advertisements of imported goods were self-referential since what was emphasized about the product was that it had been imported from Greece. The symbolism of advertisements thus assumed the readers' identification with a topos that was represented by Greek national symbols and that did not necessarily coincide with particular places of production. In this context representations of Greece were marked by a great degree of abstraction. This abstraction was cultivated through the use of iconographic material depicting Athens and Piraeus (instead of villages and provinces) and ancient Greek monuments and themes (ancient statues, deities, and the Parthenon).[43]

Advertisements of Greek commercial goods offer an insight into a mode of migrant self-conceptualization and representation that was based on everyday identification with a reality that was located "elsewhere." Conceptualizations of identity as a *heterotopic* referent were based on abstraction. The migrant was not invited to identify through reference to personal memories of his or her homeland (province or village), a mode of identification that was dominant in the case of literary production. In the case of trade and consumption of goods, identification was based on the abstraction of the referent. Yet this abstract referent was experienced in very concrete and tangible ways in everyday practices of purchase, collection, and consumption of different objects. Furthermore, the heterotopic character of the referent of identification was not grounded on any notion of insurmountable separation, as in the case of narratives of exile. Advertisements capitalized on the migrant merchants' ability to bridge commercially the distance between homeland and diasporic locations. This form of reference indicated an active disposition toward the event of separation. The mode of identification with the homeland that was presented in commercial advertisements reiterated that migrant notions of nationhood were not derived from static forms of remembrance and fixation. On the contrary, migrant modes of national identification explicitly assumed that the subject's position was always formed and transformed in relation to everyday practices and activities. Practices related to commerce, trade, banking, and travel led to the production and dissemination of ideas of nationhood that were grounded on the interrelation between migration, survival, and community networks. Migrant nationhood also relied on abstract forms of representation of homeland. However, my analysis of commercial iconography and representation indicates that abstraction on the level of signification did not imply fixity. On the contrary, the arbitrariness of abstract representations of Greece as a port, an ancient monument, or an olive branch created spaces and possibilities for intervention and change within otherwise fixed images of the nation and community.

Advertisements for commercial goods often propagated the idea that the use of particular commodities rendered the consumer an active member of the migrant community. These advertisements were usually related to different types of entertainment, such as theater, cinema, and music, as well as books, journals, association emblems, and memorabilia. In an advertisement for Greek books that was published in the newspaper *Atlantis* in 1928, the advertisers argued that books were necessary assets for every Greek American home, and urged the readers to purchase books: "Form your own library. A few books in the house show the residents' love for all the beautiful things in the world, the beauty that man's thought alone has created. The presence of books is necessary in every home. The home becomes more respectable and dear to the owners as well as to visitors. Form your own library. Buy one book a month."[44]

Activities like buying books, forming a home library, collecting music recordings, and owning association emblems were portrayed as initiation rituals that made one an active member within the Greek community in America. Commercial advertisements often instructed readers how to *perform* socially as proper members of their migrant communities. As we have seen, advertisements for goods imported from Greece stressed the importance of trade (as a form of erasure of the physical distance between homeland and diaspora) for the consolidation of the migrant community. Advertisements for activities and products related to Greek American life stressed the *performative* nature of this identity and instructed Greek migrants accordingly. In order to claim their position as social subjects, the migrants had to perform it: they had to act as migrants. Advertisements reflected the ways in which migrant subjectivity was claimed, formed, and constituted in the emerging public sphere of consumption, commodification of culture, and performance.

Entertainment and consumption of popular, national, and ethnic culture were vital for the formation and expression of migrant subjectivity. It is important to understand that forms of entertainment, such as ethnic theater, music, and the consumption of ethnic goods and services, did not constitute symptoms of parochial commitment to old-country cultural values. On the contrary, ethnic theater, music, and advertising operated as means for the production of images, symbols, and signifying tools for the realization of new ways of being a subject in an emerging transatlantic world of community life, trade, culture, and consumerism. In this sense, we can better understand these forms of communal activity as cultural enactments of subjectivity in the context of migrancy, rather than in terms of either fixation to Old World forms or assimilation to American ethnicity. Theater, music, and consumption of popular culture provided a sphere of activities where the migrants could perform their national, ethnic, and gender identities in the new context of diaspora. If identity emerges through practices of repetitive signification and enactment of rules, then, as Judith Butler and others argue, the subversion of identity is also achieved inside these signifying circuits—that is, from within national, ethnic, and community cultural values, through the introduction of variation within the process of repetitive signification. Butler has argued that

> Just as bodily surfaces are enacted *as* the natural, so these surfaces can become the site of a dissonant and denaturalized performance that reveals the performative status of the natural itself.
>
> Practices of parody can serve to reengage and reconsolidate the very distinction between a privileged and naturalized gender [or national] configuration and one that appears as derived, phantasmatic, and mimetic—a failed copy, as it were. . . . Hence, there is a subversive laughter in the pastiche-effect of parodic practices in which the original, the authentic, and the real are themselves constituted as effects.[45]

There is a subversive laughter echoing in the performances of identity and different characters that we encounter in transnational forms of Greek popular culture. Migrant self-representations were marked by the element of parody, especially as far as significations of nationhood and ethnic identity were concerned. In migrant representations of self, Greek nationhood was continuously reiterated and repetitively signified as such, but it was also explicitly presented as an effect of *mimesis* of something that existed somewhere else and that could be imitated, performed, and reenacted. However, performance and reenactment made explicit the construction of nationhood, especially in the case where the migrant performance consciously aimed at the alteration of what was performed, as in the case of theater. From this perspective, both Greek nationhood and American ethnicity were denaturalized through the enactments of what supposedly stood for the original and the authentic. These performances created the possibility for the proliferation of variations in the representation of culturally intelligible notions of nationhood and ethnicity. Thus, they operated as parody acts that opened the possibility for a subversion of naturalized notions of identity that related the nation to authenticity, ethnicity to assimilation, and diaspora to parochialism. In the emerging universe of migrant culture, the denaturalization of fixed national, ethnic, and gender identities was a necessary condition for the development of agency and subjectivity. Parody acts and practices of performance were instrumental in this process and enabled the migrants to undermine the conceptual and ideological legacies of nationalism in culturally intelligible ways.

PART THREE

MNEMONICS

FIVE

Bios and Subjectivity: Life Stories in Migration

People tell their stories (which they do not know or cannot speak) through others' stories.

—SHOSHANA FELMAN, *WHAT DOES A
WOMAN WANT? READING AND
SEXUAL DIFFERENCE*

Re-creating, narrating, and representing the lives and deeds of migrants are central aspects of the culture of migrant communities. One could even argue that life story–telling itself is an essential part of the experience of being a migrant, a practice of migration. In an effort to preserve memory, migrants produce many of these stories, either in written or in oral form. Some stories are written by their descendants or by members of the migrants' families back in the homeland in an attempt not to forget those who left. For the migrants themselves, living as migrants provides them with plenty of opportunities to narrate again and again tales of origin, migration, and settlement. State officials, community intellectuals and activists, social workers, and contemporary scholars generate and collect many stories of migration as part of projects that aim at producing knowledge about the migrant communities. Let us take the example of the migrant life stories included in the Missing Persons Files, held today at the Archives of the Greek Ministry of Foreign Affairs. Beginning in the early twentieth century, the Missing Persons Files included the life stories of those who migrated to the United States and lost contact with their families in Greece. The lack of other means of direct communication prompted families who had lost contact with family members who had migrated to America to seek the help of the state in order to find their loved ones. The remaining records of these desperate attempts include whatever information the family could provide, the results of the consulate's inquiry in locating the individual, and often the individual's response to the investigation. Thus, reading an individual file reveals a more or less complete, however epigrammatic, life story reconstructed from multiple points of view: the state, the consulate, the family, and the migrant. As the Missing Persons Files suggest, the production of social knowledge about the migrant was achieved through the engineering of multiple types of narration of migrant life stories. These files illustrate the ways in which narrative accounts of individual migrant lives consisted of fragments of stories contributed by different groups of people (family, friends, neighbors, other migrants, coffeeshop owners, and so forth) and by institutions (ministries, consulates, governments, police departments) that were implicated in the process of migration. These migrant life stories were produced through the material conditions of migration and were mediated and diffused socially by official or unofficial mechanisms of knowledge and information production.

Contemporary knowledge of past migrations derives from the generation, circulation, repetition, and diffusion of a specific body of narrative accounts of the migrants' life courses. Narration is only one of the ways in which historically lived experience is transformed into culturally learned historical knowledge. Narration of life stories—as a means by which individual and collective experience is processed and transformed on the level of representations of collectivity —plays a central role in the process of international migration and in the emergence of migrant subjectivity. Migrant life stories had many functions. The narration of the migrants' life stories was the main means of promoting migration (young villagers were often encouraged to migrate by letters or personal narrations that concerned America and the life of other Greek migrants in that country), building community support in the new land (accounts of individual migration stories were published in newspapers and magazines in order to connect newly arrived migrants to their compatriots who had preceded them), and keeping contact with family and social circles back in the homeland. More generally, biographical and autobiographical accounts can be found in many different registers of the migration experience: fiction and nonfiction; unpublished memoirs held in personal archives; serialized autobiographies published in popular magazines; obituaries; directories and bulletins; official records, such as government and consular files; oral testimonies and videotaped interviews; and historical biographies and monographs. These accounts often propagate different images of the migrant as a social subject and correspond to a broad range of levels of conceptualization: the individual and the personal, the local and the regional, the generational (age) and the historical (period), the national and the ethnic.

Life story narration constitutes not so much a form of literary representation of social experience as a fundamental practice of everyday life in migrancy. The narrativization of migrant lives followed specific patterns and included recurrent elements that partook in the creation of the social and cultural portrait of the migrant. One can trace many points of tension and rupture that characterized these biographical and autobiographical accounts. In many life stories migration was perceived as an event that interrupted the normal course of one's life. Since migration was seen as a rupture, an interruption or a diversion from a "normal" life course, telling the story of one's migration constituted a way of restoring continuity, keeping track of the diversion, mapping the collective by drawing the lines and identifying the threads of subjective experiences. From this perspective the life stories of migrants constituted *stories of migration,* since in the particular case the driving force for narrating one's own life was exactly the event of migrating. Who wrote and/or told stories of life in migrancy? What were the modes and means of production and circulation of these stories? How did "exemplary" life stories regulate subjectivity? And how did other life stories undermine hegemonic ideas about the exemplary migrant subject? How were life stories of migration circulated on various levels of cultural production, including literature, legislation, and historiography?

Some of the stories circulated in migrant culture concerned the lives of migrants themselves, while others concerned people who did not participate in migration, but whose lives represented values and ideals that were considered important for the development of individuals and migrant communities. In both categories, one can trace stories that played a hegemonic role, in the sense that they regulated the ways in which one was expected to be a migrant subject, and stories that undermined established hegemonies and pointed toward alternative and marginalized ways of being a migrant. Ideas of nationhood, citizenship, community, and selfhood played an important role in hegemonic as well as counter-hegemonic life stories that were circulated in the sphere of migrant culture.

Subjectivity and Psychobiography

Gayatri Chakravorty Spivak has posed the question: "[Regulative psychobiography] is the model narratives that give 'meaning' to our readings of ourselves and others. *We* are used to working variations on, critiques of, and substitutions for, the narratives of Oedipus and Adam. What narratives produce signifiers of the subject in other traditions?"[1] Within the Greek migrant community, life stories were often the means of propagation of exemplary versions of Greek identity. These life stories did not necessarily concern people who were migrants themselves, but were intended to function as examples for the Greek migrants in the United States. These model narratives offer an insight into the processes of cultural engineering of migrant subjectivity, since they disclose the content and the cultural references of model versions of Greek migrant identity.[2] The importance of these different cultural means of storytelling (narrative, literary, ideological, or institutional) for the study of subjectivity is the subject-effect that they have on individuals and groups, giving them a sense of their "I."[3]

Migration scholarship has analyzed the formation of a migrant sense of "I" as a process of cultural assimilation and social integration, while overlooking the subjective aspects of this process. Existing historical, anthropological, and socio-logical literature on the Greek migrant community in the United States suggests that the 1920s and 1930s constituted a period of maturation and consolidation of Greek American identity. It is often argued that in this period the Greek migrants were culturally assimilated and socially integrated in their adopted homeland.[4] Although there seems to be a consensus over the final result of this process of transformation from undesired labor migrants to assimilated members of the native society, the process itself is not usually analyzed. Assimilation is rather presented as a natural event in the context of North American cultural and so-cial history.[5] Most of the scholarly approaches to the history of the Greek mi-grant communities in America seem to focus either on the early years of life in the United States (with emphasis on the hardships caused by poverty, prejudice, and antimigrant hostility), or on the period after the late 1930s (with empha-sis on the achievements of the second generation of Greek Americans and the history of Greek American support for Greece during the period of German occupation).

We cannot, however, consider cultural assimilation as a self-evident histor-ical development. If we reject the assumption that assimilation was the result of "natural laws" of social development and address questions that concern the content of "assimilated" forms of social identification, we then need to study the forces, means, and symptoms that marked the process of transformation that took place during the 1920s and 1930s. In this period, public debates within the Greek communities in the United States often concerned the issue of compat-ibility between Greek and American culture. The origins of these debates can be traced in the early years of Greek migration to the United States, when lead-ing members of the Greek community were trying to argue against American antimigrant nativism. Nativists argued that the principles of Americanism were incompatible with the various migrant cultures. As a reaction to nativism, Greek migrant intellectuals maintained that there always had been a natural and or-ganic relation between proper Americanism and Hellenism. This reaction was not of course homogeneous. There was a lot of internal friction, often related to political differences between different representatives of the Greek American community and to antagonisms between rival elite groups for the leadership of various community institutions. In the early twentieth century, migration led to the transnationalization of Greek politics, as the Old World political divisions were transferred to the Greek communities in the United States. The political split between royalists and antiroyalists (Venizelists) that marked the political life of Greece during the 1910s also defined political alliances and antagonisms in the United States.[6] Greek communities were often divided between the royalist and the antiroyalist groups, whose political outlooks were mainly expressed by the two major daily Greek newspapers in the United States, *Atlantís* and *Ethnikós Kýrix*, royalist and antiroyalist, respectively.

The notion of Americanism was introduced into the public political discourse that was developed by these two newspapers during the second decade of the century, and it functioned as common ground between the two political poles. Americanism concerned the commitment to the cultural ideals of the United States and dedication to U.S. interests internationally. Both royalists and Venizelists claimed Americanism as a means to achieve political legitimacy and validity. During the early 1910s, *Atlantís* accused *Ethnikós Kýrix* and the Greek consulate in Washington of preaching the need to conserve Greek national identity, discouraging further migration, and exercising control over assimilation (including Americanization and change of citizenship). At the outbreak of the news about nativist attacks against Greek migrants and the launching of antimigrant policies, *Atlantís* accused Venizelists of hindering the Greeks' assimilation to American culture and thus jeopardizing the development of American Hellenism.[7]

The political turbulence caused by World War I had a great impact on Greek American politics. Royalists and the newspaper *Atlantís* were publicly accused by their rivals of anti-Americanism, since the royalist party in Greece had followed a pro-German position and delayed the country's entry into the war. The allegations made against *Atlantís* by *Ethnikós Kýrix* led to the application of the Anti-Espionage Act against the newspaper's publication.[8] According to this legislation, "the circulation in any foreign language of any news item, editorial or other printed matter, respecting the Government of the United States, or of any nation engaged in the war its policies, international relations, the state or conduct of war, or any matter relating thereto is unlawful, unless there has been filed in the form of an affidavit, a true and complete translation of the entire article containing such matter proposed to be published."[9] The political antagonism between royalists and antiroyalists resulted in long legal conflicts between the two publishers concerning issues related to libel. Each of the rivals attempted to ground its political legitimacy by claiming to be the genuine representative of true Americanism; this led to different political expressions of migrant Americanism. The cultural ideals and political principles that were foregrounded by these different expressions were often vague and undefined. Despite the antagonisms and the vagueness of the political statements they made, both royalist and antiroyalist groups agreed in their conviction that the migrant communities in the United States had to find ways to negotiate their culture and politics within the dominant Anglo-American context. Thus migrant political antagonisms were often expressed through public debates over the characteristics and the cultural profile that the community was expected to have in the future and the processes of political negotiation and cultural translation that would form this profile.

Two major fraternal associations were founded in the early 1920s in the context of the strong resurgence of antimigrant nativist movements in the United States, on the national as well as on the local level: the American Hellenic Educational Progressive Association (AHEPA) and the Greek American Progressive Association (GAPA). Despite their differences, both organizations intended to lead the Greek migrant communities in the process of the negotiation of their cultural profile and political position.[10] By the end of the 1920s, however, it was generally accepted that assimilation as such was undesirable and contradictory to the principles of proper Americanism. An article published in *Ethnikós Kýrix Monthly Illustrated* stated:

> Despite all the lectures about homogeneity and the melting of all the races into one, America remains a mosaic of races, religions, cultures, social ethics, and customs. . . . The first Greeks [migrants] wanted right from the beginning to meld with the American nationalism and were willing to be assimilated, but nowhere did they find such a separate and purely American nationalism. On the contrary, they encountered Americans, Irish, Scots, the Welsh, Germans. . . . Greeks did not find either pure Americanism or open American arms welcoming them to become assimilated, because such a pure Americanism does not exist. Thirty years of experience in this country convinced the Greeks that they had to create their own Greek American environment.[11]

Several Greek intellectuals in the United States played an active role in creating and forming this new "Greek American environment." They used biography as a means of propagation of the cultural elements that Greek Americans ought to cultivate. In 1926 the editor of the *Ethnikós Kýrix,* Demetrios Callimachos (1876–1963), published a series of articles in the journal *American Hellenic World.* His articles were biographical portraits of important figures of modern Greek history. The articles were later compiled into a book under the title *Neoellinikós Politismós* [Modern Greek culture].[12] Callimachos was born in Thrace in 1879, and as a young man he studied theology at the University of Athens. After graduation he became a journalist and contributed to Greek journals and newspapers, such as *Ellinismós* [Hellenism] and *Akrópolis* [Acropolis]. He served as a secretary to the Patriarchate of Alexandria in Egypt, where he stayed from 1906 to 1914. In 1914 he was invited to come to the United States by the Panhellenic Union. He stayed in the United States until the end of his life, where he developed both a secular and an ecclesiastical career. He became the editor of the newspaper *Ethnikós Kýrix,* and for a short time he served as a priest in Brooklyn, New York.

Callimachos was one of the most active Greek intellectuals in writing and preaching on issues of Hellenism and Greek American identity.[13] He supported the idea that the Greeks in the United States should not let themselves be assimilated by the new cultural context of their adopted homeland. He believed that the migrant community should redefine and further develop the fundamental elements of Greek culture and the principal ideals of Hellenism. He believed there were particular aspects of Greek culture that were compatible with contemporary mainstream Anglo-American culture. He held that the Greek community in the United States had the historical responsibility to retrieve these particular aspects, which he referred to as "Hellenism," to make them central elements of modern Greek culture, and thus to prove the organic relation between Hellenism and Americanism.

According to Callimachos, this process of cultural self-definition and integration was not just a Greek American affair but had a wider importance for the Greek nation, since the ultimate goal was the transformation of Greek culture both in diaspora and in the homeland. He considered the process of emergence of a "new" Greek culture in migrancy to be part of a wider process of transformation of modern Greek culture wherever Greeks lived.[14] The idea of a "new subject," that had emerged out of the historical circumstances of migration and had the ability to take a leading role in the process of transformation and elevation of modern Greek culture, was quite popular among migrant circles at the end of the 1920s and beginning of the 1930s.

> American Hellenism becomes continuously more organic, as a whole, and it acquires a consciousness of itself. Using all the available resources and positive environment of American life, which provide it with unending opportunities of development, American Hellenism can indeed create a new Greece, intellectual Greece without precedent in the history of our race. Hellenism for the first time comes collectively in contact with Anglo-Saxon life and thought, and there is no doubt that this influence will not annihilate it or assimilate it; on the contrary, Hellenism will develop into a stronger and more unique entity.[15]

Callimachos claimed for himself the role of the nation's educator. He decided to address his books mainly to Greek Americans since he firmly believed that the Greek diaspora needed to be educated by its own intellectuals so that it could take a leading role in the nation's present and future history. According to Callimachos, the Greek community in the United States was not supposed to play the role of a cultural mediator that would transplant, or translate, Americanism to Hellenism, or vice versa. He thought of the migrants not as cultural entrepreneurs, but as possible embodiments of an elevated form of modern Greek culture. Therefore, his work aimed at the education of Greek migrants so that they *would become* whom they *could be.*

Callimachos published many books, most of which were compilations of articles he had already published in the daily *Ethnikós Kýrix* and its monthly journal.[16] These books were didactic, practical, and often simplistic. He used life stories and biographies to argue by means of examples and parables. He believed that national culture had to correspond with the psychological characteristics of a people. Callimachos saw national identity and nationhood as psychological in nature.[17] Therefore, in his writings on Greek national identity and culture, he used biographies to reconstruct the psychological profile of the Greek people. Biographical portraits served to illustrate in a simple way the different constitutive elements of the Greek psyche in his own day, as well as in the historical past. He tried to point out the essential constitutive elements of Greekness (from a cultural, psychological, historical, and philosophical perspective). Historical figures were represented as personifications of different qualities and aspects of Greekness. He traced these elements through the historical past by choosing historical figures from the last three centuries of national history. Callimachos used life story, in the form of biography, as a means to conceptualize, describe, consolidate, and propagate what he considered to be the model version of the Greek migrant as a historical subject.

Callimachos's biographical sketches are *psychobiographies,* since they were intended to function as psychic references of identification for a particular Greek American readership. In these psychobiographical sketches we find traces of different disciplinary and authoritative discourses. His writings have the character of Christian preaching and evangelism. Callimachos often identified himself as an enlightened and liberal clergyman, who had decided to undertake secular duties driven by his patriotic sentiment and his commitment to the welfare of his people and his nation. In his books he often dedicated many pages to clergymen's life stories, especially when the particular individuals played an important historical role as intellectuals of the nation. He presented these figures as exemplary heroes in the struggle for Greek national independence and emphasized their altruism and the privations they willingly endured.[18]

Callimachos grounded the legitimacy of his intellectual work on the authority of historians and travelers, whom he often cited in his own books. He drew material and inspiration from the travel literature written by Western Europeans who traveled to Greece during the eighteenth and nineteenth centuries, as well as from nineteenth-century Greek national historiography and Western European historiography. Callimachos conceived the psychological profile of Greekness by means of a temporal diasporization. He portioned out the traits and constitutive elements of Greekness in three different historical periods represented by three different groups of national figures: War of Independence heroes, national benefactors, and modern migrants. For Callimachos, the War of Independence heroes constituted the nation's historical heritage. They were not models whose lives should be followed. Their life stories represented values and ideals that had the nature of genetically inherited memory. The cultural value of these biographies derived from the fact that the values and principles they represented were implanted in the national unconscious and were almost registered in the genetic code of modern Greek subjects. These figures represented heroism, bravery, irrationality, and unconditional commitment to a patriotic ethics.

The benefactors' life stories, in contrast, were intended to function as models. The benefactors were affluent individuals (merchants, intellectuals, and entrepreneurs) who lived abroad before and after the foundation of the Greek nation-state in 1932. They became benefactors because they used their financial, cultural, and material resources to benefit the Greek struggle for national independence during the first years of national political existence. What, according to Callimachos, were the distinctive features of the benefactors' life stories that rendered them archetypal and exemplary figures in the conceptualization of the constitutive elements of the modern Greek subject and modern Greek culture? First and foremost, they preserved a strong commitment to their nation despite physical dislocation and geographical dispersion. Their commitment remained strong because their financial and professional success abroad did not limit them to materialist aspirations, but inspired them to place their material resources at the service of the national and collective interests. Callimachos placed these exemplary figures against those Greeks who let themselves be distracted by their material gains and forgot their duties to their homeland.[19]

Another responsibility of the nation's benefactors was to study superior contemporary cultural and civilizational systems, and think of ways to transplant those to the homeland.[20] According to Callimachos, the benefactors were without exception lovers of Anglo-Saxon culture and ways of life. These diasporic Greeks had been living as citizens of the world, and thus they had the opportunity to experience, understand, and believe in the global superiority of Anglo-Saxon civilization and achievements. The benefactors were the ones responsible for transferring this cosmopolitan experience to their homeland. The benefactors' life stories offered useful advice concerning the social behavior of Greek subjects who lived abroad. Apart from the strength of their moral commitment to national interests, they were also dedicated to the preservation of racial integrity, mainly by avoiding marriage with people from different nationalities. Callimachos offered many examples of benefactors who forcefully took control over their daughters' lives and forbade marriage with men other than Greeks.[21] The benefactors were thus represented as guardians of female frivolity—particularly sexual frivolity—and immaturity, and thus as safeguards of the national resources.

Female figures appeared only marginally in Callimachos's biographical sketches of the national psyche, and always in abstract forms. Physical descriptions of women were absent, while physical descriptions of men were found in abundance in the section of the book that concerned the War of Independence heroes. Callimachos presented women's lives as symptoms, or indications, of the nation's overall moral advancement or degradation.[22] He argued that the nation's moral state could be evaluated by examining the degree to which female nature—which was primarily characterized by frivolity, deception, and superficiality—was successfully controlled.[23] Representations of women as the mothers of the nation were also present in Callimachos's work. In the particular context of migrancy, this traditional representation of womanhood implied that Greek migrant women had the responsibility to tame male passions, and to advise and control the male migrants, so that the men would be able to work and benefit the nation with the products of their labor. Callimachos often interrupted his biographical sketches to address readers directly, urging his compatriots to follow the examples of the benefactors and pointing out practical ways in which they could become the benefactors' successors in the course of national history.[24] He insisted on the convergence between the figure of the benefactor and that of the migrant. He made this convergence explicit through the use of the appropriate vocabulary. The Greek word for "migrant," *metanastes,* was often used with reference to benefactors and other diasporic Greeks who lived before the foundation of the Greek nation-state. This was a catachrestic use of the word, since modern migration as a concept usually relies on the existence of nation-states between which the migrants move.

Callimachos included in his book on modern Greek characters only one Greek migrant's life story. Despite the convergence between representations of benefactors and of migrants, there was at least one element that differentiated migrant biographical sketches. The benefactors' life stories had a pedagogical role; they constituted past examples that should be followed. Although their achievements were not as monumental as the life stories of the war heroes, they belonged nevertheless to a bygone era. On the contrary, the migrants' life stories functioned as explicit descriptions of contemporary historical agency. Migrant life stories were intended to function not as examples, but as proofs. Callimachos used migrant life stories to explain and prove why Greek migrants were the main acting subjects in the nation's contemporary history. The migrant life story that Callimachos included in his book was a biographical sketch of Michael Anagnostopoulos (1837–1906), director for thirty years of the Perkins Institute for the Blind. In the same chapter, which has the title "Eminent Greek Americans," Callimachos included a short biographical sketch of Samuel Howe, an American philhellene who took Anagnostopoulos under his protection and brought him to the United States. Callimachos explained that he decided to include Howe in a book about Greek identity, because Howe's life and deeds manifested in an exemplary way the truth of his arguments. Howe, like most American phil-hellenes, believed in the organic relation between Hellenism and Americanism. The life of Michael Anagnostopoulos was thus a result of an American's belief in the compatibility of the two cultures. In his biographical sketch of Anagnos-topoulos, Callimachos presented a story of success in the usual terms of lives of eminent Greek Americans in that period. He did not, however, emphasize mate-rial success, as would be expected in the story of a migrant's achievements in the New World. Instead, Callimachos dwelled on how Anagnostopoulos's life consti-tuted an explicit manifestation of the possibility and the importance of bridging American and Greek cultural ideals and principles.[25] Anagnostopoulos's life demonstrated in an incontestable way that it was possible to link Americanism with Hellenism without sacrificing either.

> The harmonious combination of Greekness with the American spirit created a great man and a model for his compatriots who chose this country as their adopted homeland. . . . Michael Anagnostopoulos's biography and career should become a textbook for all those Greeks, who assume that American-ism is without fail synonymous with the betrayal of their nationality. . . . And this is because Anagnostopoulos studied Americanism deeply and discovered that his Greek education and his Greek patriotism and his Greek virtue were attuned to the noblest elements of American culture. . . . Since Anagnos-topoulos remained a Greek without becoming any less of an American, we cannot understand why some Greeks, who do not understand in the least the American ideals, revolt even at reminders of their nationality.[26]

Anagnostopoulos represented the exemplary version of the modern Greek mi-grant. Callimachos argued that Anagnostopoulos's Americanism was not natural or genetically inherited.[27] On the contrary, it was acquired through a process of systematic effort and study in the principles of philanthropy. Anagnostopou-los studied Anglo-American culture and through his study rediscovered those elements of his own national culture that were compatible with Americanism. He thus became an exemplary representative of a hybrid culture that retained characteristics of both cultural systems. Callimachos warmly supported the idea that this hybrid new culture, whose representative was the modern migrant, was certainly defined by the principles of Americanism, since the subject had to first learn those principles and then retrieve the elements of his own culture that seemed to be compatible with them. Callimachos's support was grounded in his conviction that Anglo-Saxon Americanism was in his time the superior cultural system universally. In this biographical book Callimachos defined the content of Hellenism. In his view Hellenic subjects were endowed with a genetically inher-ited commitment to their nation, adaptability to foreign conditions and ways of life, and ability to make use of resources for the common good. The migrants needed to be educated in their national heritage so that they would realize that they had the historical duty to represent and cultivate a superior form of modern Greek culture.[28]

Migrant intellectuals like Callimachos believed that the modern migrant was a new historical subject because of the historical context that determined the social and political conditions of migrancy. This new subject needed to be educated in new forms of culture and collective consciousness. Biographical narration of life stories was used as a means of propagation of the elements that would constitute these new forms. Grounded in a belief in the advancement of American civilization, the reconstruction of life stories of Greek national heroes was overdetermined and resignified according to Anglo-Saxon cultural values and principles of racial superiority. Biographical narration operated as a means of re-imagining the nation's historicity according to the imperatives of life in migrancy. The biographical accounts that Callimachos used in his work were model psychobiographies, and their purpose was to regulate the ways in which migrant subjects would conceptualize their life stories in relation to Greek as well as American national histories. By interweaving notions of Anglo-Saxon supremacy, Americanism, and Hellenism, Callimachos's biographies propagated hegemonic versions of migrant subjectivity.

Subjectivity and Stories of Diaspora

"I was born the child of a conquered race, and sensed very early that we Greeks, under the Turks, lived in fear. What that fear was remained undefined, yet it permeated our being, and influenced our actions, because to be ruled by an alien race is to belong to the world's underprivileged."[29] This was Demetra Vaka-Brown's assessment of the Greek psyche, as given in her autobiography, published in a serialized version by the Greek American literary journal *Athene* in 1947, after her death in 1946.[30] Her husband, the American novelist Kenneth Brown, wrote a preface for the autobiography, and also edited the work. Vaka-Brown (1877–1946) was one of the best known American novelists of Greek descent.[31] She was born and brought up in a middle-class Greek family in Istanbul and received her college education in Paris. She migrated to the United States, where she spent most of her adult life, as a young woman around the turn of the century. In the United States Vaka worked as a newspaper editor and as a teacher. She was married to Kenneth Brown.[32] Vaka discovered her inclination to writing after her marriage, and she became a full-time writer. She wrote exclusively in English, and her work included novels, short stories, and political documentaries.[33] She also translated poetry from Greek to English.[34]

Her contemporaries did not consider Vaka as a Greek American author. She was rarely included in anthologies of Greek American literature. Vaka was most often included in biographical indexes of American women writers and in collections of American women's writings. Foreignness was the quality most often attributed to Vaka by those who belonged to her close social circle, the literary and intellectual circles of her time, and the broader Greek American community during her lifetime and posthumously. As Brown mentioned in his introduction to Vaka's autobiography, "she came to America in her eighteenth year without knowing a word of English, although fairly conversant with seven other languages, which included several of the Balkan tongues. . . . The gaps in her knowledge of this new world and its language were always fascinating to me."[35]

While other American authors of Greek descent became popular for their ability to express in literary form their experience of migration, Vaka was exclusively acknowledged as an author who was writing about the Orient and serving as a mediator between the Eastern and the Western world. According to her husband:

> The best way to understand the world is to understand its people. Demetra Vaka's autobiography gives us the opportunity to learn about a part of this earth which is becoming increasingly important, and which yet is little known to the people of the West. . . . There is perhaps no other writer living who has known intimately so many different types of civilization as Demetra Vaka. . . . She made us understand the Balkan peoples in her book "In the Heart of the Balkans"; she revealed intimate Turkish [life] in "Haremlik" and a "Child of the Orient."[36]

Vaka wrote numerous short stories and novels, which were both autobiographical and fictional. Most of her writing concerned everyday life and politics in Turkey and more particularly the lives of Turkish women in Istanbul and in different Balkan regions. Her autobiography was written under unknown circumstances. Brown mentioned in his preface that Vaka narrated her story to him before her death. The autobiographical text was a shorter version of *Child of the Orient,* one of her most popular books. In both the book and the autobiography, Vaka made use of numerous life stories in order to describe different aspects of life and culture in the Ottoman empire, Europe, and the United States. The autobiographical text constituted a compilation of numerous life stories in a single narrative that described the life of an "exotic American writer of Greek descent," in the editors' words. Vaka used life stories of Balkan, Ottoman, American, and European women in her fictional representation of her own experience of life between and across nation-states, oceans, and empires. My exploration is focused on her autobiography because it constituted an aftermath reconstruction and reutilization of these life stories in a coherent account of the life course of a woman whom the Greek American press of the late 1940s baptized as an "American author," recognized as a "Greek by descent," and characterized as "exotic." The case of Demetra Vaka is very important for the study of the interrelation between Americanness, ethnic descent, womanhood, and foreignness in the formation of migrant subjectivity. Three central and recurring issues emerged in her autobiography, as well as in the rest of her work: female identity, cultural differences between the Western world and the Orient, and the emergence of a "new" social subject able to cross traditional identities and cultural borders. In different parts of the autobiography, emphasis was put on one or the other of these issues separately. Conceptually, however, these three issues were always intertwined, and it is impossible to define one without referring to the others.

Many of Vaka's books were devoted to the lives of women in the Balkans and Turkey. Her main purpose was to write about conditions of life and culture in these regions from a feminine perspective. She often claimed in her work that women's lives constituted the defining point of difference between Eastern and Western culture. In her book *The Heart of the Balkans*, she narrated her experiences while traveling with her brother, a Turkish government official who had been ordered to travel around the Balkans in order to report on the political situation in the region.[37] Vaka reflected on the absence of Balkan women in any narrative of the region's politics and history. She commented that "of the women no book spoke. What were they like, the women who lived in this land of blood-feuds and never-ending killings? Were they educated at all? Were they so ignorant that they were stupefied, or were they savages? What would be the cardinal differences between them and me their sister, who, though a Greek, and a Turkish subject, did not know the terrors of constant combat?"[38]

In this book she tried to draw direct connections between the contemporary political scene and the conditions of women's lives. Some years later she followed up this theme in *The Unveiled Ladies of Stamboul*, where she gave a report on the life of Turkish women after the Kemalist movement and the change of regime in the Ottoman empire.[39] It could be argued that in general Vaka's work, including her autobiography, was a commentary on the contradictions, tensions, and transformations that women underwent in the context of different movements of modernization, expatriation, and nationalization around the turn of the century. Her autobiography is primarily a story of womanhood and female subjectivity. The first female figures that Vaka presents in it are her Greek mother and her Turkish nanny. The recurring figure of the mother represents most of the traits and qualities of traditional womanhood and femininity. Vaka rejected this maternal figure: for her, the mother represented a model that should be avoided. Her rejection of the maternal figure becomes absolute in the chapter where she describes her childhood after her father died, when she was forced to take the responsibility for herself and her mother who was trained to be a woman-wife and thus was not in position to face up to her responsibilities as the head of the family. The father figure is presented in the early part of the autobiography as the main recipient of the author's love and adoration (a role that her husband Kenneth Brown plays in later sections). However, the paternal figure never became a role model. Vaka often expressed adoration or respect for male figures, but she always positioned them in the motionless background of her narration. On the contrary, female figures are usually placed in the active foreground of social and historical developments, even when they are presented in negative ways.

Vaka never presents herself as following role models. On the contrary, in her self-representations she privileges all the elements that contributed to the uniqueness and the distinctiveness of her deeds and her character. In many migrant life stories the desire to migrate was attributed to individual psychological, physical, and intellectual traits. The connection between the desire to migrate and the migrant's nature was grounded in the assumption that migrants represented the most potent, energetic, and productive elements of the societies that they were leaving behind. In migrant life stories the migrants are often described as charismatic people who were committed to progress, believed that the United States was the most advanced country in the contemporary world, and assumed that their personal advancement would be guaranteed through expatriation and breaking away from cultural and economic constraints related to their own descent.

In Vaka's autobiography this narrative element was intertwined with her strong gender identification. The main reason for her migration to the United States was her desire to avoid the constraints that her female identity would set on her life course were she to stay in Istanbul. These constraints included having fewer opportunities for intellectual growth and feeling pressures to get married and undertake the role of a Greek wife. According to Vaka, after her return from Paris she went through a period of absolute frustration, which she later attributed to financial constraints (her family had lost most of their property after her father's death), cultural and social constraints (pressures to get married), and intellectual constraints (isolation from the Parisian intellectual circles and interruption of her college studies). Her psychological frustration led to a serious deterioration of her health. In her autobiography she related the following exchange between herself and the doctor who was trying to trace the real reasons causing the deterioration in her physical condition:

> "You look much older. Now tell me what you are worrying about. What is it exactly that you want?"
>
> "A pair of wings."
>
> "And if you got them, what would you do with them?"

"I would fly away."

"Where to?"

"To Paris, to the Sorbonne, to study."[40]

Her natural inclination to progress was coupled by natural industriousness. In the description of her early childhood, as well as in the description of her first years in the United States, she emphasized all the elements that pictured her as a hard worker. Industriousness was one of the recurrent elements in migrants' autobiographical accounts. By claiming that they offered their labor generously to the society that accommodated them, migrants often tried to legitimize their presence among the native-born Americans. Industriousness was thus considered one of the defining characteristics of the migrant. For Vaka industriousness differentiated her from traditional models of womanhood. With reference to her life as a working woman in the United States, she commented: "This new life, utterly my own, and earning money to pay for my needs, intoxicated me."[41] In *The Child of the Orient* Vaka elaborated her perception of herself as a modern "working girl." After describing the hardships that marked her life in New York, she remarked:

> I do not wish any one to suppose that I was miserable. On the contrary, I liked it: I was at last living the life I had often read about. I was one of the great mass of toilers of the earth, whom in my ignorance I held far superior to the better classes. I had romantic notions about being a working-girl, and my imagination was a fairy's wand which transfigured everything. *Besides, I was a heroine to myself. Those who have even for one short hour been heroes to themselves can understand the exaltation in which I lived, and can share with me in the glory of those days.*[42]

The model of the modern "working girl" was coupled with the imagery of the Oriental woman. With reference to her visit to Turkey after spending many years in the United States, she remarked: "With my opulent friends I lived the life of the lotus-eater. We travelled in carriages drawn by fat, well-groomed horses, and went picnicking on the shores of the Bosphorus or the Golden Horn in gay caiques. The sybarite in me gave herself up to this luxurious way of living. . . . Djimlah, whom I considered the most intelligent of them, certainly appeared happy. Yet had the choice been offered me, I unhesitatingly should have taken my hard-working life in America rather than her perfumed and easy-going existence."[43]

As noted earlier, in the first parts of her autobiography Vaka presented a dual model of womanhood, in the figures of the Greek mother and the Turkish nanny. While she rejected the model of the Greek mother as a personification of traditional versions of womanhood, Vaka was very interested in the figure of the Turkish nanny. This figure represented for Vaka emotional intimacy and her entry into a form of female interaction that was not traditional in her own culture. The figure of the Turkish nanny, which was supplemented later by numerous figures of Turkish girls and women (Vaka's friends in Istanbul), represented her potential and inclination to transgress predetermined cultural borders and to identify with social, cultural, and gender roles that did not belong to the traditional Greek roles of womanhood. Her identification with Turkish women, however, was always ambivalent, temporary, and partial. The chapters that describe her childhood are mostly devoted to her friendships with Turkish women and her experiences as a frequent guest in their houses. Her position nevertheless remained that of the observer. She never fully identified with her acquaintances. As we have seen, her migration to the United States led to a break from even this temporary and conditional identification with Turkish women. In the sections that concern her return to Istanbul for a few months' visit, she devotes many pages to descriptions of her visits to her Turkish women friends' houses. In these sections she refers to the joys of women's lives in the East, but she concludes that she has consciously chosen the life of the modern Western working woman for herself. The issues of female beauty and femininity recur often in her descriptions of her temporary return to Turkey. She narrates several incidents where relatives or friends comment on how America has made her ugly and how the working woman's life has deprived her of her freshness and femininity.

The theme of female beauty led Vaka to a discussion of alternative images of femininity and versions of womanhood that were grounded in the model of the woman laborer. In the sections that concern her early experiences as a female laborer in the United States, she makes numerous references to women coworkers, roommates, supervisors, and employees. Vaka juxtaposes the imagery of the working woman to that of the different types of Oriental women, more specifically the women who belonged to upper-middle-class Turkish harems. She keeps for herself the role of the transgressor who has the ability to enter and exit otherwise segregated terrains. As a foreigner both in the United States and in the Turkish household in her native country, the protagonist manages to feel at ease in the intellectual circles of New York, as well as in the Turkish harem. She also mentions that while a guest in Istanbul, she was often allowed to join male social gatherings, something that was not allowed to her Turkish female friends. She never explains directly her ability to transgress public and private boundaries, although she relates it to her experience of migration, continuous dislocation, and dual foreignness/nationality. Femininity is presented as the defining point and the symptom of the transformation that the subject undergoes during the experience of migration. For Vaka, femininity was also the defining point of difference between Eastern and Western cultures.

The female author-migrant through her experience of migration becomes the force, the symptom, and the sign of a reconstitution of old differences between the East and the West (and the new/old hierarchies that these differences entail). We can read this transformation in Vaka's description of her encounter with an old Turk *caïquetsi* (boatman) whom she knew before her departure to the United States and whom she met again during her visit to Istanbul:

> "*Benim kuchouk, hanoum,*" he said slowly, rubbing his eyes.
>
> "Oh! it is I!" I cried, "it is I"—and gave him both my hands.
>
> "Where have you been, all these many, many years?" he asked reproachfully.
>
> "I have been to America . . . the newest and the biggest of all countries"— and as of old I was talking, and he was listening; only this time it was not of the past, and of the people who, having done their work, were dead and forgotten, but of a country of a great present, and a still greater future.[44]

Before leaving for America, the young Greek woman had nurtured a close friendship with the old Turkish man. In this friendship the roles were very well defined. The Greek woman used to tell the Turkish man stories about the ancient glory of Greece and the superiority of ancient Greek civilization. Her American experience provided her with new ground and material to support her national pride. For her, Greek cultural and civilizational superiority did not derive exclusively from the past anymore, but was now made contemporary and subjectively conceived. It was conceived by means of her own subjective experience of migration. Vaka's experience of migration, and her knowledge and understanding of the advanced civilization that America represented, rendered her once more superior in her relationship with her Turkish friend. Migration created the possibility for the continuation of glorious national history outside the traditional territories of the nation and thus represented a moment when history was actively set in motion.

The Greek woman's ability to conceive this possibility of progress through migration was a manifestation of her cultural superiority in comparison with the Turkish man who was incapable of understanding the process of actively setting history into motion. The conceptual correlation between cultural superiority, awareness of historical progress, and migration is articulated by reference to gender-related narrative themes. The correlation is presented through a dialogue between the two friends over the issues of femininity, beauty, and America:

> Presently he asked, "But my little lady, what have you done with the roses of your face? You are pale and worn out."
>
> "One has to work hard in America," I replied. "It is a country which requires your best, your utmost, if you are to succeed." . . .

He leaned towards me, earnestness and entreaty in his kind face. "Don't go back there, my little one; don't go back there again. It is an accursed country which steals the peace from the living, their bodies from the dead, and robs a child of her roses. Say that you are not going back, my little one."[45]

. . . I looked at him, and beyond him at old Byzantium—once Greek, now full of minarets and mosques and all they stood for. A red Turkish flag floated idly against the indigo sky . . .

Why was I going back to that vast new country so diametrically different from his own? Could I explain to him? No, I could not, any more than I could have explained, years ago, to my little Turkish Kiamelé the meaning of my great-uncle's gift on my fifth birthday.[46]

"Why are you going back?" Ali Baba insisted.

No—I could not tell him. He could not understand. His flag was the Crescent—mine was the Cross.[47]

Vaka included in her autobiography, as well as in different parts of her books, numerous life stories of herself and others (the modern working woman, the industrious laborer, the Oriental woman of the harem, the Greek mother, the loving wife and daughter, the intellectual and author). It is not clear if these different stories converged in a single narrative of migration, or if they were conceived as radically divergent by the author. Can we strictly define a migrant life story? How can we differentiate between narratives of migration and narratives of alternative womanhood or cultural difference? These questions echo some of the debates that have been taking place during the last two decades in the fields of philosophy, psychoanalysis, social theory, and the humanities around issues of subjectivity. These debates sprang out of the critique of specific notions of subjectivity, such as those inherited from the philosophical tradition of Enlightenment. The critique of notions of homogeneous, unitary, solid, and centered subjectivity often led critical thinkers to view subjectivity as an empty or outmoded category "that we can happily discard along with other modern hang-ups."[48] The celebration of fragmentation of subjectivity by various postmodernist approaches to these issues eventually contributed to the theoretical and analytical foundation of yet another regulative discourse on subjectivity: the subject *has to be* and thus *is* fragmented. In the case of Vaka's autobiographical text this would mean that the different life stories that she narrates did not converge, or intersect; on the contrary, they represented the centrifugal forces that annulled the possibility of the woman-migrant subject to exist as such.

However, if we move out of the Manichean distinction between unitary and fragmented subjectivity, we can envision multiple forms of subjectivity that share their fluid character. This is a notion of subjectivity as a continuous process of becoming something that cannot fully be, because it is constantly deferred. Vaka's autobiographical text was supplemented by pictures of herself dressed in different national costumes: pictured as an Italian, Turk, Greek, or Austrian, but never able—or never desiring—to be any of these. The notion of multiple forms of subjectivity leads us away from celebratory and thus regulative (since every celebration reproduces certain norms and archetypes) conceptualizations of postmodern subjectivity, toward active forms of engagement with the historicity of different forms of selfhood and their multiplicity, mutuality, and interaction. It also moves us toward a historically sensitive study of the practices that generated and sustained multiple forms of subjectivity. Approaches that presume that subjectivity is either homogeneous or fragmented cannot give us an account of the ways in which the historical agents themselves experience different and distinct aspects of subjectivity simultaneously and intersubjectively. Neither fragmentation nor homogeneity can give us an account of the ways in which each aspect of self-representation interacts and intersects with—and is interactively determined by and differentiated from—the others.[49]

The autobiographical text offers an insight into the multiplicity and fluidity of subjectivity. Scholars of autobiography have noted that "people tell their stories (which they do not know or cannot speak) through others' stories."[50] The different aspects of subjectivity can be traced through the reading of the different stories that one can trace within the autobiographical text. In her autobiography, Vaka told many different life stories, which hardly added up to a story of migration. She referred only briefly to her identity as a migrant. Migration nevertheless was the event that set in motion all the mechanisms of subject-formation that she described. Migration gave Vaka access to the stories that she used in order to narrate her own life story; migration also created the conditions that permitted her to perceive herself as a subject who transgressed identities and cultural contexts of reference. The event of migration set in motion the stories that in their mutuality and interaction constituted subjectivity.

Although Vaka's autobiography shares this characteristic with other migrant life stories, it is also very distinct in some other respects. The main anxiety that marks most of the migrant narratives is the correlation between two apparently contradictory allegiances: homeland nationhood and the version of nationhood that the subject was compelled to acquire in the new country. Migrant narratives developed around the debate over Americanization, preservation of national (ethnic) identity, or modification of Old World national identity and culture so that they became compatible with the dominant culture of the recipient country. This debate is absent in Vaka's narrative, as are the issues of acculturation and cultural assimilation. In her autobiography, as in the rest of her work, Vaka often refers to the issue of cultural literacy rather than to acculturation or cultural assimilation. In her autobiography she refers to her ability to understand cultures different from her own and, as we have seen, it was this ability that made her famous as an author and earned her the characterization of the "exotic author."[51] Vaka was fascinated—and she made this fascination explicit in her autobiography—by her ability to pass for different nationalities. In her books, she included many references to incidents where, dressed as a Turkish woman, she actually managed to cheat strangers and pass for Turkish. In descriptions of her life in the United States she refers to her fascination when she was taken for French, or later for English. In the chapter devoted to her visit to Istanbul, Vaka presents herself as a deeply Americanized subject. She admits that she was fascinated by the idea that she could see her own world through different eyes.[52] However, she also describes how scared and shocked she was when she realized that she had forgotten the topography of her own city and that sometimes she was not recognized by her own people as one of them. The most frightening sign of her foreignness to her own place occurred when she visited her old neighborhood and her dog barked at her because it did not recognize her. She tried to bribe the dog by offering it a loaf of bread and seeking recognition in this way. Just then, an Englishman appeared and intervened in a catalytic fashion.

> From across the way an Englishman came out of a house and approached me, where I sat with Giaur's paws in my lap. "Beg pardon," he said shyly, lifting his hat. "You are a stranger here, and those fellows are dangerous. Besides, they are unhealthy." This was the last straw: *he* took me for a foreigner.
>
> "Thank you," I replied, "but I am not afraid. The fact is, we are of the same kennel, Giaur and I."[53]

Vaka resorted to solid forms of identification only when she was not recognized as whom she wished to be seen as. Passing for different nationalities might be entertaining and desirable, but not being recognized as she wanted was unsettling. Here, it led her to a definite statement of identity.[54] Narrative configurations of identity were thus subjective for Vaka, since they depended on the ways in which the subject desired to locate herself in different social settings. Multiplicity was not an essential characteristic of subjectivity, but the outcome and the symptom of the difference that marked social relations in different cultural, political, historical, and geographical settings. Multiplicity thus was not an option, but a political and contextual necessity. Vaka was brought up within an imperial society whose organization was based on the plurality, coexistence, and tolerance of ethnic and religious difference. In the process of self-identification she referred not to the form of cultural homogeneity of the nation-state, but to the cultural plurality of the empire. The absence of references to the ethnic mosaic of migrants in her descriptions of New York's Lower East Side—so common in other migrant narratives—implied that the multinational environment she encountered in the United States did not impress her. She treated this multination more as a familiar cultural norm than as a cause of estrangement. Vaka's estrangement was more related to her racial illiteracy rather than to unfamiliarity with multinational culture forms. In her autobiography (and less frequently in the rest of her books) she made anecdotal reference to "entertaining incidents" that proved her ignorance of the American cultural codes of racial hierarchy. For example, she describes how she "began to be asked out to luncheons and dinners,—partly as a freak, I am afraid—and at one of these dinners I became the victim of American humor. Happening to mention that I was surprised at not seeing any pure Americans in New York, I was asked what I meant. I explained that I meant full-blooded Indians."[55]

Elsewhere Vaka declares that she was completely ignorant about the United States before she actually migrated to this country. The few things that she admitted knowing before her arrival in the United States were related to the country's racial history.

> Of America actually I knew almost nothing. . . . The story of Pocahontas and Captain John Smith had fallen into my hands when I was twelve years old. I wept over it, and surmised that the great continent beyond the seas was peopled by the descendants of Indian princesses and adventurers. My second piece of information was gathered from a French novel, I believe, in which a black sheep was referred to as having gone to America "where all black sheep gravitate." And my third source of information was "Uncle Tom's Cabin," the book which makes European children form a distorted idea of the American people, and sentimentalize over a race hardly worthy of it.
>
> This made up my encyclopedia of American facts. That all those who emigrated succeeded easily and amassed untold wealth I ascribed to the fact that being Europeans they were vastly superior to the Americans, who at best were only half-breeds.[56]

Vaka presented the process of her Americanization as one of learning the racial grammar of the United States. Racialization in this sense was an educational issue. She viewed the issue of racial hierarchies as a matter of general knowledge and common sense. Referring to her first years in the United States, she mentioned the moment when she made herself acquainted with John Fiske's work and discovered the error of her preconceived notions about the American people and their origin. She admitted that reading Fiske's books made her look for the first time upon the American continent "as peopled by the white race." This realization filled her with "shame" for her past ignorance and a desire to learn more about America.[57]

Vaka's foreignness was thus related to her ignorance of the dominant cultural order of her new place of residence, racial hierarchy and history. How did Vaka represent her own cultural heritage? She did not subscribe to solid and fixed forms of nationhood and national identity. She thought that the quality of the cultural heritage related to her national origins helped her to navigate through the social network in the United States. She often identified herself as a "Byzantine Greek." This type of identification refers us to a form of nationhood that has a cultural content, but does not imply state or territorial political allegiances. Her perception of modern Greek cultural identity allowed her to move in and out of solid and fixed social and cultural (race, gender, class, and ethnic) identities, to expose their incompleteness and contradictory character, to change costumes, as it were, without ever becoming the costume itself. Vaka's self-representation refers us to a diasporic form of identification, in the sense that identification was never full, complete, or unconditional. The form of nationhood that she identified with was always minoritarian and elliptical, and it did not resemble nation-state forms of national identification. In her case, migration transformed nationhood into a minoritarian position that gave the subject the means to move across different lines of identification without ever fully identifying. This is the point where Vaka's life story differs from other migrant life stories. As she mentions in her autobiography, when she was working as an editor at the Greek newspaper *Atlantís* in New York, she used to read hundreds of letters to the editor sent by Greek migrants. In these letters the migrants would tell their stories of hardships related to their condition of expatriation and dislocation. Vaka tells us that she felt sorry for these poor migrants, but she never identified with them. For her, migration constituted not a forced expatriation, but a process of discovery of new ways of being at home. As noted above, Vaka's migration was related to her attempt to escape from traditional female roles and follow alternative forms of womanhood. This strongly gendered identification may have led her to disidentify from certain traditional, fixed and solid forms of nationhood. Contemporary dominant conceptualizations of the migrant subject were so gender-specific (defined by masculinity) that they could not accommodate radically different forms of identification. Diasporic conceptualizations of subjectivity, however, offered the possibility of being both inside and outside the dominant forms of migrancy and womanhood. Each of the different aspects of migrant subjectivity represented in Vaka's testimony remains incomplete, open-ended, and complex. Womanhood and migration remained the kernels around which the multiple aspects of her subjectivity were interwoven. Migration as a historical event, an individual option, and a personal risk rendered categories and identities changeable, flexible, and fluid.

Vaka's life story as narrated in her literary work and in her autobiography, as well as in the life stories of other women that she wove into the narrative of her own life, offer powerful insight into forms of early-twentieth-century female diasporic subjectivity. I characterize this form of subjectivity as diasporic because of its manifest tendency to open up otherwise closed and fixed categories, as well as social, cultural, and national identities. The term *diasporic* also refers to the subject's tendency to engage with multiple processes of identification that nonetheless remain incomplete and partial. The form of womanhood represented in Vaka's life story was socially and culturally central, since femininity was considered to be the defining point of other forms of difference; it was also minoritarian because it could accommodate conditional, multiple, contradictory, and incomplete forms of identification. In Vaka's narrative the diasporic woman was presented as an exemplary form of modern subjectivity. Yet her story was not a celebration of modern ways of being. As in other migrant narratives, we also find in Vaka's story the belief that the subjects lived at times when one was caught by the whirl of history. Dislocation was the result of personal decision and conscious choice; however, it represented not a celebrated gesture of emancipation, but a conscious acknowledgment of historical necessity. Her confession in *Child of the Orient* eloquently expresses the depth of the imprint these cultural tendencies of migrancy left on modern subjectivity:

> In order to live my own life as seemed right to me, I must flee from all I knew and loved to an unknown, alien land. It is a hard fate: it involves sacrifices and brings heartaches. After all, what gives to life sweetness and charm is the orderliness with which one develops. To grow on the home soil, and quietly to reach full blossom there, gives poise to one's life. It may be argued that this orderly growth rarely produces great and dazzling results; still it is more worth while. People with restless dispositions, people to whom constant transplanting seems necessary, even if they attain great development, are rather to be pitied than to be envied; and, when the transplanting produces only mediocre results, there is nothing to mitigate the pity.[58]

As we have seen in the case of Demetrios Callimachos, it was historical necessity that produced the migrant as a new historical subject, as it was the author's own conscious acknowledgment of the need to educate this new subject that drove his biographical writings. His biographies operated as model narratives whose purpose was to regulate the ways in which one was supposed to be a migrant. Callimachos's biographies were marked by closures and expressed a continuous attempt to contain the experience of migrancy within fixed forms of Hellenic and American subjectivity. Vaka's life stories, in contrast, maintained an open-ended perspective as the author insistently pointed toward incomplete forms of the migrant state of being. Both tendencies coexisted in the making of Greek migrant culture of the early twentieth century, and the unresolved issues that arose during this coexistence marked the Greek diaspora for decades.

SIX

The History of Migration: Autobiographical Writing and Historiography

Although migration has been a formative process of modern and contemporary societies during the last two centuries, it has not constituted a central area of historical research. With the exception of American historiography—a case where migration is considered to be an important element of national history—historical research has attributed a rather peripheral role to the study of people's movements and relocations. Partly due to the conceptual hegemony of national concerns, professional historians have treated migration mainly in terms to its impact on the nation-state. As a result, the history of migrants themselves has occupied a secondary role in relation to the history of processes *related* to migration, such as assimilation, integration, or national security; more important, the historical analysis of these processes has almost ignored the subjective aspects of migration and the relation between transnational movements and the emergence of new forms of subjectivity. And yet the historiography of migration has relied on certain assumptions about the subjectivity of migrants—assumptions that derive from representations and images produced and circulated in the broader cultural sphere of migrant and homeland communities. On the other hand, and in the context of the lack of professional historical research in migrant subjectivity, autobiographical and biographical accounts of migration have played an important role in the formation of the cultural plots and assumptions underlying the development of historical knowledge about migration and its role in national, social, and economic history.

New "Good Old Stories" of Migration

Most of the autobiographies and memoirs written by first-generation Greek migrants were published during the two decades that followed World War II. Most of these autobiographies were written in Greek, by male migrants and repatriates, and were published in Greece.[1] Migrant autobiographies were aimed at a wide readership that included the Greek communities in the United States, as well as the general public in Greece. Autobiographies also addressed the growing numbers of prospective migrants in the years that followed World War II. The reasons why an individual decided to write his or her autobiography

determined the readership as well as the content and the character of the narrative. Most of the autobiographies had a didactic tone, and some were particularly practical and utilitarian. They provided information that concerned the
current opportunities of migration and advice intended to help future migrants.
Repatriated migrants often decided to write their autobiographies as a way to
explain the reasons for their repatriation to their compatriots who were still in
the United States. These autobiographies included advice concerning the status of repatriates in Greece, state policies, legal issues, and social perceptions.
Finally, migrant autobiographies were intended to provide the younger generations of Greek Americans with knowledge of the history of their community in
the United States.

The primary goal of migrant autobiographies, however, was to make the past
and present history of Greek communities in the United States known in Greece.
The autobiographical text was communicative. The authors addressed their
readers directly and explicitly expressed their intention to share their individual experiences and thus transform them into common social knowledge. The
autobiographical narrative was grounded in the assumption that the migrants'
subjective experience in the United States, like their wages, could be "remitted"
to Greece, and that it could supplement and become part of the contemporary collective political experience in the homeland. Autobiographical narratives
constituted a communicative means of self-conceptualization. The analysis included in autobiographies offers an insight into the self, as well as into the social
alterity that the migrant represented. As a result, migrant autobiographies vary
greatly. The subject of the autobiography used his or her life story as a starting
point in order to narrate the stories of relatives, friends, and compatriots. Most
subjects used the first person plural of narration ("we") to describe their personal experiences as migrants in the United States. Autobiography is in general
considered one of the most individualistic modes of representation.[2] Scholars of
minoritarian autobiographical writing have pointed out, however, that subjects
often vacillate between the individual self and the collective subject, between
the first person singular and the first person plural of narration.[3] The individual
subject of the migrant autobiography is part of a group that forms the collective subject of migration. The contemporary reader of migrant autobiographies
often finds it difficult to distinguish between the individual and the collective
story, since the main narrative is intertwined with multiple other stories that
present the lives of other migrants in the United States.

The autobiographies written by Greek migrants in the United States often
included a foreword written by a widely known public figure, usually an intellectual, a politician, or a journalist. The purpose of this foreword was to evaluate
the book and to underline its pedagogical value. Forewords often indicated how
the public was to receive migrant autobiographies. The writer of the foreword

introduced the author of the autobiography to the public as an example for the younger generation of modern Greeks, with emphasis on the national and social importance of the migrants' moral input to modern Greek culture. As Spyros Demenagas remarked in his foreword to the autobiography of Karolos Manos, published in 1964, migrants usually were not educated and lacked the means of scholarly or systematic reflection on their own lives. The value of the migrant autobiographies derived from how they allowed the communication of experience by means of subjective forms of representation.[4] In the process of *auto-bio-grafein* the migrant operated as a living container of unprocessed experience. At least, this seemed to be how Greek migrant autobiographies were viewed in Greece.[5] Autobiographical texts written in the 1950s and 1960s included almost all the cultural elements that grounded contemporary images of the Greek migrant subject in Greece. Autobiographical texts thus operated as a form of cultural remittance of migration in a period marked by increased Americanization of state politics, popular culture, and everyday ways of life. The 1950s and 1960s were also marked by new waves of migration from Greece to Western Europe, Australia, and the United States. Since many of these autobiographies addressed prospective migrants, the autobiographical text recorded the imagery of early twentieth-century migration as it was inherited by post–World War II generations of Greek migrants.

In 1954 Nina Ladoyianni published a semifictional biography of "Uncle Charlie," a Greek migrant to the United States who returned to Greece in the beginning of the 1950s.[6] The book was published privately in five hundred copies. As Ladoyianni mentioned in the introduction, she met Uncle Charlie—who had left Greece at the start of the twentieth century as an "illiterate village boy" and returned in the 1950s as an "illiterate old migrant"—at a social gathering, where she heard him narrating his life story to a group of curious friends and relatives. The author—who possessed the skill of writing—decided to write Charlie's autobiography for him. The narrative itself repeated many elements of stereotypical representations of migrant life, including references to the adversities of the first years, the poverty, the struggle, the exploitation, the injustice, as well as the determination to survive and succeed, willingness to work, intelligence, and social adaptability. There was, however, a particular characteristic in Uncle Charlie's story. The reference to the scarcity of all kinds of resources (such as wealth, skills, education, and social and cultural familiarity with the recipient country)—a stereotypical element in all accounts of migration—was related to the issue of generational difference. According to Ladoyianni, the old migrant belonged to an already bygone era and generation, and he thus represented Greek qualities and virtues that were quickly disappearing in post–civil war Greece. Older generations were deprived of resources, but they were endowed with such qualities as determination, faith, and courage. These characteristics were preserved and

developed under conditions of migration and were personified by Uncle Charlie. The presence of the old migrant guaranteed the possibility of rejuvenation
of the Greek psyche. Ladoyianni decided to write this mediated autobiography
because for her, migration had already become "history," and the experiences of
the Greek migrants seemed to constitute part of the nation's cultural tradition.[7]

The issue of scarcity of resources was a recurring element in migrant autobiographies, one that allowed for the representation of other qualities that marked
migrant life. In the autobiography of Karolos Manos, the author explained that
his survival under very adverse conditions in America was due to the principles
he followed in his life. Thus the migrant's moral qualities compensated for the
lack of knowledge and other resources. Here again, the lack of material and educational resources was related to the issue of generation.[8] The Greek migrant
represented old and well-preserved Greek values that had perished in post–civil
war Greece, but had been cultivated under the conditions of migrancy. Migrant
autobiographies propagated the idea that endurance and patience in conditions
of economic deprivation, social inequality, and political depredation were essential characteristics of the Greek psyche and that the cultivation of these virtues,
combined with hard work, was the only way to progress and improvement. As
migration was being inscribed in the nation's cultural heritage, it was also related to particular work ethics as well as to stereotypes of Greece as the nation
struggling against all kinds of adversity.

In other autobiographies the theme of scarcity of resources grounded claims
to the migrants' need for guidance and protection. In Emmanuil Polenis's autobiography, published in Athens in 1945, migrants were presented as children in
need of parental protection and care.[9] Polenis argued that in the United States
the government played the role of the protecting father for the migrants. Forms
of self-conceptualization that stressed the scarcity of resources and the impossibilities that characterized migrant life were often combined with perceptions
of America as the protective power. "Those of us who went to America, we were
poor and unprotected kids, we found there great moral and material support,
and as true inheritors of descendants of the ancient Greek spirit, we adapted
immediately to the American environment, and we were greatly helped to do so
by the local laws of the American government and the enlightened interest of the
great American philanthropic foundations and associations."[10]

Similar images of the American state were almost always juxtaposed with representations of the Greek state as inherently and incurably inefficient. By juxta-
posing the two states, many authors expressed political opinions that favored
American intervention in Greek political life and argued in favor of protection-
ism in international politics. The theme of scarcity often functioned as an introduction to references to the virtues of Greek identity and the importance
of these virtues in the context of migration. Despite the scarcity of resources,

the Greek migrant had supposedly always been naturally diligent, frugal, and progressive. These were the qualities that had permitted the integration of the Greek migrant in the recipient American society.[11] In his autobiography, Polenis did not construct an entirely positive picture of the Greek migrant in the United States. He portrayed eloquently his misgivings over the migrants' social behavior, and he gave advice to future migrants, especially concerning the bohemian life led by some. Bohemian life included illicit relationships with women and often resulted in contraction of contagious diseases, gambling, and alcoholism, all of which the migrants had to avoid if they were committed to survival and progress. According to Polenis, despite the dangers and the hardships involved, migration offered the Greek people the opportunity to overcome the limitations and the scarcity that was imposed on them by their national and cultural origin. Migration was the result of economic underdevelopment, civilizational delay, and cultural inferiority.[12] But migration also provided the subject with an opportunity to transcend historical and geographical determination and improve his position in the international division of labor and in the international hierarchy of civilizational advancement. As Polenis mentions, his initial decision to migrate was strengthened when one of his close friends informed him about the possibility of improving his status as a worker by moving to India, a place where his European background would give him some advantage within race and class hierarchies of the labor market.[13] Although he finally migrated to the United States rather than to India, he remained convinced that migration was the way to overcome the economic and cultural time lag that was related to the underdevelopment of the migrant's birthplace and to his national origin.

The issues of personal self-improvement; moral, physical, and psychic well-being; and professional progress were central and recurrent in migration narratives. Self-improvement and well-being often constituted elements of the process of Americanization. We have already encountered this interrelation between Americanization and personal improvement in the regulative psychobiographies. In the individual autobiographies we can trace this interrelation in the sections where the authors give advice on how to achieve happiness and how to progress in the new homeland. Almost all autobiographies featured "how-to" chapters that offered detailed discussion of the "virtues of American life." Most of these "virtues" concerned the private sphere of everyday life, such as family life and more specifically the raising of children. The "American ways" included rationalization of family life and personal relationships. "It is about time that these ideas become dominant in Greece. In America, where everything is arranged according to wise experience and scientific psychology, the education of the youth does not constitute a simple or secondary issue. The Americans are practical and civilized people, and as such they have given freedom to the child and they support every good initiative that he takes and they guide children in every step of their lives." [14]

The virtues of American ways of life were also manifested in the public spheres of international and domestic politics. Many migrants thought that their mission to transplant American qualities of life to Greece was a continuation of a long process of U.S.-Greek exchange and international relations. The subject's individual history of migration thus found its way into the collective history of the nation. Polenis started his autobiography with a reference to the history of U.S.-Greek relations and more specifically to the American philhellenism during the period of the Greek War of Independence. Migrants often represented themselves as the successors of nineteenth-century American philhellenes.

The theme of the emergence of new forms of subjectivity in the United States was very popular in Greek migrant autobiographies. The application of American ways of life and the expansion of these ways around the world was generally expected to lead humanity toward progress and civilizational advancement. This belief was expressed most impressively in the ways in which the intermixing of ethnicities and populations in the United States was expected to produce a "new race" of American people who would be superior to existing European races. [15] How then did the authors of autobiographies deal with the debate that concerned the antithesis between Americanization and preservation of Greek national culture? A great part of Polenis's autobiography concerned the issue of double national allegiance. He began with the assumption that migrants are de facto "people without a homeland." "Having a homeland" could be detrimental for the migrant, since it imprisoned him in an unproductive state of nostalgia. This condition concerned mostly the first generation of Greek migrants in the United States, people who for years felt "that [they] were under arrest, that [they] were exiles, deprived of good luck, and that now after so many years [they] were at last liberated." [16] Taking his own experience as a starting point, he advised other migrant Greeks to develop more positive forms of self-understanding and representation. He also argued that the migrant community needed to develop new, alternative ways to relate to their country of origin. First, nationhood should be disconnected from notions of territoriality and civic allegiances. "Dear compatriots, our patriotism and our love for the ones we choose to love are alive no matter where we live and no matter what kind of citizenship we have. . . . On the contrary, as we all well know, some of our nation's most important benefactors were Greeks who lived abroad." [17]

In his attempt to define the relation between location and national feeling, Polenis often used the examples of travel and tourism to argue in favor of a cosmopolitan idea of nationhood. Migrant autobiographies written in the 1950s and 1960s—a period marked by the development of mass tourism and organized traveling—often used elements typical of travel literature. In the narration of his wanderings in the United States and in Greece, Polenis included detailed descriptions of scenery, landscapes, and historic monuments. The new, cosmopolitan idea of nationhood that the author advocated was certainly inspired by a tourist's disposition toward culture, peoples, and places. In his view, migrant nationhood should have a cultural and moral content, while remaining free from territorial references and civic constraints. The cultural content of migrant nationhood would be the result of an eclecticism that would allow the migrant to keep all those elements that were compatible with his everyday life in a different country and ignore all the rest. Furthermore, the application of the model of tourism to migrant nationhood privileged a voyeuristic approach to national culture. Much like the tourist-voyeur, the migrant desired and often demanded a prearranged scene and a fixed image of the nation. In the autobiographical text this desire was expressed through an insistence on the definition and description of essential and inherited constitutive elements of Greek identity. To carry the metaphor of the tourist-voyeur a bit further, we could argue that in voyeuristic relations the voyeur holds a position of authority that allows him to enter and exit the scene according to his own will. The voyeur has no commitment to the scene, or to its protagonists. In the same way the migrant-tourist, through a process of fixation and objectification of national culture, took the place of the observer and kept the privilege to enter and exit nationhood at will. Polenis remained aware that the migrant could not afford to follow the tourist model of nationhood, because of social, political, and economic constraints. He pointed out the difference between the traveler and the migrant, whenever he included descriptions of monuments or landscapes in his autobiography, by commenting that only few times in his life had he managed to "transform for a while to a traveler." Although he desired and provisionally did undertake the role of the traveler, he nevertheless identified consciously with what he called "the world's migrants."

The autobiographical accounts of Greek migrants in the post–World War II period reveal the retreat of older controversies over ethnic American versus Greek cultural identification and the emergence of new, transnational forms of identification. These new forms emerged after some fifty years of controversies over issues of cultural identity and its transformation in the context of thickening transnational movements and exchanges. The rise of transnational economic, political, and social structures was accompanied by the expressions of subjectivity that were manifested in new modes of identification, no longer based on the idea of inherited culture, territorial origins, or civic allegiances, but instead grounded in individual preferences, initiatives, principles, possessions, and activities. The autobiographies written by migrants and repatriates privileged essentialist definitions of Greekness and folkloric notions of nationhood. By disconnecting nationhood from territorial references and civic attachments, they propagated depoliticized notions of nationhood. At the same time, the autobiographical accounts demonstrated the migrants' self-appointed position in the context of the emerging transnational political scene. The subjects considered migration a result of their country's civilizational time lag due to unequal international development. They also saw migration as the only way to compensate for this time lag, and in this way they incorporated their individual subjective stories of migration into the historical narrative of the Greek nation.

Writing the Chronicles of Hellenism in America

The first historical accounts of the experiences of Greek migrants in the United States appeared in community guides and directories that were published during the first two decades of the twentieth century with the intention of facilitating communication between Greek migrants and ethnic businesses in different American cities. They included the names and addresses of all Greeks in each American city, as well as information on their occupations, enterprises, and family status.[18] The guides also included information about the history of the United States, as well as practical information on cultural practices and legal matters. One of the most famous guides was the one written by Seraphim Canoutas, a Greek lawyer in New York. Canoutas's guide included a long discussion of the phenomenon of migration in general and Greek migration in particular. He made a special effort to define migration and to differentiate it from other kinds of movements of population, and with this purpose he drew a line between the transatlantic migration of Greeks in his time and earlier phases of Greek migration in Europe and Africa. Canoutas made reference to Greek statutes and state-commissioned reports on the phenomenon of migration, and his views echoed the official positions on the issue at the time. He differentiated between migration and cosmopolitan traveling for business or entertainment. Canoutas was disposed against migration, which he considered to be detrimental to Greece's national interests. He noted that although in general the causes of migration were economic, in the case of the Greeks the increase of migration was due to other factors: "the advancement of civilization and the development of modern modes of transportation created among the [Greek] people a tendency for cosmopolitanism, profiteering and greed, which people thought that they could satisfy only by immigrating to a different place."[19]

The guides provided statistical and other information on the contemporary status of Greek migration, explanations and interpretations of the causes of the increase of migration, references to its advantages and disadvantages, and discussion of how the United States differed from previous destinations of Greek migrants. Finally, the guides included accounts and descriptions of the status of Greek migrants in the United States from the first years of migration onward.

The guides resembled historical sketches, and as such they included life stories of early Greek migrants who had achieved wealth and fame in America. The guides constituted a personal as well as cultural *Who's Who* for the Greek migrant community. In this context of defining, bounding, and mapping the Greek presence in the United States, life stories operated as landmarks to facilitate navigation in the territory of migrant culture.

The first historical accounts of Greek migration to the United States were intended to serve certain practical needs. Similarly, another category of chronicles was commissioned directly or indirectly by religious organizations whose purpose was to gather information that would facilitate proselytizing and interaction between different churches. In this case the writers' purpose was to provide information about the Greek migrant community to "outsiders."[20] As the first quasi-systematic studies on Greek migrants, these commissioned historical accounts served as references for practically all the subsequent books on the same topic written by Greek or American scholars. The importance of these accounts was that very early on they constructed certain images of the first years of Greek migration in the United States, and they bequeathed those images to future studies. These images echoed the ecumenism that marked the writers' strongly Christian point of view. They breathed a missionary air that was very apparent in the propagation of the idea that the negative opinions of the Greeks held by many native-born Americans were the result of misunderstandings, that the migrants were actually available for assimilation by the religious and cultural establishment of the American polity, given the right methods of proselytizing and cultural education.

The first systematic accounts of the history of Greek migration in the United States were given by American social scientists.[21] Greek migration was studied in the context of the general debates over the problem of the "new immigration." American scholarly studies on Greek migrants sought to gather information that would help determine the extent to which the migrants could be assimilated into American culture. In 1911 Henry Pratt Fairchild completed his doctorate in anthropology at Yale University, with a dissertation on Greek migration to the United States.[22] Although his work was generally despised by Greek American intellectuals, who considered that it constituted an unfavorable representation of Greeks, it was later widely cited in historical and sociological studies of the Greek migrant communities. Fairchild set out to study the effects of migration both on Greece and on the United States. His inquiry was driven by two major sets of questions. First, he wanted to address issues that concerned the American nation's power to assimilate different national cultures and peoples. The project was based on the assumption that "as the country is filling up and as conditions are coming not so distantly to resemble those of older lands . . . the issues surrounding the contact of races are bound to be vital and perhaps determinative of the destiny of the nation."[23] As the myth of the western frontier was ceasing to form contemporary dominant conceptualizations of the American nation, and as the issue of proximate interracial social interaction was brought into the foreground, migration was increasingly discussed in terms of "quality" of migrant races.

Second, Fairchild set out to study the character of Greek people and the causes of Greek migration, in order to reach some conclusions regarding the value that the assimilation of the Greeks would have for American culture and civilization. Fairchild began the discussion with a general discussion of how difficult it was to foresee immediately the effects that the presence of "peculiar classes of people amidst the American people" could have on Anglo-America. Fairchild's basic reference in this discussion was the "case of the negroes in the United States." During the first years of the slave trade, Fairchild argued, Anglo-Americans failed to foresee that they were creating a major problem for themselves that would "work irreparable injury to the American stock by the annihilation of the flower of southern manhood." Migrants constituted a problem of the same order as the race problem.

> There is much similarity between the case of the negroes and that of the modern immigrants. To be sure, the newcomers are for the most part white-skinned instead of colored . . . yet in the mind of the average American, the modern immigrants are generally regarded as inferior peoples—races which he looks down on, and with which he does not wish to associate in terms of social equality. Like the negroes they are brought in for economic reasons, to do hard and menial work to which an American does not care to stoop. The business of the alien is to go into the mines, the foundries, the sewers, the stifling air of factories and workshops, out on the roads and railroads in the burning sun of summer, or the driving sleet and snow. If he proves himself a man, and rises above his station, and acquires wealth, and cleans himself up—very well, we receive him after a generation or two. But at present he is far beneath us, and the burden of proof rests with him.[24]

Accordingly, Fairchild argued, the assimilation of Greeks would be very difficult and not of any particular value for the United States because of the adverse social circumstances of migration and the great difference in cultural background. The essential condition under which both Greeks and Americans could benefit from the Greeks' integration into the native society would be closer contact and familiarization with each other's culture. Fairchild, however, did not think of contact and interaction in terms of equality and mutual commitment. He rather believed that it was the migrants' own responsibility to raise themselves to a level of culture that would permit them to interact with native-born Americans. Although some scholars of that period expressed more liberal views and insisted more on the migrants' achievements in the process of assimilation, in general the intervention of American social scientists in the debate over migration led to a hardening of notions of cultural and racial hierarchy by endowing them with a scientific aura.[25] Led by an explicit confidence in social science's abilities to render social groups transparent by means of application of sophisticated research techniques, as well as to engineer culture, American scholars propagated the idea that social subjects were divided between those who had the ability to know and those who had the opportunity to become knowable. In this particular case, this separation was defined in ethnic and racial terms.

Most Greek intellectuals opposed Fairchild's views, but the book had a great influence on later historical and sociological accounts as Greek writers set out to refute Fairchild's conclusions. Subsequent accounts written by Greek migrant authors stressed the achievements of Greeks in the United States and tried in this way to oppose the idea that assimilation was difficult and not valuable to the United States. As a result, these subsequent accounts conformed to the logic of assimilation by opposing Fairchild's arguments in his own terms. The first chronicles written by Greeks in the United States appeared in the late 1910s and were the outcome of the migrants' engagement with nativist antimigrant propaganda.[26] Driven by the immediate and urgent political need to confront antimigrant American nativism, migrant intellectuals defended their own positions from within a framework of reference that admitted the historical inevitability and naturalness of cultural and racial inequality and hierarchy at that time. Early histories of the Greeks in the United States adopted quasi-apologetic modes of writing, where the subject of the story was always being (self-) represented in the presence of an outsider that did not need to be represented since he occupied the position of the knowing subject.

Most of these early chronicles documented the local history of Greek communities in the United States. The first overall account was written by Canoutas: "Hellenism in America, or the History of the Greeks in America from the Early Days to the Present Time with an Appendix of what America has done for the Greeks during their War of Independence in 1821 and afterwards and with a treatise in English, regarding the Greek contribution to America in the past and in the present war, the success and the progress of the Greeks in business, letters etc. and certain remarks and suggestions for a better understanding and appreciation of the non-English speaking migrants."[27] Canoutas's purpose in writing this book was twofold. First, he pointed out the migrants' achievements during this early period of migration. He also stressed the Greek migrants' devotion to the ideals represented by the U.S. government, with emphasis on what he saw as the migrants' eagerness to enlist in the U.S. Army during World War I. While internalizing and essentializing the cultural hierarchy that defined American culture as superior to migrant culture, Canoutas stressed the progress that

Greek migrants had made in assimilating and in proving themselves devoted to the ideals of "true Americanism." This process of internalization was not direct or unmediated; rather, it eventually altered the assumptions that were internalized. Canoutas wrote the second section of his book in English because, as he stated, it was addressed to Americans. In that section he refuted the false Americanism that was advocated by antimigrant nativists and demonstrated the ways in which the migrants represented ideal examples of proper Americanism. He argued that "if Americans look down with contempt upon the migrant because he is poor, uneducated, or cursed with certain faults he acquired while living in a poor or ill-governed country, they cannot make him believe that America stands for democracy, justice and general brotherhood. . . . The word 'Americanization' applies not only to the foreigners, but to the natives too, because Americans can and need to become better Americans."[28]

Although the cultural hierarchy that structured Americanism was internalized in this migrant self-representation, the concept itself was modified, since it was presented more as a cultural ideal than as an inherited characteristic. In this way the migrants were given access to the symbolic order of representation of the American nation. However, the organizing role in this order was still held by the native-born subject to which the migrant subject reported and was self-represented. Canoutas concluded with a prophetic argument: "When Americans, in their struggle to instruct the foreigners have acquired for their own part a better knowledge of the characteristics of each race, when they rightly attribute the faults of the foreigners to the painful conditions under which they lived in their own country, when they patiently bring to light the better qualities of those whom they aspire to educate, then that unity so desirable, so necessary for this great nation will be perfected."[29]

Canoutas accepted the logic and the conceptual economy that put the migrants in a position of inferiority and then tried to write a history of how they succeeded in changing this position. He argued that migration was not a new element in Greek history, but had constituted an integral part of the national past from ancient to present times. His chronicle was addressed to Greeks in America as well as to Greeks in Greece, and his purpose was to trace the history of Hellenism in America from the colonial period until his own time. His project was inscribed in the logic that the presence of the Greeks in contemporary America would be legitimized if it were proved that they had been an integral part of the nation's history for a long time. To prove this, Canoutas claimed that Greeks had always been "a venturesome people having irresistible inclination for sea and travel."[30] He also made the assumption that Greek people must have participated in the process of Western expansion, but their participation had been concealed because of the historians' "prejudice and [the] lack of interest prevailing in those days among other Europeans for the people of a nation supposed to have disappeared forever from the face of earth."[31] As a consequence of this discrimination, Greeks themselves often concealed their own nationality or race by changing their names and adopting European ones. To counteract this systematic concealment, Canoutas retrieved from the colonial archives numerous cases where the participation of individuals of Greek origin in the process of colonization was documented. As a result, Canoutas's narrative is a compilation of brief individual life stories and biographies. According to the author, the life stories of these individuals were offered twofold proof. First, they proved the connection between the history of Greek migration and the history of the American nation. Second, they proved the connection between the history of Greek migration and that of the Greek nation. Apart from Greeks' "irresistible inclination to sea and travel," it was also the political and historical circumstances—Ottoman occupation in particular—that made migration a quasi-essential element of Greek history and culture. The stories of the migrants were related to the history of the nation, in such a way that the biographical stories became the history of the nation. In this early type of chronicle of Greek migration we can trace the first articulation of representations of Greece as a nation of migrants. We can also trace the ways in which the history of the homeland—transcribed as the history of a nation of migrants—was brought into interaction with the history of the American nation. For Canoutas and other migrant intellectuals, the early twentieth-century history of the Greek nation, as seen from the perspective of migration, had changed direction, in the sense that Greece was now entering the group of the civilized nations having participated in the process of colonization and Western expansion. The urge to travel and the capacity to adapt were the two main characteristics of advanced races, and Canoutas argued that Greeks shared those characteristics with the rest of the civilized imperialist nations. The intervention of the history of migration in the symbolic order of the Greek nation's representation introduced in this order elements of the conceptual order of Americanism and imperialism, notions of racial and civilizational hierarchy in particular.

Histories of migration relied on evolutionist, teleological, holistic, and hierarchical schemes of human history. The insertion in the schema of world history was made possible through evolutionist understandings of historical process. According to these understandings, each nation occupied a different position in the scale of historical progress, at the top of which stood the developed nations of the European West and the American North. This hierarchical understanding of human history determined the position the migrant intellectual took regarding the issue of cultural assimilation. In his attempt to represent the history of Greek migration in the context of world history, Canoutas noted in 1907 that "Greeks are not assimilated by other peoples . . . in Egypt, Turkey and in general in places where the native people are considered to be inferior in comparison with the foreigners in matters of civilization, developments, wealth or social position. This is a general rule and it applies to all the people and all the rest of the nations and not only to the Greeks. . . . One loves to imitate and to be assimilated by individuals or peoples whom one considers to be somehow more developed, superior or at least equal."[32]

The formation of modern historical consciousness in the West has been based on evolutionary as well as other ways of conceptualizing historical time.[33] Evolutionary temporality coexisted with religious circular understandings of historical process, or nationalistic revivalist conceptualizations of collective culture. Migrant histories, however, relied almost exclusively on evolutionary temporality and made evolution the main discursive element in representations of the migrant as a historical subject. Migrant self-representations attributed a particular gravity and everyday cultural value to the notion of historical evolution, in the sense that they related evolutionary temporality to the migrants' position in terms of whether or not to internalize Anglo-American ways of life.

Migrant chroniclers claimed that migrant histories were the mediators between particularistic histories of the nation and universalistic histories of the world. What was the role of migrant life stories in this process of conceptual mediation and amalgamation? Life stories were used excessively in early chronicles. While Fairchild justified his reliance on life stories by claiming that all other sources on migration were unsatisfying and poor, Canoutas and other Greek migrant intellectuals claimed that they resorted to life stories because official history—Greek and American alike—had concealed or misrepresented the histories of Greek migration. Canoutas reconstructed the history of Hellenism in America by citing long lists of biographies because he considered this to be the only narrative strategy that would allow him to refute negative stereotypes of Greek migrants and the inferior position attributed to Greek migrants by official national histories. It could thus be argued that early migrant chronicles of migration constituted a more subjective version of history, since they voiced experiences excluded from traditional history. A close reading of the kinds of life stories chosen to represent the "real" migrant experience, however, reveals that this subjective version of history was in its turn quite regulative and exclusionist. Canoutas cited those biographies that represented the two historical plots that interested him. He used life stories of successful scholars, scientists, and businessmen, on the one hand, and life stories of patriotic laborers committed to the ideals of Americanism, on the other. The authentic protagonist in the course of migration history was represented as a homogeneous collective subject, defined according to the principles and representational order of racial and social hierarchy, and expressed by means of reference to stories of individual achievement. Broad areas of migrant experience, such as the migration of women, were completely obliterated from this reconstructed image of Greek migrant subjectivity, while certain aspects of the experience of migration, such as sickness, death, poverty, and lunacy, were pathologized as abnormal, unfortunate, and exceptional. The reliance on life stories introduced subjectivity in the history of migration, but then the subject quickly vanished under the pressure of regulative representations of life in migrancy.

Stories of antimigrant discrimination, mob riots, lynchings, and violence were strictly omitted or systematically suppressed in mainstream chronicles of Greek migration to the United States, which presented cases of violent forms of discrimination as isolated events and self-inflicted misfortunes. In 1909 Greek communities around the United States were struck by the news of a violent anti-Greek riot that had taken place in Omaha, Nebraska, and had resulted in the destruction of properties owned by Greek migrants and the physical expulsion of the Greeks from the town. The riot followed an incident between a Greek migrant and an American policeman that resulted in the policeman's death. As it was reported, the policeman attempted to arrest John Massaourides because the latter was seen socializing with a white woman. Massaourides resisted his arrest, stabbed the police officer, and escaped. Following the policeman's death, part of the American population of Omaha chased Massaourides with the intention of lynching him. The Greeks resisted, and in response the mob destroyed their properties and injured several of them. This incident led to a long international and legal dispute as the Greeks whose properties had been damaged claimed their right to be indemnified by the U.S. government for their losses.[34] In 1918, forty thousand dollars was paid to the Greek government as indemnity for the losses suffered by Greek citizens in the United States "as a matter of grace and without reference to the question of liability."[35] The reaction of the Greek press to this incident illustrates how official representations registered violence and anti-Greek racism as a self-inflicted phenomenon. As the editor of *Atlantís* argued, "the revolt against the Greeks was the natural consequence of the general condition of the Greeks. . . . For sixteen years *Atlantís* has repeatedly counseled that all the Greeks who have come here to find work and improve their condition should become American citizens . . . [and] associate as much as possible with the American people."[36]

Antimigrant violence was thus attributed to the migrants' behavior and their failure to integrate themselves into American society. Similarly, experiences of discrimination were suppressed in hegemonic constructions of memory as isolated incidents of failure of Americanization. Mob action was presented as a justified act undertaken by Americans in order to protect the high ideals of Americanism to which Greek migrants had not yet adjusted. The Omaha riots were presented in this way in all subsequent mainstream historical reconstructions of the early years of Hellenism in the United States. Memories of discrimination were effectively erased or suppressed from representations of migrant subjectivity as signs of personal failure and misconduct. A Federal Writers Project interviewer who attempted to collect life histories of Greek migrant residents in Omaha in 1939 commented on this erasure of memory:

> Whenever there is a conflict, a riot, a strike, a war, or engagement of any
> kind, there are always two or more causes that have brought it about. . . . The
> remote causes are generally the more important. The immediate causes are
> generally excuses manufactured at the time to incite bitterness, prejudice, and
> hatred. . . . The remote causes, the real causes, have never been published;
> and they probably never will be published because they dealt with matters
> that respectable papers refuse to print. . . . Although the actual provocations
> were no profound secret at the time of the riot, they were of such a nature
> that those who knew them spoke in whispers, and even at this late date, while
> there are many "old timers" who know, and will talk about it in confidence,
> they will not consent to give one permission to quote them. ~~DO YOU WANT
> THE REST OF THIS STORY?~~[37]

The early chronicles of the history of Greek migration to the United States played an important role in the production of hegemonic, regulative, and exclusivist representations of migrant subjectivity. Moreover, they rigidified fixed and homogeneous notions of national and transnational subjectivity. They reproduced Anglo-American civilizational hierarchies and elaborated the axiomatic subordination of Greek national history to the teleological schema of Western civilizational and historical advancement. A certain degree of ambivalence was nevertheless present in these historical narratives. The insertion of the figure of the migrant in the representational order of the nation necessarily modified this order even though its fundamental principles were reproduced. Processes of reproduction, subordination, insertion, and integration did not go unhindered, and were not without contradictions. Early historical narratives of Greek migration to the United States insisted on the global dimension of the idea of nationhood and moved away from conceptualizations of nationhood as primordial. The explicit presupposition that commitment to the American nation constituted a political expression of the Greek migrants' commitment to the principles of civilizational progress and advancement brought into the foreground one of the hidden contradictions of nationalism as a modern Western political ideology: the ambivalent reliance on the international structure of racial and civilizational hierarchy, on the one hand, and, on the other, the reliance on the idea of the essential uniqueness of different national cultures and subjects, and the consequent impossibility of multiple national alliances. In the early chronicles of Greek migration to the United States, this internal paradox of nationalist ideology was explicitly treated as the main presupposition for the reconstruction of histories of migration.

Writing the Histories of Hellenism in America

The ambivalence of the early chronicles was maintained in the following decades in popular literature and amateur historical writing.[38] It was gradually abandoned in the more academic historiographical accounts that started appearing in the late 1950s. The first professional historical accounts of Greek migration were written by second-generation Greeks in the United States. By that period the assimilationist framework of understanding migrant culture and history had become dominant in the field of social science. However, the hegemony of assimilation—meaning the prevalence of the native Anglo-American conceptual economy in the signifying processes of migrant subjectivity and identity—was never a completed process. Assimilation set the terms of negotiation but did not bring to an end the process of definition and signification of migrant culture. In the 1950s and 1960s second-generation migrant historians set out to reconstruct the history of Greek migration in the United States and to redefine the role of the migrant ethnic subject in the political and social scene of the post–World War II United States. These accounts were marked by the postwar context of conflict and heated negotiations over race, ethnicity, civil rights, identity, and representation in the United States and globally.

The works of two postwar Greek American historians of Greek migration to the United States represent two main frameworks of conceptualization of migrant subjectivity in that period. Coming from different perspectives and pursuing different research projects, the historical works of Theodore Saloutos (1910–80) and Helen Papanikolas (b. 1918) are generally considered definitive contributions in this field. These two contributions constituted a systematic reworking of the cultural imagery of the Greek migrant that the earlier decades of the twentieth century had already produced. These professional histories of Greek migration produced disciplinary knowledge on the migrant, and by endowing already existing representations with academic legitimacy and authority, they provided definitive narratives of how migrant subjectivity came into being. Critical analysis of these historical narratives is thus indispensable because of their important role in the formation of contemporary Greek conceptualizations of migration and migrant subjectivity.

Although Papanikolas and Saloutos followed very different methodologies in their work, they shared an interest in and reliance on migrant life stories as the main source of historical knowledge on Greek migration. Helen Papanikolas was the daughter of first-generation Greek migrants. She grew up in Utah in a community of Greek migrants, miners, and laborers. She began publishing historical articles in journals such as the *Utah Historical Quarterly* during the 1950s. In terms of genre her work varies from autobiographical narration to oral and local history. She combined research and writing with participation in community projects that were directed toward the preservation of ethnic heritage and memory. She conducted interviews with Greek migrants in Utah and contributed this material to the Oral History Archive at the Marriott Library, University of Utah. These interviews constituted the main material for her numerous books and articles, which addressed different aspects of migrant life, the position of women in Greek communities, the labor movement and unionism, ethnic family traditions, antimigrant nativism, and the impact of the Great Depression on the Greek communities. Papanikolas wrote on labor and the history of the Greek migrant community.[39] She also wrote an autobiographical book on the stories of her parents, Aimilia and George Papanikolas.[40]

Papanikolas wrote within the field of ethnic American history. The history of the ethnic community constituted an element of the history of contemporary America. Her narrative, however, maintained a tone of dissent. Papanikolas set out to write about the histories of Greek migrants because she wanted to document an aspect of recent history that was rapidly disappearing. Her stories on Greek migration constituted not a narrative of how mainstream America came into being, but rather a story of how certain elements of past life were fading away in contemporary collective memory. The stories of migration that Papanikolas retrieved from Greek migrants' life story narratives exuded a sense of interruption, silencing, loss, and disappearance. They were stories about lives frozen in time and bound in the confined space of American Greektowns. They were stories about the knowledge that was erased from collective consciousness during the process of the migrants' transformation into members of an American ethnic group; knowledge related to the experiences that marked the first years of Greeks' life in the United States; knowledge about the kinds of social consciousness, ideas, mentalities, ways of living and understanding the world—and themselves in the world—that the migrants carried with them. Papanikolas was aware of the process of disappearance of the material traces of this knowledge. Her work was dedicated to the preservation of these traces, the echoes of the migrant voices and lives. Papanikolas soundly expressed her awareness of disappearance in the book she wrote on her parents' story of migration: "I think as I drive home how quickly immigrant life vanished, Greek towns long since gone, the young matriarchs and patriarchs sick to death or dead already. . . . I think of them, my parents, in the early mornings when the grieving call of the mourning dove beyond the hollow comes with the fresh scent of water and greenness. I think of them at night when in the blackness a diesel whistle sounds across the Salt Lake Valley, its blare mitigated by distancing. It is not the haunting call of the old steam engines, but it is better than nothing."[41]

The end of the era of the "young matriarchs and patriarchs" meant the disappearance and the gradual oblivion of the old migrants' forms of identification. Papanikolas decided to write about her parents' story of migration after her unexpected identification with her Greek cousin while traveling for the first time in Greece. She described this incident of unexpected identification: "As I walked up the road of her [my mother's] village, a woman came to me, as tall as I but thinner, wearing a faded brown kerchief with which village women still covered their heads. With a little leap in my heart I looked into eyes identical with my own. She was my mother's sister's daughter. Her name, like mine, was Eleni and we were the same age."[42]

External traces of sameness and proximity made her aware of an identity and sense of community that had been erased from her consciousness. She decided to write the history of this identity, which was actually the history of migration. Although Papanikolas treated the Greek migrants as members of an American ethnic group, and insisted on their Greek American identity, she touched upon the issue of homeland nationhood in an indirect and special way. In her descriptions of Greek migrant life, Papanikolas referred to a split notion of nationhood. This notion included, on the one hand, a kind of group social consciousness that was grounded in shared beliefs, mentalities, dispositions, and experiences, and an almost primordial sense of connectedness, belonging, and spiritual bonding. This was an esoteric version of nationhood that could be traced in everyday private life and personal interaction. On the other hand, Papanikolas referred to another version of nationhood that was more civil, political, public, obligatory, and exoteric. The migrants' Americanness was a social consciousness of belonging to the broader social scene of America. It constituted a necessary background that allowed them to enact their stories in the contemporary political and cultural context. Papanikolas's stories of migrant life always communicated a sense of separation and distancing between the two spheres of collective identification, as seen in the following passage, where she reconstructs in summary the story of the community where she grew up, by leafing through her family's photo album:

> Later, I saw a black man's picture as I idly turned the pages of a staple in
> Greek homes, the photograph album. The mothers screaked on in the room
> dimmed by rubber and basil plants at the windows. I scrutinized the pictures
> of weddings, baptisms—naked boy babies propped against pillows, their
> penises like ridged buttons, girl babies in demure embroidered baptismal
> dresses—picnics with squatting men turning lambs on spits and dancing
> in rounds against the mountain pines, and on the last page a black man
> dangling from a tree and under him men, women and children, arms crossed,
> smiling at the photographer. In this house my mother and we four sisters
> stood at the kitchen window and looked in silence at a Ku Klux Klan cross
> burning on the blackness of a mountain slope and across the valley the
> migrants' circle of fire flaming in answer.[43]

This text is marked by ambivalence. The separation between the two spheres of life—the public and the private, the migrant household and the American mob, the kitchen and the mountain, the hanging black body and migrants' bodies stranded in the kitchen, the inside and the outside of the window—is made explicit, but it is also erased through references to their connectedness, their intersection, their fusion. The pictures of lynching included in the family album, the children's gaze through the window, the window's transparency, the sight of the mountain marked by the Ku Klux Klan cross or by the dances of Greek men: these functioned as a semiosis of the fusion between esoteric and exoteric forms of identification in the textual representation of migration history. But these pictures were also the traces of the author's own consciousness as a second-generation Greek migrant, since her scrutinizing gaze was captured by these particular pictures and not others. Papanikolas's historical writing represented types of consciousness and forms of identification that included unresolved ambivalence. This ambivalence concerned notions of belongingness, the inside and the outside of the bound community, the disjunctive histories of the native society and the migrant community, the individual's investment in her differentiation from the nation's history. And finally, which is the *nation* that operates here as a magnetic pole of identification? Is it the Greek nation, the American nation, the black nation, the Klan nation, the migrant nation, the nation of the men dancing on the mountain slope, or the nation of the women gathering around the kitchen table, the nation of the exposed and photographed penises, or that of the female bodies covered by woman-made embroidery and imposed demureness?

Papanikolas described the effect on her of this ambivalence by referring to her constant feeling of always "wanting to be somewhere and not wanting to be there."[44] Papanikolas's historical representation of the formation of migrant subjectivity illustrates the open-endedness of the process of subjectification and the inherent lack of finitude. Hers was not a narrative of accomplished assimilation, rebirth, progress, or success. In her stories of migrant life, the subject's success derived from her ability to escape the grasp of history not by struggling against it, but by distancing herself and making herself an observer (an insider/outsider) of history, as it were. The migrants' success did not derive from their fight against fate or from their success in assimilating and progressing according to the rules and the norms of the local society. This was made explicit in her historical reconstruction of the life of a Greek migrant midwife, Magerou. According to Papanikolas, Magerou was a midwife who migrated to America and became very famous there by offering help and comfort to Greek women in the migrant communities. Gradually, Magerou started offering her services also to other migrant women, and thus her fame crossed over the boundaries of the Greek communities. Papanikolas's description of Magerou's character combines many of the qualities and traits that the historian attributed to the migrant as a social and historical subject: "Magerou was not diminished by the prejudice she found in America. She had faith in time's solution to problems. The many pictures of her show a smiling serene woman appearing much younger than she was. The Mideastern ache and hand-wringing against fate had barely brushed her nature. She was stoic over the deaths of her own infants and family reverses. She endured without knowing that she did."[45]

A quite different representation of the history of Greeks in the United States was given by Theodore Saloutos. Saloutos is considered to be the main historian of Greek American history, and his work is generally treated as the definitive contribution in the field of Greek American historical studies. Like Papanikolas, Saloutos was also a second-generation Greek American, a trained historian, and a professor at the University of the City of Los Angeles, where he specialized in the history of agriculture.[46] Early in his career, Saloutos developed a strong interest in Greek American history, but he did not feel comfortable pursuing it, since he thought that migration history was a marginal field of study. He devoted himself to the study of the Greek American community only after he had become an established historian and university professor.[47] Saloutos's books constitute the only example of a general and comprehensive history of the Greeks in America, written by a professional historian and grounded in secondary sources as well as in primary archival sources. He published two major books on the history of Greek migration to the United States: *They Remember America: The Story of the Repatriated Greek Americans* (1956), and *The Greeks in the United States* (1964).[48] Saloutos also published numerous articles on the topic, and was treated as the authority on the Greek American case among his migration history contemporaries.[49]

For Saloutos the starting-point for the study of Greek migration was his interest in post–World War II Greek American political relations. In 1951 he applied for a Fulbright scholarship, proposing to study the influence of returning migrants on Greece: first, as a "phase in Greek American relations"; second, as a "material factor in helping the weak Greek social economy"; third, as an aid in "appraising anew the attitudes of these people toward the United States" after they settled in Greece; fourth, as a "cultural and spiritual force"; and fifth, as an "agency for promoting understanding and good will" between the United States and Greece.[50] In a letter to Oscar Handlin, the famous historian of migration, Saloutos admitted that he chose this topic because he thought he had more chance to be funded, since the Fulbright Foundation was likely to express interest in a project that concerned Greek American political relations, given the contemporary political circumstances.[51] More generally, we could argue that Saloutos's interest in the history of Greek migration to the United States sprang out of his conviction that the migrant was a transnational figure who could and should play an active role in the context of Greek American political relations. Saloutos's project and his historiographical insight were embedded in his contemporary political context of the expansion of American influence on Greek politics and culture.

We must also contextualize Saloutos's work in terms of American domestic politics. His personal archive includes numerous, rich files concerning the civil rights movement and the so-called "awakening of ethnic consciousness" in the 1960s and 1970s. The material that he gathered on ethnic and race struggles— newspaper clippings, notes, essays, and photographs—mainly concerns relations between the American white ethnic communities and the African American communities. The political contextualization of Saloutos's work, as well as the analysis of the gradual formation of his academic interests, indicates that Saloutos's intellectual motivation grew from two important political settings: first, domestic racial and ethnic politics in the context of the civil rights movement and the arrival of new migrants after the 1950s; and second, Cold War U.S. politics in Greece and the search for the particular social groups (in this case repatriated migrants) that would become the vehicle of U.S. politics and culture in the process of consolidation of Cold War political balances. Saloutos's reconstruction of the history of Greeks in the United States cannot be understood outside this twofold political context.

Saloutos used personal narratives and interviews in his work. His book on the repatriated Greeks was based primarily on oral material that he collected by interviewing repatriates in Greek villages, as well as in Athenian coffeeshops and social clubs. During the 1960s and 1970s Saloutos traveled around the United States visiting Greek communities and collecting interviews given by prominent Greek Americans. The numerous interviews that he collected offer information on community matters, recent migration from Greece, and interracial relations. The dates of the interviews indicate that Saloutos started this project after he had completed his first project on the repatriated Greeks. He used this material for background information. While he based his account of the history of the Greeks in the United States mostly on official records and archives, he used the information that he derived from the migrants' testimonies to frame his historical understanding and to render his account cohesive and politically intelligible. Saloutos employed traditional historical research methods in order to safeguard the objectivity and academic legitimacy of his work. However, since his topic was migration history, he also relied on migrant life stories, which had constituted for half a century the most culturally intelligible form of representation of the experience of migration.

After receiving the Fulbright scholarship, Saloutos traveled from the United States to Greece in September 1952 on a steamship. While on board, he started his research on repatriated Greeks by interviewing fellow passengers who were returning to Greece for a temporary or permanent stay. He kept notes of these interviews in his shipboard journal, which contained a lot of information on the historian's expectations and personal dispositions toward his subjects of study: Greek American relations, Greek culture, mentalities, and attitudes. As becomes clear in his journal, Saloutos used the method of interview in order to construct a categorization of Greek migrants. His effort was to isolate certain views, mentalities, reasons of repatriation, and cultural attitudes, which he then arranged in groups and attempted to relate each group to a particular and identifiable type of migrant. He used a similar kind of typology later in his book in order to construct a representative migrant figure and to argue for the role that this social figure could play in the context of Greek American relations. Thus, Saloutos's use of life stories resulted in an erasure of subjectivity and particularity, and the consolidation of internally homogeneous and coherent images of the migrant subject. In his book on repatriated Greeks, he studied the cultural traits, social attributes, and political potential of the migrant as a social subject.

> In going from an advanced to a retarded social economy, they [the Greek repatriates] took with them money, higher standards of living, a spirit of optimism, reformist attitudes, and pronounced pro-American sentiments. They had come into contact with a different language, with different customs and attitudes. They could hardly have failed to acquire new skills and techniques; their tempo of life had quickened; they had seen people worship in different churches, for better or for worse they were exposed to the American press, periodicals, and literature; they had seen women treated differently; and they had sensed the pulsating effects of living in a strong and wealthy country. What they brought back often filtered down into the poverty-stricken areas of the country, and many of the services they and the expatriated rendered were of a character normally furnished by local governments in America. . . . Their devotion to Greece was more altruistic than that of their voluble critics or of the Athenian who flocked to the sidewalk cafes. [52]

Saloutos argued that the repatriates constituted a psychological and material benefit for Greece. [53] Their national devotion was progressive and healthy because it was consistent with American principles of progress and development. This "healthy" type of nationalism was manifested on the level of everyday life, where the repatriated Greek American "besides emphasizing the utilitarian as against the impractical and sentimental, . . . reflected a greater sense of timeliness, industry, and orderliness." [54] Saloutos argued that the internalization of the cultural principles and values represented by the United States constituted a form of completion of the Greek national psyche. As he also argued consistently in his shipboard journal, he believed that migrant culture was an exemplary form of Greek national culture, in terms of both future potential and preservation of tradition. The Greek communities of urban America constituted an organic depository of Greek folk culture that was gradually disappearing in Greece. [55]

Regarding the role that the Greek migrants could play in the context of Greek American political relations, Saloutos argued in his shipboard journal that Greek public opinion of the United States, and more specifically Greek anti-Americanism, was directly related to the impression that the Greek repatriates made on their compatriots, an argument that he supported in later works. He argued that Greek American migrants represented the United States in Greece, although the truth was that Greeks were not well informed about the progress that their compatriots had achieved in the United States. Reading through the pages of Saloutos's shipboard journal, we can trace the origins of his next project: a comprehensive history of the Greeks in the United States. As he responded to another Greek passenger's remark that the Greek migrants had made little progress in America:

> [I told him that] the sons and the daughters of immigrant parents have made considerable [progress] professionally and academically and that I thought he was misinformed. . . . My belief is that an account of the accomplishments of the Greeks in the United States is in order for the benefit of the now-migrating compatriot. Much of the misinformation about the U.S. can be erased. If Americans can only hear what Europeans have to say about them, their behavior, their standards and their general outlook on life. There seems to be unanimity of opinion regarding the mechanical and technical progress of the U.S. and its wealth of course, but serious doubts are expressed about other matters.[56]

As his personal notes indicate, Saloutos conceived his intellectual project as part of a wider project that sought to normalize U.S. foreign relations, and he supported the propagation of the qualities of American ways of life, culture, and civilization abroad in the context of Cold War politics, the Marshall Plan, and the consolidation of U.S. political influence over Greece after the end of the Greek civil war and the defeat of the left. As the passage quoted above indicates, Saloutos was also preoccupied with the phenomenon of contemporary (1950s and 1960s) Greek migration to the United States. His historical account of the early period of Greek transatlantic migration was to a certain extent addressed to prospective Greek migrants. In the face of as yet undefined transformations of the Greek American community, the historian of migration sought to consolidate a definitive version of the story thus far.[57]

In this context, Saloutos reconstructed the history of Greek migration to the United States as a normalizing process of unidirectional development, integration, and irreversible progress. In *They Remember America*, he described the social characteristics of the Greek migrant subject who came out of this progressive process. He described the Greek repatriate as a model national type and commented on the ways in which the nation would benefit by the migrants' psychological and material progress. In *The Greeks in the United States,* he projected this image of the migrant as the model national type in the past tense and traced those aspects of migration stories that converged with the main narrative of migration as a process of material benefit and spiritual and ethical elevation. Saloutos used migration life stories in order to reconstruct a unidirectional history of the migrant as a temporally (historically) and spatially (socially) homogeneous subject. As part of this reconstruction, he narrated a story of the Greek nation as seen from a present-day hegemonic point of view. Saloutos's work is a definitive representation of the history of the Greek migration to the United States and has contributed to the cultural proliferation of representations of the experience of migration that empowered discourses of social and cultural hierarchy, as well as images of Greek migrant subjectivity that erased and silenced whole aspects of the experience of migration. In *The Greeks in the United States,* Saloutos insisted on the "pioneering spirit" of the Greek peasants who decided to migrate to the United States, and noted that it was this spirit that put them on the same civilizational level as other European nations. He also insisted on inherent Greek "individualism that was to blend admirably with the native American variety."[58] Saloutos restricted his genealogical account of Greek history in the United States to matters that concerned the public sphere of social activity, mainly party politics and the politics of community organizations. He presented the absence of women migrants from the history of Greek migration as a natural "matter of fact" and grounded this naturalization in the low numbers of female migrants in comparison with male migrants. In the same vein, he presented racist discrimination against the migrants as another natural matter of historical fact and attributed this discrimination to cultural misunderstandings and lack of communication that were meant to be overcome with the passing of time. These are illustrative examples of the ways in which Saloutos constructed a unidirectional and homogenizing representation of Greek migrants in the United States, which naturalized historical subjectivity and omitted the historicization of the studied categories and concepts.

Life story narration constituted the most prominent means of cultural communication, knowledge production, and migrant representation during the first half of the twentieth century. Individual life stories were used on different levels of cultural production as well as social interaction in order to communicate the experiences of migration and to reflect on the conditions of transnationalism that marked the establishment of transatlantic communities in that period. In this sense, the life story formed the basic unit of accumulated experience that was used in the process of cultural production of knowledge about migration and the migrant. Individual life stories played this important role in migrant culture especially during the first two decades of the century, a period when the migrant had not yet become a recognizable figure in Greek, American, or transatlantic culture. As older notions of territoriality that defined culture, political identities, and subjecthood were modified under the thickening of transnational and transcontinental cultural, economic, and demographic exchanges, the life story appeared as a particularly powerful means of communication in the sphere of migrant culture and politics. Particular plots of migrant life stories were diffused widely and propagated certain cultural ideals, principles, and social traits that were in different ways attributed to the migrant as a social and historical subject. As my analysis of different forms of life story narration has shown, these cultural ideals, principles, and social traits that were related to migrant lives were often contradictory or split. The interplay of gender, class, race, and geopolitical hierarchies that defined culture on both sides of the Atlantic during the first half of the twentieth century maintained the internal contradictions and the irreducible multiplicity of the emerging migrant subjectivity. The gradual normalization of the life stories that defined our knowledge of migration history—a process that culminated in the post–World War II period and in the context of Cold War resignification of transatlantic politics and culture—also marginalized particular aspects of the experience of migration in the cultural register, thus creating an opening for new elaborations of migrant subjectivity after the 1950s.

History in Future Anterior

The conceptualization and organization of this book were based on the assumption that historical research can function as an exercise in contemporary critical thinking and cultural criticism. The questions that were addressed took shape at the intersection of three areas of intellectual engagement: (1) research in the archive of migrant cultural production; (2) theoretical and methodological debates in the fields of cultural history and history of subjectivity; (3) contemporary cultural politics and debates over sovereignty, transnationalism, and cultural representation that have developed under the impact of recent (post-1989) migrations.[1]

The study of the emergence of migrant subjectivity as a distinct form of sociality took the form of an exploration of different expressions and representations of subjectivity that were produced within native and migrant communities in the United States and in Greece. The research that I conducted indicated that during the first half of the twentieth century the migrant emerged as a socially and politically recognizable figure on different levels of social interaction. In that period, migration was given a central place in political debates over the so-called "social problem." Migration became a central public issue at a time when politics on both sides of the Atlantic were marked by visions of social engineering and by various scientific and ideological attempts to imagine ways of managing effectively modern societies of difference. In this context, the emergence of the migrant as a discernible social subject was made possible through the dissemination of information, narratives, and images that claimed to represent the experience of migration, the state of migrancy, and migrant subjectivity itself. Diverse social, cultural, and political references were employed in the articulation of these representations, as migrants, politicians, native and migrant intellectuals, legislators, historians, writers, and artists all constituted different versions of subjectivity in migrancy. For migrants and those who lived in the context of transnational movement and exchange, there was never one single way of becoming a subject. On the contrary, becoming a subject—as a result of the continuous negotiation and interplay between different types of fantasy and imagination—remained tentative and performative. Thus the ambivalence, self-irony, and contradiction that often characterized the different performances of subjectivity that we discussed in the previous chapters. The study of the history of subjectivity has to account for the interaction—always situated historically and politically—between these different ways of becoming a subject.

Historical research in the archive of migrant cultural production revealed the conditions of generation of the narratives that eventually constituted the conceptual material for the emergence of migrant subjectivity within the intersecting cultural economies of Greek and American nationalisms. The historical formation of migrant subjectivity was explored on different levels of cultural production and sociopolitical interaction. The different levels of cultural production and the various types of materials that were analyzed did not suggest that the different forms of migrant subjectivity that emerged on these different levels eventually were conflated into an all-inclusive "subject." On the contrary, this analytical option foregrounded the "openendedness" of the process and the fluidity of concepts that were often perceived as fixed and stable (such as "the migrant," "the national subject," and "the nation"). Certainly, the history of migrant subjectivity during the first half of the century was also marked by moments of fixation when certain versions of how one was expected to be a migrant subject were hardened and became hegemonic. Reconstructing the history of subjectivity often requires keeping a double perspective: exploring both the cultural engineering of notions of subjecthood that become hegemonic, and the simultaneous operation of performative acts of subjectivity that attempt to defer fixation and maintain a certain degree of self-reflection and creativity.

Research in the cultural archive of Greek migration revealed the impossibility of a concrete narrative historical reconstruction of migrant culture and resulted in a discontinuous genealogical account of different aspects of that culture and its impact on how one became a subject in the context of transatlantic movement. My main aim was to trace the ways in which the history of migration was mediated by culture at different historical moments. How did the experience of migration become part of the nation's history? How was Greece transformed into a "nation of migrants"?[2] The focus of the historical reconstruction that I have pursued in this book has been continuously shifting in order to follow the changing intersection among different levels of temporality in culture. Culture constituted the terrain through which the history of migration was mediated and the site through which the past returned and was remembered, however fragmented, imperfect, or disavowed. Through that remembering and recomposition, new forms of subjectivity and community were thought and signified.[3]

The historical experience of Greek migration to the United States during the first half of the twentieth century resulted in the formation and generation of powerful representations of migrant subjectivity that were gradually reinscribed in culture as representations of nationhood and national identity. The representations of migrant subjectivity that we studied in the previous chapters constituted forms of resignification of already existing conceptualizations of Greek nationhood under the impact of the experience of migration. As my analysis has shown, these representations were diverse, fluid, and often contradictory, and they included elements and cultural references that varied depending on the level of cultural production. The stories of migration cannot be characterized as progressive or conservative, for one can trace both progressive and conservative, nationalist and alternative, regulative and emancipatory cultural elements in popular and official representations of migrant subjectivity.

Contrary to the claims that have been made recently in public debates over racism in countries like Greece and Italy—countries that have been transformed during the last decade from traditional senders of emigrants to new receptors of immigrants—the cultural heritage of the experience of migration cannot by itself function as a vaccination against contemporary racism and xenophobia. As I have shown, the experience of migration often led to the internalization of hierarchical discourses of racial and cultural inequality and superiority in migrant culture and self-conceptualizations. Furthermore, representations of migrant subjectivity were often grounded in the exclusion of certain aspects of the experience of migration from their representational order. The exclusion of women's experiences and the demonizing of images of womanhood often operated as a sine qua non condition for the articulation of culturally intelligible migrant self-representations. Representations of migration in Greek culture recapitulate both reactionary and progressive conceptual references. The history of migration is thus not by definition a progressive or alternative narrative.

In this book, I did not seek to renarrate the history of migration as an opposition to other versions of national narratives. Quite differently, through the study of the history of cultural representations of Greek migration in the twentieth century, I attempted to retrieve the modalities of self-conceptualization and the forms of cultural engineering of notions of nationhood and subjectivity. By focusing on the analysis of representations of migrant subjectivity, I sought to retrieve expressions of the long encounter of situated forms of sociality with modernity. The enactment and rearticulation of this type of historical knowledge in contemporary culture could create references for the formation of visions and practices of subject and community not governed by nationalist modes. My exploration thus constituted an engagement with the past that aimed at the creation of the space for this type of cultural enactment.

The history of Greek migration can indeed operate as an enactment of difference in the contemporary culture of the nation. This study of migrant representations of subjectivity attempted to locate practices of disidentification and resignification that the "outside-within" condition of migrants made possible. The enactment of difference within national culture does not constitute merely an attempt to articulate oppositional forms of identification against nationalist imperatives. On the contrary, disidentification allows for the exploration of alternative political and cultural subjectivities that emerge within the continuing effects of displacement.

Let me conclude by pointing out three possible ways in which the history of Greek migration may enact difference in the culture of the nation.

First, contrary to historical studies of national formations that have embraced the notion of an immutable link between cultures, peoples, or identities and specific places, my study of Greek migration offers a historical grounding for the conceptual dissociation between culture and closed spaces. As contemporary scholars of diaspora have argued, the study of migrant culture undermines the confidence in the permanent join between a particular culture and a stable terrain that has grounded modern notions of nationhood and subjectivity.[4] The physical migration and dislocation of Greek populations led to the formation of multiple shapes of Greek culture in different social and cultural contexts. In many cases, migration displaced the nation-state as the exclusive space of production of national culture, and thus migration enacted difference and heterogeneity in Greek national culture.

This form of differentiation was brought into the foreground under the impact of the repatriation to Greece of ethnically Greek populations that had been residing in former socialist countries. The arrival of repatriates, however, often led to the emergence of even more rigid nationalist modes of understanding subjectivity and community. The repatriates were either considered to represent the homogeneity and organicity of Hellenism beyond national borders, or were perceived as foreign elements within the national body, whose Greek heritage was to be denied. In *Ν' Ακούω Καλά τ' Ονομά Σου* [May I always hear good things about you], a novel published in Greece in 1993 that narrated the story of a Greek repatriate from Albania, the protagonist comments on his interaction with Greek natives in Greece: "We did not mingle with the local people in public. Once or twice that we met with locals at a house they were looking at us as if they were waiting for us to leave. . . . Only when we were singing they wanted us. Only then I was saying to myself that we were of the same blood. . . . One day a local kid threatened his female friends that he would give them to the Albanians. They were screaming jokingly and they were laughing and they did not care that we listened."[5]

Nationalist discourses and cultural practices tend to transform Albanian Greeks into Albanians, Russian Greeks into Russians, Romanian Greeks into Romanians, in the same way that American Greeks were transformed into Greeks (in the United States) or Americans (in Greece). Histories of migration and diaspora do not lead automatically to differentiation within the national culture. History needs to be mediated through culture; differentiation needs to be actively enacted in contemporary culture by cultural practitioners, critics, and educators.

Second, the study of the process of cultural engineering of migrant subjectivity foregrounds the ways in which linear representation of the nation as a homogeneous sociocultural entity were grounded in the exclusion of certain experiences from the representational order of culture. Pointing out the exclusion and misrepresentation of women's experience in mainstream narratives of Greek migration provides a challenge to the legitimacy of these narratives and signals the need for the writing of *different* histories—of nonelites, of insurgencies, of women—that would render representation and linear narrative as problematic categories. The introduction of *different* stories in historical representations could provide references for the articulation of alternative practices of community, subjectivity, and cultural politics.

Finally, the study of the history of migration illustrates the ways in which conceptualizations of the nation are always produced in the context of historical phenomena, social interactions, and cultural exchanges that transcend the territories of the nation-state. Migrant conceptualizations of subjectivity explicitly expressed the idea that culture and nationhood are always determined by historical experiences of encounters between situated forms of sociality and the imperatives of global economy and internationally dominant forms of culture. Migrant subjectivity was developed in the context of the migrants' "outside-within" position in relation to intersecting cultural settings. The reenactment of the history of migration may thus lead to the introduction of the "outside-within" condition as a constitutive element of contemporary culture in Greece. The transnationalization of our understanding of "our own" culture may provide the possibility for practices of community and politics that oppose nationalist modes of perception of ourselves and others, and claim difference as a reference for construction of political alliances and community.

From the perspective of a transnational understanding of national culture, the contemporary phenomenon of foreign migration to Greece would not be perceived as a threat to social bonds. On the contrary, migration would be perceived as an opportunity to insert new elements in national culture, as it were, to extract knowledge out of information and to create alternative social networks, political alliances, and interest groups that would enhance the vitality of contemporary culture in Greece and in Europe more generally.

The issue of enactment of memories of migration in the context of countries that are currently being transformed into recipients of migration was invoked in the Italian film *Lamerica*, by Gianni Amelio.[6] Amelio narrates the story of a young Italian businessman who travels to Albania with the goal of buying a former state-run industry and of appropriating in this way economic development funds. To fulfill this goal, the Italian businessman is advised by an Albanian middleman to use an old, wretched, and almost crazy Albanian man who would be presented to the authorities as the Albanian partner in the investment. A series of complications in the original plan forces the Italian businessman to come in close contact with the old Albanian as they wander together around a distressed Albania overflowing with people who are always on the move trying to find a way to flee the country. In the course of their adventures, it is revealed that the old man is in fact Italian, a World War II soldier, who after the defeat of Mussolini remained in Albania and changed his identity. As the old man regains memory of his origin and his personal history, his mind is caught in a historical time-lag; he relives his history as a young Sicilian man growing up in the economically distressed Italy of the interwar period. The association between social conditions in Italy at the beginning of the century and contemporary social conditions in Albania leads the subject to continuous temporal intersections. Memory blocks out reality, and history abolishes contemporaneity. On board a boat full of Albanian migrants heading to Italy, the old Italian thinks that he is actually on a steamboat heading for America. The young Italian businessman also aboard the same boat listens to the old man's delirium, speechless. Italy's history of migration is projected on Italy's present of xenophobia and racism. The clash between these intersecting orders of reality is catalytic and disorienting. The old man is trapped in the realm of insanity, the young Italian is muted, and contemporaneity is postponed.

Lamerica operates as a cultural form of mediation of history. The history of migration can challenge (or postpone) contemporary realities only if it is mediated by culture in ways that illustrate the connections between past and present, and enact the historicity of contemporary culture. Currently, the responsibility for the materialization of this cultural mediation lies with historians, educators, artists, cultural practitioners, and critics whose competence does not concern primarily the elaboration of truth claims about history but the participation in its making. After all, today history as such must also be written in the future anterior tense; history must also be written as *it will have been*. This book is intended as a contribution to the wider project of cultural mediation of history, enactment of the history of migration in contemporary culture, and production of historical knowledge that may create the possibility for alternative forms of subjectivity, community, and cultural politics to emerge.

Introduction

1. Mary Vardoulakis, *Gold in the Streets* (New York: Dodd, Mead, 1945), pp. 107–8.

2. Arjun Appadurai, "Patriotism and Its Futures," in *Modernity at Large: Cultural Dimensions of Globalization* (Minneapolis: University of Minnesota Press, 1996), p. 158.

3. Avtar Brah, *Cartographies of Diaspora: Contesting Identities* (London: Routledge, 1996), p. 211.

4. For a critique of this expansive use of the concept of diaspora and migrancy, see Pheng Cheah, "Given Culture: Rethinking Cosmopolitan Freedom in Transnationalism," in *Cosmopolitics: Thinking and Feeling beyond the Nation,* ed. Pheng Cheah and Bruce Robbins (Minneapolis: University of Minnesota Press, 1998), pp. 290–328.

5. Gayatri Spivak, "Foundations and Cultural Studies," in Questioning Foundations: Truth/Subjectivity/Culture, *ed.* Hugh J. Silverman (New York: Routledge, 1993); Etienne Balibar, "Is There a Neo-racism?" in *Race, Nation, Class: Ambiguous Identities* (London: Verso, 1991). For a critical review of theories of travel, diaspora, and exile, see Caren Kaplan, *Questions of Travel: Postmodern Discourses of Displacement* (Durham: Duke University Press, 1996).

6. Michael Hardt and Antonio Negri attempt to historicize the new global form of power in their book *Empire* (Cambridge, Mass.: Harvard University Press, 2000). Hardt and Negri develop Foucault's notion of biopower in order to trace the stages that have marked the evolution of global forms of power from nineteenth-century European imperialism and colonialism to contemporary forms. The vivacity of the debates that this book has caused since its publication is partly the result of scholars' and activists' need to find points of entry into the historicity of globalization.

7. In Europe migration is often dealt with as a "new" and "massively invasive" phenomenon. This is related to the lack of knowledge and research concerning the impact of migration on European politics and culture during the last two centuries. European historiography has addressed the issue of transatlantic migration only recently, during the last two decades; in countries such as Italy and Greece, whose twentieth-century history was significantly marked by emigration, the historiographical production on this topic remains very marginal. See Dirk Hoerder, *Labor Migration in the Atlantic Economies: The European and North American Working Classes during the Period of Industrialization* (Westport, Conn.: Greenwood Publishing Group, 1985); Dirk Hoerder and Leslie Page Moch, eds., *European Migrants: Global and Local Perspectives* (Boston: Northeastern University Press, 1996). New migrations to Europe during the last two decades have stirred academic debates and have produced excellent scholarship, especially concerning the migration of women.

8. Dirk Hoerder has argued in favor of a comparative approach that would view migration from the point of view of continental networks of exchange. See Dirk Hoerder, "From Euro- and Afro-Atlantic to Pacific Migration System: A Comparative Migration Approach to North American History," in *Rethinking American History in a Global Age,* ed. Thomas Bender (Berkeley: University of California Press, 2002), pp. 195–235. Shifting from a national to a continental perspective, Hoerder urges us not to approach systems of migration solely on the macro-historical level, but to reconsider, on the micro-level where agency is located, the multiple origins of American history as an "all people's history" that remains "at the same time many distinct people's histories."

9. American historians have recently undertaken the project to globalize the writing of American history. Thomas Bender, editor of an inspiring collection of essays, *Rethinking American History in a Global Age,* has asked important questions concerning the future orientation of historical research and writing: "Can we imagine an American historical narrative that situates the United States more fully in its larger transnational and intercultural global context? Can such a narrative reveal more clearly than the histories we have at present the plenitude of stories, timescales, and geographies that constitute the American past? Can we historicize the nation itself in such a way that its historical career and its making and unmaking of identities, national and otherwise, can be better understood outside of itself, as part of a larger history than that of the bounded nation?" ("Historians, the Nation, and the Plenitude of Narratives," in *Rethinking American History in a Global Age,* ed. Bender, p.10). This recent reorientation toward continental and transatlantic historical perspectives was introduced by scholars of the African diaspora in particular, who insisted on the need to take the Atlantic—and not the nation-state—as the basic unit of analysis in the exploration of modernity, migrations, and diasporas. See Paul Gilroy, "Cultural Studies and Ethnic Absolutism," *Cultural Studies,* ed. Lawrence Grossberg, Cary Nelson, and Paula A. Treichler (New York: Routledge, 1992), p. 192. Drawing on a long tradition of thinkers, including C. L. R. James, W. E. B. Du Bois, and Richard Wright, Gilroy further developed this idea in *The Black Atlantic: Modernity and Double Consciousness* (Cambridge, Mass.: Harvard University Press, 1993).

10. For a comprehensive account of American historiography on immigration, see Edward Saneth, *American Historians and European Immigrants 1875–1925* (New York: Russell and Russell, 1965 [1948]).

11. On the history of European historiography see Georg Iggers, *Historiography in the Twentieth Century: From Scientific Objectivity to the Postmodern Challenge* (Hanover, N.H.: Wesleyan University Press, 1997 [1993]); and Iggers, *The German Conception of History: The National Tradition of Historical Thought from Herder to the Present* (Middletown: Wesleyan University Press, 1968).

12. Saskia Sassen, *Guests and Aliens* (New York: New Press, 1999), p. 5.

13. Rey Chow, *The Protestant Ethnic and the Spirit of Capitalism* (New York: Columbia University Press, 2002), pp. 32–33. Chow proposes a shift of paradigm in the study of ethnicity when she replaces the notion of the resisting subject with that of the protestant ethnic subject. She argues that to be an ethnic subject is to protest, "but perhaps less for actual emancipation of any kind than for the benefits of worldwide visibility, currency, and circulation . . . because protesting constitutes the economically logical and socially visible vocation" for ethnics to assume (p. 48). Although I find this a path-breaking analytical move in the study of ethnic and transnational subjects, the question remains: if ethnic protest, as an act that renders one a subject, is determined by economic logic and social visibility, then who determines the latter? If the terms of visibility are imposed by "US politicians, businessmen, missionaries, media personalities, and academics" who "do the human rights story," as Chow seems to imply, then are we prompted to understand ethnic subjectivity as overdetermined and imposed by these groups rather than as a product of continuous negotiation—even though unequal—between people occupying shifting subjective positions?

14. Luisa Passerini has criticized the use of adjectives before the term *subjectivity* because the multiplication of subjectivities refers us to the stiffness of some identity politics and reduces subjectivity drastically, depriving it of its doubleness and privileging exclusively its empirical contents. Passerini argues that instead of pluralizing subjectivity, we should talk of different locations that people as groups and as individuals can have within the field of

subjectivity. See Luisa Passerini, "Becoming a Subject in the Time of the Death of the Subject," paper given at the Fourth European Feminist Research Conference, Bologna, September 2000, available online at: <www.women.it/cyberarchive/files/passerini.htm>. My use of the term *migrant subjectivity* refers exactly to these different locations that those who migrate take within the field of modern subjectivity. At the same time, *migrant subjectivity* refers to the new modes of becoming a subject and subjectivation that emerged in the context of migration and the transnational movement. Aiwa Ong has argued that these new modes of subjectivation are drastically shaped by the conditions of transnational mobility and consist of "flexible practices, strategies and disciplines associated with transnational capitalism," related to "new modes of subject making and new kinds of valorized subjectivity" (Aiwa Ong, *Flexible Citizenship: The Cultural Logics of Transnationality* [Durham: Duke University Press, 1999], pp. 18–19).

15. Passerini, "Becoming a Subject in the Time of the Death of the Subject."

16. Michel Foucault, "Nietzsche, Genealogy, History," in *Language, Counter-Memory, Practice,* ed. Donald F. Bouchard (Ithaca, N.Y.: Cornell University Press, 1977 [1971]), pp. 139–40.

17. Ibid., p. 154. See also Foucault's discussion of "differentiations" in *The Archaeology of Knowledge* (London: Tavistock, 1974 [1969]).

18. Passerini has stressed the importance of intersubjectivity and has argued that processes of recognition are necessary for the constitution of subjectivity, since recognition assumes both self-reflection and conflict. See Passerini, "Becoming a Subject in the Time of the Death of the Subject." See also Luisa Passerini, ed., *Identitá culturale Europea: Idee, sentimenti, relazioni* (Florence: La Nuova Italia, 1998).

19. For the use of the notion of circuit in a framework of cultural analysis of the nation, see Richard Johnson, "Towards a Cultural Theory of the Nation: A British-Dutch Dialogue," in *Images of the Nation: Different Meanings of Dutchness 1870–1940,* ed. Annemieke Galema et al. (Amsterdam: Rodopi, 1993), pp. 159–218; Johnson, "Frameworks of Culture and Power: Complexity and Politics in Cultural Studies," *Critical Studies* 3, no. 1 (1991).

20. For example, under the impact of the dominant political doctrine of forced "Americanization" in the United States in the 1920s, the Greek communities engaged in a broad debate concerning the need to separate—as efficiently as possible—the private from the public sphere of the community's social interaction as a way of retaining at least a part of the migrant self "unassimilated."

21. Mainly in Gilles Deleuze and Félix Guattari, *A Thousand Plateaus: Capitalism and Schizophrenia* (Minneapolis: University of Minnesota Press, 1987 [1980]).

22. Stuart Hall's article "Cultural Identity and Diaspora" remains a powerful inspiration for imagining identity as difference. Hall also turned to the continental concepts of "American," "European," and African "presences" in order to unpack diasporic identities and avoid reducing them to minoritarian versions of nationhood. Stuart Hall, "Cultural Identity and Diaspora," in *Identity: Community, Culture, Difference,* ed. Jonathan Rutherford (London: Lawrence & Wishart, 1990), pp. 222–37.

23. David Roediger, ed., *Towards the Abolition of Whiteness: Essays on Race, Politics and Working Class History* (London: Verso, 1994); Noel Ignatiev, *How the Irish Became White* (New York: Routledge, 1995); Matthew Frye Jacobson, *Special Sorrows: The Diasporic Imagination of Irish, Polish and Jewish Immigrants in the United States* (Cambridge, Mass.: Harvard University Press, 1995); Jacobson, *Whiteness of a Different Color: European Immigrants and the Alchemy of Race* (Cambridge, Mass.: Harvard University Press, 1998); and Jacobson, *Barbarian Virtues: The United States Encounters Foreign Peoples at Home and Abroad, 1876–1917* (New York: Hill and Wang, 2000).

Chapter One

1. Hannah Arendt, *On Revolution* (London: Penguin Books, 1990), pp. 181–82.

2. Ibid., p. 180.

3. Jon Stratton and Ien Ang, "Multicultural Imagined Communities. Cultural Difference and National Identity in the USA and Australia," in *Multicultural States: Rethinking Difference and Identity,* ed. David Bennet (London: Routledge, 1998), p. 141.

4. On the racial character of the 1790 Naturalization Act, see Matthew Frye Jacobson, *Barbarian Virtues: The United States Encounters Foreign Peoples at Home and Abroad, 1876–1917* (New York: Hill and Wang, 2000), p. 191.

5. In Matthew Frye Jacobson, *Whiteness of a Different Color: European Immigrants and the Alchemy of Race* (Cambridge, Mass.: Harvard University Press, 1998), p. 25.

6. Daniel Rodgers, "An Age of Social Politics," in *Rethinking American History in a Global Age,* ed. Thomas Bender (Berkeley: University of California Press, 2002), pp. 250–73.

7. Daniel Rodgers, *Atlantic Crossings: Social Politics in a Progressive Age* (Cambridge, Mass.: Belknap Press of Harvard University Press, 1998).

8. Thomas Peyser, *Utopia and Cosmopolis: Globalization in the Era of American Literary Realism* (Durham: Duke University Press, 1998).

9. See Lewis Mumford, *The Story of Utopias* (New York: Boni and Liveright, 1922). The close connection between utopian thought, visions of social engineering, and social reform projects is documented in the work of personalities like H. G. Wells who combined the roles of social reformer, publicist, utopian thinker, and science-fiction author. For an elaboration of the relation between social reform, utopian thought, and notions of globality, see Ioanna Laliotou, "Visions of the World, Visions of America: Science Fiction and Other Transatlantic Utopias at the Turn of the Century" in *Across the Atlantic: Cultural Exchanges between Europe and the United States,* ed. Luisa Passerini (Brussels: P.I.E.–Peter Lang, 2000), pp. 99–115.

10. Rey Chow has taken up Foucault's notion of biopolitics in order to interpret ethnicity and racial discrimination as a "logical manifestation of biopower, the point of which is not simply to kill but to generate life, to manage and optimize it, to make it better for the future of the human species" (Rey Chow, *The Protestant Ethnic and the Spirit of Capitalism* [New York: Columbia University Press, 2002], p. 7). My aim in this chapter is to show how, during the first decades of the twentieth century, "biopolitics" in this sense was expressed through projects of cultural and racial engineering that concerned the so-called "immigration problem" and that sought to "produce" the migrants as social subjects.

11. Jeremiah Jenks et al., *The Immigration Problem: A Study of American Immigration Conditions and Needs* (New York: Funk & Wagnalls, 1912), pp. 24–25 (my emphasis).

12. On the role of the Immigration Commission, see M. F. Behar, *Our National Gates: Shut, Ajar or Open?* (New York, 1916). The commission had nine members, three appointed by the Senate, three by the House, and three by the president. On the conflict between the Senate and the president over the control of the commission, see Oscar Handlin, *Race and Nationality in the United States* (Boston: Little, Brown, 1957), p. 99.

13. Jenks et al., *The Immigration Problem,* p. xv.

14. U.S. Immigration Commission, *Reports of Immigration Commission,* vols. 1–42 (Washington, D.C.: U.S. Government Printing Office, 1911).

15. On the tasks of the Immigration Commission, see also Ronald M. Pavalko, "Racism and the New Immigration: A Reinterpretation of the Assimilation of White Ethnics in American Society," *Sociology and Social Research* 65, no. 1 (1980): 56–77.

16. John Higham, *Strangers in the Land, Patterns of American Nativism, 1860–1925* (New Brunswick, N.J.: Rutgers University Press, 1988), p. 189.

17. Such organizations included the Immigration Restriction League, the Eugenical

Association, the Patriotic Order, Sons of America, the Junior Order, United American Mechanics, the Farmers' Educational and Cooperative Union of America, and the Council of Jewish Women; see Pavalko, "Racism and the New Immigration," p. 60.

18. Jenks et al., *The Immigration Problem*, p. 1.

19. Ibid, pp. 1–2.

20. Roland Robertson, " 'Civilization' and the Civilizing Process: Elias, Globalization and Analytic Synthesis," in *Cultural Theory and Cultural Change*, ed. Mike Featherstone (London: Sage Publications, 1992), pp. 211–27.

21. Jenks et al., *The Immigration Problem*, p. 5.

22. Ibid.

23. Ibid.

24. Dr. Daniel Folkmar and Dr. Elnora C. Folkmar, *Dictionary of Races and Peoples*, U.S. Immigration Commission Reports, 61st Cong., 3d sess., Senate, vol. 5, doc. 662 (Washington, D.C.: U.S. Government Printing Office, 1911). The use of the term *race* in this period was quite loose and flexible. It is difficult to distinguish the cases when reference was made to ethnic, national, or racial origin. In the *Dictionary of Races and Peoples* the term was used in place of the terms *nationality* and *ethnicity*. Nevertheless, as it has been noted, "whether such official definitions create or reflect public conceptions of reality is difficult to ascertain and certainly debatable. The point is that they were part and parcel of the rhetoric used to discuss and debate the issue of immigration" (Pavalko, "Racism and the New Immigration," p. 61).

25. Ibid., p. 62. On the *Dictionary of Races*, see Handlin, *Race and Nationality in the United States*, pp. 101–8.

26. Higham, *Strangers in the Land*, p. l33; Thomas Gossett, *Race: The History of an Idea in America* (Dallas: Southern Methodist University, 1963), p. 133.

27. Nevertheless, the argument concerning the lack of "sharp physical differences between native Americans and European immigrants" breathes an air of anachronism, since a closer study of the imagery of migrants in this period shows that these physical differences were more than apparent to the Anglo-Saxons as well as to the migrants from Southern Europe. For a very vivid iconographic account of the starkness of physical differences, see Edward Steiner, *On the Trail of the Immigrant* (New York: Fleming H. Revell Company, 1906), especially pp. 282–91 concerning Greek migrants. On the interrelation between the visibility of physical differences and anti-Greek nativist attacks, see John G. Bitzes, "The Anti-Greek riot of 1909—South Omaha," *Nebraska History* 51, no 2 (Summer 1970): 199–224; Helen Zeese Papanicolas, "The Greeks of Carbon County," *Utah Historical Quarterly* 22 (1954): 143–64.

28. Jenks et al., *The Immigration Problem*, p. 6.

29. According to this argument the black race was dying out because of high incidence of tuberculosis, venereal disease, and other life-threatening diseases closely related to inherent immorality. See Carol M. Taylor, "W. E. B. Dubois's Challenge to Scientific Racism," *Journal of Black Studies* 11, no. 4 (1981): 451. As Taylor shows, the vital place that the argument had in the articulation and support of white supremacist racial discourse is proved by the fact that distinguished scholars and political activists such as W. E. B. Du Bois often undertook the task of publicly denouncing it, even by use of statistical data suggesting the contrary.

30. Jenks et al., *The Immigration Problem*, pp. 124–25.

31. Ibid., p. 172.

32. Ibid., p. 173.

33. For an interesting approach to the position that American trade unions held on the issue of immigration and literacy, see A. T. Lane, *Solidarity or Survival? American Labor and European Immigrants, 1830–1924* (New York: Greenwood Press, 1987).

34. On the role that the commission's position on this issue played in the political developments (especially in terms of the pre-election political battles) in this period, see Higham,
Strangers in the Land, p. 189.

35. Jenks et al., *The Immigration Problem*, p. 6.

36. On the deepening and culmination of these political attitudes in more lasting forms of
political and social consciousness in the 1920s, see Paul L. Murphy, "Sources and Nature of
Intolerance in the 1920s," in *Nativism, Discrimination, and Images of Immigrants*, ed. George E.
Pozzetta (New York: Garland Publishing, 1991).

37. Jenks et al., *The Immigration Problem*, p. 6.

38. Ibid., p. 124.

39. Ibid., p. 6.

40. Ibid., p.7.

41. Ibid., p. 172.

42. Stuart Hall has demonstrated in an exemplary way the discursive association between
migration and criminality in the late twentieth century. See Hall et al., *Policing the Crisis:
Mugging, the State, and Law and Order* (London: Macmillan, 1978).

43. Kenneth M. Ludmerer, "Genetics, Eugenics, and the Immigration Restriction Act of
1924," in *Nativism, Discrimination, and Images of Immigrants*, ed. Pozzetta, p. 367.

44. See Pavalko, "Racism and the New Immigration," p. 60; Kenneth M. Ludmerer, "American Genetics and Eugenics Movement: 1905–1935," *Journal of the History of Biology* 2, no. 2
(Fall 1969): 337–62.

45. Francis Galton, *Hereditary Genius: An Inquiry into Its Laws and Consequences* (London:
Macmillan, 1869); *Inquiries into Human Faculty and Its Development* (London: Macmillan,
1883).

46. Cited in Nancy Stepan, *The Idea of Race in Science: Great Britain 1800–1960* (London:
Macmillan, 1982), p. 111.

47. For eugenic notions of survival as a genetic racial merit, see Paul Crook, *Darwinism,
War and History* (Cambridge: Cambridge University Press, 1994), pp.130–52.

48. Stepan, *The Idea of Race in Science: Great Britain 1800–1960*, p. 113.

49. For example, in Brazil eugenics "instead of being overly racialist, appears to have taken
from the beginning a somewhat non-racialist, environmentalist orientation; infant and family
hygiene and nutrition were the concerns, so that the inherent genetic worth of the individual
had the best chance of full expression" (ibid., p. 124).

50. Higham, *Strangers in the Land*, pp. 150–53, 191, 201; James Allen Rogers, "Darwinism
and Social Darwinism," *Journal of the History of Ideas* 33, no. 2 (1986): 265–80; Ludmerer,
"American Genetics and Eugenics Movement," pp. 337–62.

51. See Robert Young, *Colonial Desire: Hybridity in Theory, Culture and Race* (London:
Routledge, 1995).

52. Elazar Barkan, *The Retreat of Scientific Racism: Changing Concepts of Race in Britain
and the United States between the World Wars* (Cambridge: Cambridge University Press, 1992),
p. 17.

53. On the notion of "preconceptual plane," see David Theo Goldberg, "The Social Formation of Racist Discourse," in *Anatomy of Racism*, ed. Goldberg (Minneapolis: University of
Minnesota Press, 1990), p. 298.

54. Ludmerer, "American Genetics and Eugenics Movement," pp. 352–55.

55. Stepan, *The Idea of Race in Science: Great Britain 1800–1960*, p. 128.

56. From the late 1920s the appeal of eugenics diminished within the scientific community. It has been suggested that the surrender of scientific racism in the interwar period had a

twofold origin: (1) the realization that current genetic knowledge promised no quick hereditary improvement of the human race; and (2) the Nazi terror. Anti-eugenicism often was not inspired by antiracism. On the contrary, its main thrust was the conviction that the Americans and the British "knew better" how to manage their social problems. It could be said that anti-Germanism led to adoption of humanitarianism and cultural racism, by ostracizing modernity's terrifying aspect—fascism—as a distinctively German monstrosity (a German technology of supremacist politics of domination). The scientists who denounced eugenicism at the dawn of German fascist racial policies were driven by a sort of humanitarianism expressed through and combined with anti-Germanism. On the connection between the decline of eugenics and the rise of anti-Germanism, see Barkan, *The Retreat of Scientific Racism;* Ludmerer, "American Genetics and Eugenics Movement," pp. 352–62.

57. I use the term *politicization* not in the sense of *rendering political,* since racial perception cannot be anything but political in any case. I refer here to the process through which at that time these perceptions became a first priority political issue.

58. Kenneth Roberts, *Why Europe Leaves Home* (Indianapolis: Bobbs & Merrill, 1922).

59. The Immigration Restriction Act of 1924 aimed at the restriction of migration by imposing a national quota system as a mode of regulation of the numbers of new arrivals of migrants to the United States. The act's sponsor, Rep. Albert Johnson, was chairman of the committee and one of the protagonists of the antimigration campaign. It has been observed concerning the Immigration Restriction Act of 1924 that "the national origins system offered a direct implementation of racial nationalism and an answer to all charges of discrimination. It gave expression to the tribal mood, and comfort to the democratic conscience" (Higham, *Strangers in the Land,* p. 323). On the issue of the Immigration Restriction Act of 1924 see also William S. Bernard, ed., *American Immigration Policy: A Reappraisal* (New York: Harper, 1950). On the relation between the act and racial politics see Mae Ngai, "The Architecture of Race in American Immigration Law: A Re-examination of the Immigration Act of 1924," *Journal of American History* 86 (1999): 59–86.

60. Higham, *Strangers in the Land,* p. 313.

61. Roberts, *Why Europe Leaves Home,* p. 4.

62. On the distinction between the notion of the migrant and that of the nomad, see Gilles Deleuze and Félix Guattari, *A Thousand Plateaus: Capitalism and Schizophrenia* (Minneapolis: University of Minnesota Press, 1987 [1980]), p. 381. They argue that what defines the difference between the two is their different disposition toward the concept of origin: "whereas the immigrant leaves behind a milieu that has become amorphous and hostile, the nomad is the one who does not depart, does not want to depart, who clings to the smooth space left by the receding forest, where the steppe, or the desert advances." In this sense, the migrant is connected—in positive or negative ways—with a point of departure, whereas the nomad *does not have* any point of departure, or origin as such; the nomad is always already in motion and for this reason, according to Deleuze and Guattari, escapes subjectivation.

63. Roberts, *Why Europe Leaves Home,* p. 23.

64. Ibid., pp. 5–6.

65. In terms of narrative structure, it is interesting to note that ten of the thirty-three pages of Roberts's introductory chapter are dedicated to Jewish populations of Europe and Jewish immigration to the United States. Considering the number of ethnicities covered in the book, this representation is disproportionate, and in this sense it indicates the particular gravity that Jewishness acquired in the context of negative representations of Europe.

66. Roberts, *Why Europe Leaves Home,* p. 17.

67. Ibid., pp. 17–18.

68. Ibid., p. 14.

69. Ibid., p. 22. Here Roberts refers to the conflict between eugenicists and anthropologists who were arguing that migrants may belong originally to racial stocks different than the dominant Anglo-Saxon stock, but nevertheless the racial traits that constituted their difference tended to disappear within a certain period of time after their establishment in the United States because of the transformation of the environmental and sociocultural conditions. This conflict was central in the debates over migration. Roberts makes a direct reference to anthropologist Franz Boas who in 1908 was entrusted with the investigation of the physical characteristics of migrants. In his report, *Changes in the Bodily Form of Descendants of Immigrants,* Senate Doc. 208, 61st Cong., 2d sess. (Washington, D.C.: U.S. Government Printing Office, 1911), he argued that the differences between first- and second-generation Americans born of different ethnicities were smaller than between the respective European populations. Boas refuted the very notion of permanence of physical types or characteristics that was the basis of racial theories and politics in this period. His opinion remained marginal in the circles of the Immigration Commission, since they went against the fundamental principles that were dominant among members of the commission. Later, Boas testified at the Supreme Court in favor of the Armenians' case that they belonged to the white race and should be thus allowed to migrate to the United States.

70. Roberts, *Why Europe Leaves Home,* p. 2.

71. Ibid., pp. 3–4.

72. Ibid., p. 5.

73. Ibid., p. 3.

74. Slavoj Žižek, *For They Know Not What They Do: Enjoyment as a Political Factor* (London: Verso, 1991).

75. The psychoanalytical framework of analysis of racism is very instructive. However, its general application may lead to the construction of a totally "empty," and thus passive and homogeneous, figure of the racial "other." This mechanistic employment of the framework often results in undermining the historical complexity of racism by means of a totalizing gesture of interpretation that obliterates differences and diversity. On the role of psychoanalysis in the study of racism, see Stepen Frosh, "Psychoanalysis and Racism," in *Crises of the Self,* ed. Barry Richards (London: Free Association Press, 1989).

76. Henry Fairfield Osborn, "Shall We Maintain Washington's Ideal of Americanism?" in *The Alien in our Midst,* ed. M. Grant and Chas. Stewart Davison (New York: Galton Publishing Co., 1923), pp. 204–9.

77. Gossett, *Race,* p. 388.

78. Osborn, "Shall We Maintain," p. 207 (emphasis in original).

79. Ibid., pp. 207–8.

80. Ibid., p. 209.

81. See Barkan, *The Retreat of Scientific Racism;* Stepan, *The Idea of Race in Science: Great Britain 1800–1960.*

82. The shift from biological to cultural racism can be documented on different levels of cultural, political, and intellectual discourse in that period. Susan Koshy has very persuasively traced this shift in the politics of cultural representation in the work of D. W. Griffith and especially in the difference in the director's disposition toward race politics between his two films *The Birth of a Nation* (1915) and *Broken Blossoms* (1919); see Koshy, "American Nationhood as Eugenic Romance," *Differences* 12, no. 1 (Spring 2001): 50–78.

83. Horace Kallen, *Culture and Democracy in the United States* (New York: Boni and Liveright, 1924).

84. Ibid., p. 64.

85. Walter Michaels, *Our America: Nativism, Modernism, and Pluralism* (Durham: Duke University Press, 1995), p. 140.

86. Randolph Bourne, "Trans-national America," *Atlantic Monthly* 118 (July 1916): 86–97.

87. Matthew Frye Jacobson traces the connection between U.S. domestic and international politics in relation to "foreign peoples" in *Barbarian Virtues: The United States Encounters Foreign Peoples at Home and Abroad, 1876–1917* (New York: Hill and Wang, 2000).

88. Emory S. Bogartus, *Essentials of Americanization* (Los Angeles: University of Southern California Press, 1920), p. 14.

89. Julius Drachsler, *Democracy and Assimilation: The Blending of Immigrant Heritages in America* (New York: Macmillan, 1920), p. 191.

90. Ibid., pp. 20–23.

91. Ibid., p. 184.

92. Ibid., pp. 233–34. See also Winthrop Talbot, *Americanization, Principles of Americanism, Essentials of Americanization, Technic of Race-Assimilation: Annotated Bibliography* (New York: H. W. Wilson Co., 1917).

93. Robert Park, *The Immigrant Press and Its Control* (New York: Harper & Brothers, 1922), pp. 70–71. This book was published in the "Studies in Methods of Americanization" series, which included books that dealt with the role of education, industrial life, community life, neighborhood, and health services in the Americanization of new immigrants. According to the editors of the series, Americanization meant "the union of native and foreign born in all the most fundamental relationships and activities of national life. . . . Such americanization should perpetuate . . . growing and broadening, national life, inclusive of the best wherever found" ("Publisher's Note").

94. Drachsler, *Democracy and Assimilation*, pp. 211–23.

95. Ibid., p. 218.

Chapter Two

1. Saskia Sassen, *Guests and Aliens* (New York: New Press, 1999), p. 2.

2. Ibid., pp. 68–69.

3. R. J. B. Bosworth, *Italy and the Wider World, 1860–1960* (London: Routledge, 1996), p. 123.

4. Dino Cinel, *The National Integration of Italian Return Migration, 1870–1929* (Cambridge: Cambridge University Press, 1991).

5. Pasquale Verdicchio, *Bound by Distance: Rethinking Nationalism through the Italian Diaspora* (London: Associated University Presses, 1997), pp. 90–91.

6. Ira Emke-Poulopoulou, *Προβλήματα Μετανάστευσης-Παλιννόστησης* [Problems of migration and repatriation] (Athens: Institute for the Study of Greek Economy, Greek Association of Demographic Studies, 1986), p. 39.

7. Ibid., p. 33.

8. Artemis Leontis has traced the literary mappings of the Greek homeland from the 1880s to the 1960s in her book *Topographies of Hellenism: Mapping the Homeland* (Ithaca: Cornell University Press, 1995).

9. On the history of merchant communities, see Traian Stoianovich, "The Conquering, Balkan, Orthodox Merchant," *Journal of Economic History* 20 (1960): 234–313. On the history of Greek diasporic communities in the Ottoman period, see "Ο Ελληνισμός στη Δύση" [Hellenism in the West], in *Ιστορία του Ελληνικού Έθνους* [History of the Greek nation], vol. 1 (1453–1669) (Athens, 1980), pp. 230–45; Olga Katsiardi-Hering, *Η Ελληνική*

Παροικία Τεργέστης, 1751–1830 [The Greek community in Trieste, 1751–1830] (Athens, 1984).

10. On the history of the politics of the "Great Idea" in the broader area, see Antonis Liakos, *Η Ιταλική Ενοποίηση και η Μεγάλη Ιδέα* [The Italian unification and the great idea] (Athens: Themelio, 1985).

11. Alexander Kitroeff, "The Transformation of Homeland-Diaspora Relations: The Greek Case in the Nineteenth and Twentieth Centuries," in *Proceedings of the First International Congress on the Hellenic Diaspora: From Antiquity to Modern Times*, ed. John M. Fossey, vol. 2, *From 1453 to Modern Times* (Amsterdam: J.C. Gieben, 1991), p. 238; I. K. Chasiotis, *Επισκόπηση της Ιστορίας της Νεοελληνικής Διασποράς* [A review of the history of modern Greek diaspora] (Thessaloniki: Vanias, 1993).

12. On the idea that the state constitutes the nation's political workshop, see Ion Dragoumis, *Ελληνικός Πολιτισμός* [Greek culture] (Athens, 1927 [1914]); and Periclis Yiannopoulos, *Νέον Πνεύμα* [New spirit] (Athens, 1906).

13. G. Maurogordatos and Ch. Chatziosif, eds., *Βενιζελισμός και Αστικός Εκσυγχρονισμός* [Venizelism and civic modernization] (Heraklion: Crete University Press, 1988); Thanos Veremis, *Μελετήματα για τον Βενιζέλο και την Εποχή του* [Studies on Venizelos and his era] (Athens: Philippotis, 1980); Antonis Liakos, *Εργασία και Πολιτική στην Ελλάδα του Μεσοπολέμου. Το Διεθνές Γραφείο Εργασίας και η Ανάδυση των Κοινωνικών Θεσμών* [Labor and politics in interwar Greece: The International Labor Office and the emergence of social institutions] (Athens, 1993).

14. On the impact of "refugeeness" on Greek culture, see Grigorios Dafnis, *Η Ελλάς Μεταξύ Δύο Πολέμων 1923–1940* [Greece between two wars] (Athens: Ikaros, 1955). On the ethnic homogenization of the Greek population in that period, see Athanasios Protonotarios, *Το Προσφυγικό Πρόβλημα Από Ιστορικής, Νομικής και Κρατικής Απόψεως* [The refugee problem from historical, legal and state perspectives] (Athens: Pyrsos, 1929); see also Dimitri Pentzopoulos, *The Balkan Exchange of Minorities and Its Impact upon Greece* (Paris: Mouton, 1962).

15. Ioannis Tournakis, *Μετανάστευσις και Μεταναστευτική Πολιτική* [Migration and migration policy] (Athens, 1923), p. 17.

16. Andreas Andreadis had already published a series of articles on the Greek migration in which he compared the emergent Greek communities in the United States with older Greek diasporic communities in the Orient. See Andreas Andreadis, "Les émigrants grecs aux Etats-Unis," *Bulletin d'Orient* 212 (12 January 1908), 213 (25 January 1908), 220 (14 March 1908), 222 (28 March 1908), 226 (25 April 1908).

17. Andreas Andreadis, *Η Ελληνική Μετανάστευσις* [The Greek migration] (Athens, 1917).

18. The questionnaire consisted of nine main questions concerning the chronological development of migration in different provinces; causes of migration; conditions of migrant life abroad (destinations, professions, ways of life); number, age, and social background of migrants; economic consequences of migration for the places of origin; moral consequences ("Did the migrants progress in terms of culture and education and to what extent? Did they contract contagious diseases which they spread in their homelands?"); national consequences of migration ("How is the migrants' national consciousness threatened by migration?"); and legislation on migration and its effectiveness.

19. See *Πρακτικά της Βουλής* [Parliamentary proceedings], Athens, Greece, for the period 1910–20.

20. Ioannis Tournakis, *Μετανάστευσις και Μεταναστευτική Πολιτική* [Migration and migration policy] (Athens, 1923); see also his book *Διεθνής Μεταναστευτική Κίνησις* [International migration movement] (Athens, 1930).

21. Tournakis, *Μετανάστευσις και Μεταναστευτική Πολιτική* [Migration and migration policy], p. 9.

22. Ibid., pp. 22–23.

23. Ibid., p. 15.

24. This position was also held by antimigrant nativists in the United States at the same time, though they reached it from a radically different point of view.

25. In this respect he also suggested that migration policy as a public affairs issue should be considered alongside other emerging fields of public interest, such as tourism. This position was later adopted in the period of the dictatorship of Ioannis Metaxas (1936–40). See "Τύπος και τουρισμός" [Press and tourism], in *4 Αυγούστου 1936–4 Αυγούστου 1940. Τέσσερα Χρόνια Διακυβέρνησης Ιωάννη Μεταξά* [4 August 1936–4 August 1940: Four years of Ioannis Metaxas governing] (Athens, 1940).

26. Tournakis, *Μετανάστευσις και Μεταναστευτική Πολιτική* [Migration and migration policy], p. 23.

27. Chr. Christophis, *Ύλη προς Σύνταξιν Νομοσχεδίου περί Μεταναστεύσεως* [Material for a migration bill] (Piraeus, 1905); *Η εξ Ελλάδος Μετανάστευσις. Η Έκθεσις της Επιτροπής της Βουλής και Σχετική Πρότασις Νόμου* [Migration from Greece: The report prepared by the Parliamentary Committee, accompanied by relevant bill] (Athens, 1906); Emmanuel Repoulis, *Μελέτη περί Μεταναστεύσεως μετά Σχεδίου Νόμου* [Study and bill on migration] (Athens, 1912).

28. *Η εξ Ελλάδος Μετανάστευσις. Η Έκθεσις της Επιτροπής της Βουλής και Σχετική Πρότασις Νόμου* [Migration from Greece: The report prepared by the Parliamentary Committee, accompanied by relevant bill], p. 1.

29. S. Balanos, *Έκθεσις του Αποσταλλέντος εις Ιταλίαν Τμηματάρχου της Μεταναστεύσεως προς τον Υπουργόν Εσωτερικών* [Report on the Italian Migration, submitted by the head of the Migration Office to the minister of Domestic Affairs] (Athens, 1911), p. 129.

30. On the restrictions that applied to the migration and repatriation of Greek slavophone Macedonian subjects, see Christos Mandatzis, "Μετανάσταση και Ταυτότητα. Η Περίπτωση των Μακεδόνων Ελλήνων Μεταναστών" [Migration and identity: The case of Macedonian Greek migrants], in *Ταυτότητες στη Μακεδονία* [Identities in Macedonia], ed. Yiorgos Angelopoulos et al. (Athens: Papazisis, 1997), pp. 197–228.

31. "Περί τροποποιήσεως του Β. Διατάγματος 'Περί Μεταναστεύσεως'" [Amendment to the Royal Decree on Migration], *Εφημερίς της Κυβερνήσεως* [Government Gazette] 25 (18 February 1921).

32. Doris Weatherford, *Foreign and Female: Immigrant Women in America, 1840–1930* (New York: Schocken Books, 1986), p. 187; see also International Labor Office, *Emigration and Migration: Legislation and Treaties* (Geneva, 1922), pp. 13–24.

33. Agni Roussopoulou, *Οδηγός Ιδρυμάτων Κοινωνικής Πρόνοιας* [A guide to social welfare institutions] (Athens, 1936), p. 146.

34. Epitropi tis Voulis, *Η εξ Ελλάδος Μετανάστευσις. Η Έκθεσις της Επιτροπής της Βουλής και η Σχετική Πρότασις Νόμου* [Migration from Greece: Report by the government-appointed committee and bill proposal] (Athens, 1906), p. 19.

35. "Τα ταξείδια των μεταναστών" [The migrants' travels], *Ανεξάρτητος Αθηνών* [Athens Independent] 5 (4 February 1911): 310.

36. *Πρακτικά της Βουλής* [Parliamentary proceedings, Athens, Greece], 27.1.1920, p. 1, and 21.5.1920, pp. 1, 8; Public Law 1920–2475. See also Xenophon Zolotas, *Μετανάστευσις και Οικονομική Ανάπτυξις* [Migration and economic development] (Athens, 1966), p. 72.

37. Epitropi tis Voulis, *Η εξ Ελλάδος Μετανάστευσις. Η Έκθεσις της Επιτροπής της Βουλής και η Σχετική Πρότασις Νόμου* [Migration from Greece: Report by the government-appointed committee and bill proposal], p. 29.

38. Ion Dragoumis, *Ο Ελληνισμός μου και οι Έλληνες* [My Hellenism and the Greeks] (Athens, 1927 [1903–9]), p. 20.

39. I. D. Asimakopoulos, "Μετανάστασις εις Αμερικήν" [Migration to America], *Η Σφαίρα* [The Globe], 12 May 1882, pp. 2–3.

40. For later uses of this theme, see Emmanuil Likoudis, *Οι Μετανάσται* [The migrants] (New York: Proskopos Press, 1919), pp. 1, 15, 16; Vasileios Valaoras, *Ο Ελληνισμός των Ηνωμένων Πολιτειών* [The Hellenism of the United States] (Athens, 1937), p. 57.

41. "Πώς θα σωθώμεν από της ερημώσεως" [How are we going to be saved from desolation?], *Η Σφαίρα* [The Globe], 17 March 1907, p. 1; Asimakopoulos, "Μετανάστασις εις Αμερικήν" [Migration to America], pp. 2–3.

42. Konstantinos Amantos, "Το Αιγαίον και η Γεωγραφική Διάσπασις του Ελληνισμού" [The Aegean and the geographic fragmentation of Hellenism], *Ημερολόγιον της Μεγάλης Ελλάδος* [Almanac of Great Greece] (1923): 345–46.

43. Yeoryios Skliros, *Τα Σύγχρονα Προβλήματα του Ελληνισμού* [The contemporary problems of Hellenism] (Alexandria: Grammata, 1919), p. 54.

44. M. Dendias, *Αι Ελληνικαί Παροικίαι ανά τον Κόσμον. Ήτοι οι Έλληνες εις Ρωσσίαν, Ρουμανίαν, Αίγυπτον, Ηνωμένας Πολιτείας και πάσας τας Άλλας Χώρας. Η Εξέλιξις Αυτών, η Σημερινή Κατάστασις, το Μέλλον των* [The Greek colonies around the world: The Greeks in Russia, Romania, Egypt, United States, and in general in all the other countries: Their development, contemporary situation, and future] (Athens, 1919), p. 11.

45. Ibid.

46. S. Vlavianos, "Ψυχολογία του Σύγχρονου Ελληνικού Λαού" [Psychology of modern Greek people], *Ψυχιατρική και Νευρολογική Επιθεώρησις* [Psychiatric and Neurological Review] (1903): 219.

47. Periklis Yiannopoulos, *Έκκλησις προς το Πανελλήνιον Κοινόν* [Call to the panhellenic public] (Athens, 1907), p. 21.

48. Dragoumis, *Ελληνικός Πολιτισμός* [Greek culture], p. 190.

49. Epitropi tis Voulis, *Η εξ Ελλάδος Μετανάστευσις. Η Έκθεσις της Επιτροπής της Βουλής και η Σχετική Πρότασις Νόμου* [Migration from Greece: Report by the government-appointed committee and bill proposal], pp. 16–17.

50. *Ιστορικά Αρχεία Υπουργείου Εξωτερικών* [Athens, Greece, Historical Archives of the Ministry of Foreign Affairs], Φάκ. Μετανάσται [File: Migrants], 1900–1911; Φάκ. Μετανάστασις-Παλιννόστησις [File: Migration—Repatriation], 1911–1922.

51. *Ιστορικά Αρχεία Υπουργείου Εξωτερικών* [Historical Archives of the Ministry of Foreign Affairs], Φάκ. 1921 Β/Πολιτική Β/45 2 Φάκ. Περί Μεταναστεύσεων [File: 1921 B/Politics B/45 2; File: On Migrations], Υπουργείον επί των Εξωτερικών προς την Πρεσβείαν Ουάσιγκτον, Ρίον Ιανάρον, Λονδίνον, Παρισίου, Βερολίνου, Μαδρίτης, Ρώμης, Βαρσοβίας, Πράγας, Βιέννης, Βουκουρεστίου, Βελιγραδίου, Σόφιας, Καΐρου, Στοκχόλμης, Βέρνης, Χάγης, Βρυξελλών, Τοκίου, Κων/πολιν [The Ministry of Foreign Affairs to the Consulates of Washington, Rio de Janeiro, London, Paris, Berlin, Madrid, Rome, Warsaw, Prague, Vienna, Bucharest, Belgrade, Sofia, Cairo, Stockholm, Verne, the Hague, Brussels, Tokyo, Istanbul], 1 December 1922.

52. Christos Mandatzis, "Μετανάστευση και Ταυτότητα. Η Περίπτωση των Μακεδόνων Ελλήνων Μεταναστών" [Migration and identity. The case of Macedonian Greek migrants], in *Ταυτότητες στη Μακεδονία* [Identities in Macedonia], ed. Angelopoulos et al., pp. 197–228.

53. *Ατλαντίς* [Atlantis], 8 November 1909.

54. *Ιστορικά Αρχεία Υπουργείου Εξωτερικών* [Historical Archives of the Greek Ministry of Foreign Affairs], Φακ. Β 35.3 Πολιτική. Φάκ. Ελλήνων Αμερικής [File: Politics. Greeks in the United States], Greek Royal Legation to Ministry of Foreign Affairs, 4/17 March 1918, no. 772, p. 1.

55. *Καταστατικόν Πανελληνίου Ενώσεως* [General laws of the Panhellenic Union] (Boston: Cosmos, 1910), p. 1.

56. *Πανελλήνιος Ένωσις* [Bulletin of the Panhellenic Union].

57. *Ιστορικά Αρχεία Υπουργείου Εξωτερικών* [Historical Archives of the Greek Ministry of Foreign Affairs], Φακ. Β 35.3 Πολιτική. Φάκ. Ελλήνων Αμερικής [File: Politics. Greeks in the United States], Greek Royal Legation to Ministry of Foreign Affairs, 4/17 March 1918, no. 772.

58. Ioakim Alexopoulos, *Μελέτη περί Εκκλησιαστικής Διοργανώσεως του εν Αμερική Ελληνισμού* [Study of the ecclesiastic organization of Hellenism in America] (New York, 1919); and Alexopoulos, *Οι Κίνδυνοι του εν Αμερική Ελληνισμού και τα μέσα Διασώσεως Αυτού* [The dangers threatening Hellenism in America and the means for its salvation] (Boston, 1926).

59. *Ιστορικά Αρχεία Υπουργείου Εξωτερικών* [Historical Archives of the Greek Ministry of Foreign Affairs], File: 1908 A/B 12, 13, 14, 16, 18. Δραπέται-Μετανάσται [Fugitives-Migrants], Έκθεσις του εν Αγίω Φραγκίσκω της Καλιφορνίας, των Ηνωμένων Πολιτειών Προξένου της Α.Μ. προς το επί των Εξωτερικών Υπουργείον [Report submitted by the San Fransisco Greek Consulate to the Ministry of Foreign Affairs], 20 August 1907.

60. Ibid.

61. Poulopoulou, *Προβλήματα Μετανάστευσης—Παλιννόστησης* [Problems of migration and repatriation], p. 33.

62. As an indication of the importance of repatriation, the first postwar scholarly historical work on the topic of Greek migration to the United States concerned exclusively the phenomenon of repatriation. See Theodore Saloutos, *They Remember America: The Story of the Repatriated Greek-Americans* (Berkeley: University of California Press, 1956).

63. *Ιστορικά Αρχεία Υπουργείου Εξωτερικών* [Historical Archives of the Ministry of Foreign Affairs], Φάκ. Β/45.2 Μεταναστεύσεων [File: Migrations], 1921, Η Παλιννόστησις των Μεταναστών [The repatriation of migrants], p. 3.

64. Ibid.

65. *Ιστορικά Αρχεία Υπουργείου Εξωτερικών* [Historical Archives of the Ministry of Foreign Affairs], Φάκ. Β/45.2 Μεταναστεύσεων [File: Migrations], 1921, Ρούσσος προς Ελληνικόν Υπουργείον [Roussos to Greek Ministry], p. 4.

66. *Ιστορικά Αρχεία Υπουργείου Εξωτερικών* [Archives of the Ministry of Foreign Affairs], Φάκ. Β/45.2 Μεταναστεύσεων [File: Migrations], 1921, Υπουργείον των Εσωτερικών προς το Υπουργείον των Εξωτερικών [Ministry of Domestic Affairs to the Ministry of Foreign Affairs], 7 August 1919, no. 25417.

67. *Ιστορικά Αρχεία Υπουργείου Εξωτερικών* [Archives of the Ministry of Foreign Affairs], Φάκ. Β/45.2 Μεταναστεύσεων [File: Migrations], 1921, Ελληνικόν Προξενείον εν Σηάτλ προς το Υπουργείον των Εξωτερικών [Greek Consulate at Seattle to the Ministry of Foreign Affairs], 23/5 November 1920, pp. 1–2.

68. "Τα Ταξείδια των Μεταναστών" [The migrants' travels], p. 310.

69. Early official reports made special reference to the problem of repatriated migrants who were suffering from tuberculosis. Special recommendation was made for a department to be created at the main hospital for contagious diseases in Athens at the time, Sotiria Hospital.

This department would be devoted to the treatment of repatriated Greek migrants. See *H εξ Ελλάδος Μετανάστευσις*. *Η Έκθεσις της Επιτροπής της Βουλής και σχετική Πρότασις Νόμου* [Migration from Greece: The report prepared by the parliamentary committee, accompanied by relevant bill] (Athens, 1906). On the history of the Sotiria Hospital, see Nikos Makridis, *Αι Υπηρεσίαι Υγιεινής εν Ελλάδι* [Health services in Greece] (Athens, 1933), p. 17.

70. George Catsainos, *Η Σύφιλις και οι Συγκακούργοι της. Κοινωνία, Πολιτεία και Ιατρός* [Syphilis and its collaborators: The society, the state, and the doctor] (New York: Cosmos, 1922), p.79.

71. Thodoros Chatzipantazis and Lila Maraka, *Η Αθηναϊκή Επιθεώρηση* [Athenian Revue], 3 vols.: A1, A2, A3 (Athens: Estia, 1977).

72. Ibid., A1, 208–9.

73. Ibid., A1, 70–76.

74. The only full text that has survived was that of 1911, which does not include skits about migrants. See "Παναθήναια, 1911" [Panathinea, 1911], in Chatzipanatazis and Maraka, *Η Αθηναϊκή Επιθεώρηση* [Athenian Revue], A3, 275–342.

75. Ibid., A1, 72.

76. Αρχείο Θεάτρου [Athens, Greece, Theater Archives], *Χειρόγραφα Επιθεωρήσεων* [Revue Manuscripts], *Παναθήναια 1908* [Panathinea 1908], Act III, scene 1, "Μετανάσται και Νικολέτος" [Migrants and Nikoletos].

77. Αρχείο Θεάτρου, [Athens, Greece, Theater Archives], *Χειρόγραφα Επιθεωρήσεων* [Revue Manuscripts], *Παναθήναια 1910* [Panathinea, 1910].

78. Valaoras, *Ο Ελληνισμός των Ηνωμένων Πολιτειών* [The Hellenism of the United States], pp. 58, 62.

79. On the history of the Near East Relief Foundation, see Dimitra Giannouli, "American Philanthropy in the Near East: Relief to the Ottoman Greek Refugees, 1922–1923 (Greece, Turkey, Missionaries)," Ph.D. diss., Kent State University, 1992.

80. *Εφημερίς της Κυβερνήσεως* [Government Gazette], 24 June 1922, Gennadeios Library Scrapbook.

81. Ιωάννης Γεννάδειος [Ioannis Gennadeios], *Νέος Κόσμος* [New World], 13 July 1924, in Gennadeios Library Scrapbook.

82. Dean Alfange, "Speech Given by the President of AHEPA," *AHEPA Bulletin* (May–June 1928).

83. Vasileios Valaoras, "Κληρονομικότητα και Περιβάλλον" [Heredity and environment], *Επιστημονική Ηχώ* [Scientific echo] (April 1936): 50–54 (emphasis in original).

84. During the 1950s the U.S. government invited intellectuals from foreign countries to visit the country through different programs of academic exchange. These official visitors were also encouraged to publish books on American society, culture, and politics; many of these books were translated into numerous languages. For an analysis of these cultural and academic exchanges as part of the "intellectual Cold Wars" conducted by the United States in that period, see Volker R. Berghahn, *America and the Intellectual Cold Wars in Europe: Shepard Stone between Philanthropy, Academy, and Diplomacy* (Princeton: Princeton University Press, 2001).

85. Manolis Triantafillidis, *Έλληνες της Αμερικής. Μια Ομιλία* [Greeks of America: A speech] (Athens, 1952), p. 36.

86. Ibid., pp. 25–26.

87. Yiorgos Theotokas, *Δοκίμιο για την Αμερική* [An essay on America] (Athens: Ikaros, 1954).

88. Ibid., p. 224.

89. Ibid., pp. 235–36.

90. Chrisanthi Sotiropoulou, *Η Μετανάστευση στον Ελληνικό Κινηματογράφο* [Migration in Greek cinema] (Athens, 1994).

91. Michel Saunier, *Το Δημοτικό Τραγούδι της Ξενιτιάς* [Folksongs about migrancy] (Athens: Hermes, 1990), p. 7.

92. Ibid., p. 8. The Greek word *xénos* is translated in English as "foreigner," "stranger," "immigrant," "emigrant," and "guest."

93. Ibid., pp. 295–96.

94. Opposition to migration was also expressed by popular feminist poetry that was published in the interwar period in women's periodicals. See the poem written by Marika M. Falanga, "Οι Φθισικές" [The consumptives], *Ελληνίς* [Greek Woman] 12 (1932): 255.

95.   Μάνα Τούρκοι, μάνα Φράγκοι

μάνα τρεις Αμερικάνοι

ήρθανε για να με πάρουν

στο Τσικάγο να πάγουν

μάνα πάρτω και παθαίνω

στο Τσικάγο δεν πηγαίνω

(Saunier, *Το Δημοτικό Τραγούδι της Ξενιτιάς* [Folksongs about migrancy], p. 297)

96.   Μη με στέλνεις μάνα στην Αμερική

εγώ θα μαραζώσω, θα παθάνω εκεί.

Δολλάρια δε θέλω, πώς να σου το πώ ;

Θέλω ωλιές, κρεμμύδι κ' εκείνον που αγαπώ,

Με έχει φιλημένη μεσ' τις ρεματιές

και αγκαλιασμένη κάτω από τις ιτιές.

Γιώργο μου, σ' αφήνω, φεύγω μακριά,

παν να με παντρέψουν μες στην ξενιτιά.

Σαν αρνί με πάνε να με σφάξουνε,

κι από τον καημό μου θα με θάψουνε

(Ibid.)

Chapter Three

1. This is especially true for the first period, when regional associations and societies of mutual aid were not yet established. One of the most important services that the first newspapers offered the migrants was the publication of missing persons advertisements. The newspaper office also received letters for people whose address was unknown, or for others who had their mail addressed to them care of the newspaper offices. Migrants seeking assistance in dealing with particular problems, including legal woes, would frequently write to the newspapers for help.

2. Within the field of ethnic studies, the literature of ethnicity acquires a privileged position mainly as a result of the growth of interest in issues that concern subjectivity, identity, and difference. See Werner Sollors, *Beyond Ethnicity: Consent and Descent in American Culture* (Oxford: Oxford University Press, 1986); Sollors, *Neither Black nor White and Yet Both: Thematic Explorations of Interracial Literature* (New York: Oxford University Press, 1997); William

218   NOTES TO PAGES 94–95

Boelhower, *Autobiographical Transactions in Modernist America: The Immigrant, the Architect, the Artist, the Citizen* (Udine: Del Bianco, 1992); A. Singh, J. Skerrett, and R. Hogan, *Memory, Narrative, and Identity: New Essays in Ethnic American Literatures* (Boston: Northeastern University Press, 1994). For a literary approach to these issues in the field of American studies, see Priscilla Wald, *Constituting Americans: Cultural Anxiety and Narrative Form* (Durham: Duke University Press, 1995). However, the focus in this chapter is not on literary analysis, but on the literary process and the ways in which it operated as an information mode for the dissemination of narratives of migrant subjectivity. For the use of the concept of the information mode in the analysis of subject formation, see Mark Poster, *The Information Subject* (New York: Routledge, 2001).

3. Almost all the sociological, anthropological, and historical accounts of the history of Greeks in the United States include extensive references to the history and the role of the Greek press. For a concise account, see Victor Papacosma, "The Greek Press in America," *Journal of the Hellenic Diaspora* 5, no. 4 (Winter 1979).

4. See, for example *Ethnikós Kýrix, Τιμοκατάλογος 1916. Βιβλιοπωλείον Εθνικού Κήρυκος. Βιβλία—Εικόνες—Δελτάρια—Μουσική* [Price list, 1916. Ethnikós Kýrix Bookstore. Books—pictures—postcards—music] (New York: Ethnikós Kýrix, 1916); *Atlantís, Τιμοκατάλογος Βιβλιοπωλείου Ατλαντίδος* [The Atlantis Bookstore price list] (New York: Atlantis, 1917). Both companies were publishing and distributing similar listings of their books and publications almost once a year. These catalogues were mailed all over the country and abroad, and included mail order forms. In this chapter I refer mostly to the publications of these two publishers. Although they were both located in New York, their publications were distributed in many states, as well as in cities of Greece and in other locations with strong Greek communities throughout Asia Minor, Western Europe, North and South Africa, and Australia.

5. I use in the text the transliterated version of the titles of the newspapers *Εθνικός Κήρυξ* (Ethnikós Kýrix, or National Herald) and *Ατλαντίς* (Atlantís).

6. *Μηνιαία Εικονογραφημένη Ατλαντίδα* [Atlantis Monthly Illustrated] 1, no. 1 (January 1910), through 23, no. 12 (December 1932); *Μηνιαίος Εικονογραφημένος Εθνικός Κήρυξ* [National Herald Monthly Illustrated] 1, no. 7 (July 1915), through 25, no. 9 (September 1939).

7. *Μηνιαίος Εικονογραφημένος Εθνικός Κήρυξ* [National Herald Monthly Illustrated] (April 1925): 50.

8. Ibid.

9. Ibid.

10. As the editor remarked, the monthly magazines had the highest circulation outside the United States of all periodical publications (including newspapers, weekly editions, and almanacs). Ibid., p. 49.

11. Some of these short stories were later compiled into books published by the same company.

12. See also the special issue of the *Journal of Modern Greek Studies, Empowering the Minor,* 8, no. 2 (1990). On Greek American literature see Yiorgos Kalogeras, "Greek American Literature: Who Needs It? Some Canonical Issues concerning the Fate of an Ethnic Literature," in *New Directions in Greek American Studies,* ed. Dan Georgakas and Charles Moskos (New York: Pella Publishing, 1991), pp. 129–41; Kalogeras, " 'The Other Space' of Greek America" *American Literary History* 10, no. 4 (1998): 702–24.

13. Gilles Deleuze and Félix Guattari, "What Is a Minor Literature?" in *Out There: Marginalization and Contemporary Cultures,* ed. R. Ferguson, M. Gever, Trinh T. Minh-ha, and Cornel West (Cambridge, Mass.: MIT Press, 1990), pp. 59–69.

14. Ibid., pp. 60–61.

15. See Matthew Schneirov, *The Dream of a New Social Order: Popular Magazines in America 1893–1914* (New York: Columbia University Press, 1994), p. 86.

16. Robert Park, *The Immigrant Press and Its Control* (New York: Harper & Brothers, 1922), pp. 70–72. This book was published in the "Studies in Methods of Americanization" series, which dealt with the role of education, industrial life, community life, neighborhood, and health services in the Americanization of new migrants.

17. Ibid., pp. 69–79.

18. Editorial, *Μηνιαία Εικονογραφημένη Ατλαντίδα* [Atlantis Monthly Illustrated] 17, no. 1 (January 1926): 16.

19. In the introductory notes to dictionaries of Greek or English, the editors of *Atlantís* and *Ethnikós Kýrix* often claimed that many of the Greek migrants, who were illiterate when they came to the United States, actually learned how to read and write through their reading of Greek-language newspapers and magazines.

20. "Κουβέντες με τους Συνεργάτες μας" [Discussions with our contributors], *Πρωτοπόρος* [Pioneer] 2, no. 7 (September 1936): 17. Older workers' newspapers, such as *Η Φωνή του Εργάτου* [The Worker's Voice] and *Εμπρός* [Forward], had been publishing short stories of migration since the early 1920s. In this chapter I refer specifically to *Protoporos* because of its more literary and educational character.

21. In the same period the daily publications often organized contests in which readers were asked to submit short answers to a variety of questions that concerned the experience of Greeks as migrants in the United States. As a typical example I refer to the announcement of a contest for the best short "Γνώμη περί Αμερικής" [Opinion about America]. The contests had a definite canonizing and educational function, since they provoked writing on particular, predetermined issues and involved competition and evaluation of produced writing. Each contest lasted for approximately two months, and the winning responses were published in the Sunday issue with comments on the value and the importance of this kind of contest for cultivation of appreciation of the value of America, its people, civilization, and culture, for the advancement of the migrants who had been living in this country for over a generation by that time. According to the editorial, these contests also encouraged the migrants' participation in mediated public debates. See "Διαγωνισμός ῾Γνώμης Περί Αμερικής᾽" ["Opinion about America" contest], *Ατλαντίς* [Atlantis], 2 January 1930, p. 4.

22. As we will see, most of these stories present images of rural landscapes and locations. The representations of homeland that we find in the short stories are in this sense different from those we find in travel memoirs and articles in the same period. Travel articles were also very popular in the monthly magazines. At this time contributors and journalists were traveling in Greece and returning with fresh memories—not from the rural areas that constituted the place of origin for the majority of the migrants, but from the major urban centers and mainly Athens. In the same period, the magazine correspondents in Athens were also writing articles describing the developing and "rapidly modernizing" Athens. These articles breathed a nostalgic air, and they sought the *a posteriori* creation of an urban memory of homeland. Descriptions of Greek urban centers are never encountered in the stories that we are studying in this section.

23. Ioanna Pappa, "Εξαγνισμός" ["Expiation," first prize winner, Second Short Story Contest], *Μηνιαία Εικονογραφημένη Ατλαντίς* [Atlantis Monthly Illustrated], May 1927, p. 31.

24. I purposely use the masculine form here since the migrant was always represented by a male protagonist.

25. Thanos Yiouroukopoulos, "Το Ευλογημένο Χέρι" ["The blessed hand," third prize winner, Fifth Short Story Contest], *Μηνιαία Εικονογραφημένη Ατλαντίς* [Atlantis Monthly Illustrated], November 1927, p. 36.

26. For a sociological approach to the relation between labor, "redemption," and conceptualizations of ethnicity, see Bernard Rosen, "Race, Ethnicity, and the Achievement Syndrome," *American Sociological Review* 24, no. 1 (February 1959): 47–60.

27. Yiorgos Evrotas, "Η Επιστροφή" ["The return," commendation, Third Short Story Contest], *Μηνιαία Εικονογραφημένη Ατλαντίς* [Atlantis Monthly Illustrated], July 1927, p. 36.

28. A. Fokion, "Δουλεύουμε στα Τενεκετζίδικα" [We work at the tin factory], *Πρωτοπόρος* [Protoporos] 2, no. 5 (July 1936): 15.

29. Ibid.

30. The account of immigrant labor has often been omitted from "mainstream" histories of Greek migration, in which exploitation of immigrant labor was seen as a necessary stage in the economic advancement of Greek migrants and was often attributed to the migrants themselves ("low level of formal education" and "lack of industrial skills"). On the undermining of history of labor in foundational historical accounts of Greek migration to the United States, see Dan Georgakas, *Greek America at Work* (New York: Smyrna Press, 1992).

31. The "private" sphere of migrant life has been studied by social scientists and anthropologists. Sociological and anthropological research has provided useful accounts of the history of institutions and social spaces that accommodated and sustained the private/public separation. On the role of Greek coffeehouses in this context, see James Patterson, "The Unassimilated Greeks of Denver," *Anthropological Quarterly* 43 (October 1970): 245–49.

32. The principles and internal organization of various fraternal associations that were founded in this period are indicative of this tendency. Separate sections were established for men and women, and although the male sections tended toward the use of the English language and the integration of Greek males in the American business world, the female sections were focused on cultural activities and philanthropy as a means of preserving the character and welfare of the Greek migrant communities. On this aspect of the history of the American Hellenic Educational Progressive Association, which has been one of the most important associations of this kind, see Vasilios Chebithes, *AHEPA and the Progress of Hellenism in America* (New York, 1935); and Daughters of Penelope, *The 50th Anniversary of the Daughters of Penelope, 1929–1979* (Washington, D.C.: AHEPA, 1979[?]). On women's benevolent associations, see Stella Coumantaros, "The Greek Orthodox Ladies Philoptochos Society and the Greek American Community," in *The Greek American Community in Transition,* ed. Harry J. Psomiades and Alice Scourby (New York: Pella, 1982), pp. 191–96.

33. The 1920s saw the transformation of Greek migrant communities from predominantly male to family communities. In this period the number of Greek women who were migrating to the United States as picture-brides increased and so did the numbers of weddings and family establishments. On the first generation of Greek women migrants in the United States, see Constance Callinikos, *American Aphrodite: Becoming Female in Greek America* (New York: Pella Publishing, 1990).

34. The observance of the religious holidays was difficult because of the difference between the Greek Orthodox and other religious calendars. One of the first references to this theme occurs in an early fictional account of migration in the form of a novel: Eustratios (Theophilakes) Lumas, *Οι Περιπλανώμενοι* [The Vagrant people] (New York: Stamatakis Ch. M., 1918).

35. P. Nikas, "Η Αποκατάσταση του Κλεάρχου" [The restoration of Klearchos], *Πρωτοπόρος* [Protoporos] 1, no. 11 (January 1936): 15.

36. During the first and second decades of the century newspapers of various Greek cities often published articles about consumptive repatriates from the United States wandering the streets and waiting for their inevitable death.

37. Elias Janetis, *Η Αυτού Μεγαλειότης, ο Μετανάστης* [His majesty the migrant] (New York: NYL Anatolia Press, 1946), p. 27.

38. On literary representations of homosocial relations, see Eve Kosofsky Sedgwick, "The Beast in the Closet: James and the Writing of Homosexual Panic," in *Speaking of Gender,* ed. Elaine Showalter (New York: Routledge, 1989), pp. 243–68; and Sedgwick, *Between Men: English Literature and Male Homosocial Desire* (New York: Columbia University Press, 1985). For a contemporary account of the housing conditions of early Greek migrants, see Milton Hunt, "The Housing of Non-family Groups of Men in Chicago" *American Journal of Sociology* 16 (1910): 145–71; Jett Lauck, "Industrial Communities," *Survey,* 7 January 1911, pp. 585–86.

39. For an early commentary on the scarcity of Greek women in the United States and the character of the male migrant communities (including accounts of male entertainment), see Maria Economidou-Sarandidou, *Οι Έλληνες της Αμερικής, Όπως τους Είδα* [The Greeks of America as I saw them] (New York: Divry, 1916).

40. Janetis, *Η Αυτού Μεγαλειότης, ο Μετανάστης* [His Majesty the migrant], p. 184.

41. Ibid., pp.186–87.

42. Ibid., p. 65.

43. Other, less common pictures portrayed Asian women in traditional costumes and naked African tribal women. Most of these pictures were published repeatedly over long periods of time. In the case of *Atlantís,* these pictures belonged to the newpaper's extensive photographic archive, today held at the Balch Institute for Ethnic Studies. The pictures had mainly a "decorative" function in the monthly publications, although the subtitles often offered general cultural and anthropological information.

44. Similar opinions were often expressed about other non–Anglo-Saxon feminist movements; see "Τουρκικός Φεμινισμός" [Turkish feminism], Μηνιαίος Εικονογραφημένος Εθνικός Κήρυξ [National Herald Monthly Illustrated] (January 1921): 25.

45. *Μηνιαία Εικονογραφημένη Ατλαντίς* [Atlantis Monthly Illustrated] (June 1921): 1.

46. In the 1930s daily newspapers, weekly special issues, and monthly magazines were publishing various articles on fashionable dressing as well as skin care (emphasis was put on "whitening" methods, that is, ways in which certain homemade remedies could prevent the darkening of the skin during the summer months). See Mary K. Takideli, "Ο Κόσμος των Γυναικών. Η Ελληνίς της Αμερικής και τα Ζητήματά της. Νοικοκυριό και Κουζίνα. Υγιεινή και Ωραιότης" [Women's world: The Greek woman in America and her problems: Housekeeping and cuisine, health and beauty], Ατλαντίς [Atlantis], 10 September 1936, p. 4.

47. For an indication of the importance of family relations for Greek women's access to the publishing world, see the biographical information on its contributors that the newspaper *Ethnikós Kýrix* published in a special issue in 1925; Μηνιαίος Εικονογραφημένος [National Herald Monthly Illustrated] (April 1925): 41–50. As these biographical accounts indicate, most of the women contributors were members of families that were already very active in the publishing world.

48. Theano Papazoglou, "Η Γυναίκα στη Σοβιετική Ένωση. Δεκαοχτώ Χρόνια Ισότητος και Λαυτεριάς" [Women in the Soviet Union: Eighteen years of equality and liberty], *Πρωτοπόρος* [Protoporos], November 1935, pp. 5–6. On Papazoglou see Yiorgos Kalogeras, "Suspended Souls, Ensnaring Discourses: Theano Papazoglou-Margaris' Immigration Stories," *Journal of Modern Greek Studies* 8, no. 1 (May 1990): 85–96.

49. These stories included the following: "Η Ελπίδα" [Hope], Πρωτοπόρος [Protoporos], February 1937, pp. 16–18; "Η Κόνα Κατίγκω και τα Κατινάκια" [Mrs. Katigo and the Little Katinakia], Πρωτοπόρος [Protoporos], April 1937, pp. 7–9; "Ένα Μονάχο" [A single child], Πρωτοπόρος [Protoporos], May–June 1937, pp. 13–14.

50. Theano Papazoglou-Margaris, Χρονικό του Χώλστεντ Στρητ: Ελληνοαμερικανικά Διηγήματα [Chronicle of Halsted Street: Greek-American Short Stories] (Athens, 1962). Halsted Street was one of the main streets in the Greektown of Chicago during the first part of the century. For contemporary descriptions of the Greektown in Chicago, see Grace Abbot, "A Study of the Greeks in Chicago," American Journal of Sociology 15, no. 3 (November 1909): 379–93; and Philip Morris Hauser, Local Community Fact Book: Chicago Metropolitan Area (Chicago, 1938).

51. Charles Moskos, Greek Americans: Struggle and Success (Englewood Cliffs, N.J.: Prentice-Hall, 1980), p. 98.

52. Dimitris Michalaros, "The Chronicle of Halsted Street," Athene 24, no. 1 (Spring 1963): 44.

53. The process of "patriarchalization" of Greek ethnicity in the United States has often been described in autobiographical accounts written by second-generation Greek women. For such an account written in English, see "The Forgotten Generation," Athene 10, no. 4 (Winter 1950).

54. Many of the stories about repatriation used the narrative device of daydreaming.

55. Sigmund Freud, The Interpretation of Dreams, trans. James Strachey (New York: Basic Books, 1955), pp. 48–65.

56. Ibid., p. 314 (my emphasis).

57. That many of the migrants to the United States came originally from multiethnic empires or nation-states has been in general ignored by scholars of ethnicity and migration. Greek migrants from Asia Minor had, before their migration, been living in a multiethnic environment and were accustomed to a notion of nationhood based on cultural and religious difference rather than on political representation.

58. The division of time according to private and public, and the encirclement of national ("ethnic") culture in the sphere of the private contributed to the development of notions of fixity. Different aspects of Greek life in Ameriki (such as festivals, folklore, religious services, cooking) involved ritualistic performances of national culture. Although rituals were subject to changing social circumstances, they propagated notions of fixity, unchangeability, and repetition.

59. Chr. Christovasilis, "Το Όναιρο του Ξενητεμένου " [The migrant's dream], Μηνιαίος Εικονογραφημένος Εθνικός Κήρυξ [National Herald Monthly Illustrated], January 1918, p. 30.

60. Pol. Papachristodoulou, "Ο Μετανάστης" [The migrant], Μη νιαία Εικονογραφημένη Ατλαντίδα [Atlantis Monthly Illustrated], August 1929, p. 31.

61. Descriptions of Athens became very popular in the late 1920s. This fascination can be understood in the context of the rapid urban development that the city underwent after the massive arrival of refugees from Asia Minor in 1922, the construction of public service systems, and the establishment of various American organizations (Near East Relief, YMCA, American College). As relevant advertisements in the Greek press indicated, when Greek migrants to the United States started visiting Greece as tourists at the end of the 1930s, Athens was their primary destination.

62. On the importance of national community networks, see Charles Tilly, "Transplanted Networks," in Immigration Reconsidered: History, Sociology, and Politics, ed. Virginia Yans-McLaughlin (New York: Oxford University Press, 1990), pp. 83–84.

63. Scholars of Balkan nationalisms have commented on the ways in which nationalist ideological discourses in the Balkans are based on a series of negative identifications ("what we are not"). For a compelling analysis of the relation between negative self-identifications and negative European perceptions of the Balkans, see Maria Todorova, *Imagining the Balkans* (New York: Oxford University Press, 1997).

Chapter Four

1. *Εθνικός Κήρυξ. Μηνιαίος Εικονογραφημένος* [National Herald Monthly Illustrated], August 1918, p. 3 (in English in the original).

2. Ibid., p. 14.

3. Ibid.

4. Ibid., p. 22.

5. Ibid., p. 15 (in English in the original).

6. Jacques Lacan, *The Four Fundamental Concepts of Psychoanalysis* (New York: W. W. Norton, 1981 [1973]), p. 183.

7. Ibid., p. 178.

8. Ibid., p. 181.

9. *Goumenos* is the Greek word for "abbot."

10. Nikos Lambropoulos, *Οι Φωστήρες* [Leading lights] (San Franscisco, 1925), pp. 12–13. The words *woma* and *gierl* are in English in the original.

11. *Εθνικός Κήρυξ. Μηνιαίος Εικονογραφημένος* [National Herald Monthly Illustrated], February 1922.

12. The use of Gringlish was part of negative stereotypes of Greek Americans also in Greece.

13. Greek Archives, *The Rebetiko Song in America 1920–1940*, vol.1 (FM Records SA, 1993).

14. Ibid.

15. "*Το Σιγαρέτο*" [The cigarette], in Aman Amerika Orchestra, *Cafe Aman Amerika: Greek-American Songs Revised and Revisited* (Music World Productions, 1995).

16. See Rhoda Kaufman, "The Yiddish Theater in New York and the Immigrant Jewish Community: Theater as Secular Ritual," Ph.D. diss., University of California, Berkeley, 1986.

17. On the Greek American amateur theater, see Nikos Rozakos, *Το Νεοελληνικό Θέατρο στην Αμερική, 1903–1950* [Popular modern Greek theater in America, 1903–1950] (San Francisco: Falcon Associates, 1985).

18. See Angel Alex, *Καρδιές που Ραΐζουν* [Hearts that break] (New York: Divry, 1926); Nikos Lambropoulos, *Ιερείς και Παπάδες* [Priests and fathers] (San Francisco: California Greek Newspaper, 1935); Lambropoulos, Ο *Κακός Δρόμος* [Going astray] (San Francisco: Prometheus Publishing, 1928).

19. Lambropoulos, *Ο Κακός Δρόμος* [Going astray].

20. Lambropoulos, *Ιερείς και Παπάδες* [Priests and fathers].

21. Angel Alex, *Το Φουστάνι της Γυναίκας μου* [My wife's skirt] (n.p., n.d.).

22. Ibid., p. 8.

23. Ibid., pp. 7, 11.

24. Ibid., p. 11.

25. See Xenophon Zolotas, *Μετανάστευσις και Οικονομική Ανάπτυξις* [Immigration and economic development] (Athens, 1966); see also *Statistique du commerce spécial de la Grèce avec les pays étrangers pendant l'année . . .* (Greek Ministry of the National Economy, Office of Statistics), vols. 1905–20 and 1921–40.

26. Seraphim Canoutas, *Ελληνο-αμερικανικός Οδηγός* [Greek-American guide] (New York, 1907); *United States and Canada Greek Business Directory* (New York, 1907).

27. For a convincing refutation of this position, see Liz Cohen, *Making a New Deal: Industrial Workers in Chicago, 1919–1939* (Cambridge: Cambridge University Press, 1990), p. 101.

28. See in particular John Clarke, C. Critcher, and Richard Johnson, *Working-Class Culture: Studies in History and Theory* (New York: St. Martin's Press, 1980). See also Angela McRobbie, *Feminism and Youth Culture* (London: Macmillan, 1991).

29. Cohen, *Making a New Deal*, p. 101.

30. John Brewer and Ann Berminham, eds., *The Consumption of Culture 1600–1800: Image, Object, Text* (London: Routledge, 1995), p. 4.

31. Artemis Leontis's ethnographic research on Greek women's embroidery in the United States illustrates the instrumental role that objects played for individual, family, and collective histories of Greek migration. Leontis demonstrates how objects that belonged to a particular family, such as embroidery, represented collective histories of travel, adventures, struggles, movement, and successive reestablishments. See Artemis Leontis, "Women's Fabric Arts in Greek America," *Laografia. A Journal of the International Greek Folklore Society* 12, no. 3 (May–June 1995): 5–11.

32. Dick Hebdige, *Subculture: The Meaning of Style* (London: Methuen, 1979), p. 126.

33. Robert E. Park, *The Immigrant Press and Its Control* (New York: Harper & Brothers, 1922).

34. See Booras Bros., *Ημερολόγιον Θερμοπυλών* [Thermopylae almanac] (New York, 1904).

35. See Helen Phiambolis Jannopoulo, *And across Big Seas* (Caldwell, Idaho: Caxton, 1949).

36. See Edward Steiner, *On the Trail of the Immigrant* (New York: Fleming H. Revell Co., 1906), especially his descriptions of social stratification and the different classes of travelers in the steamships.

37. *Ατλαντίς* [Atlantis], 23 December 1911, p. 4; *Ελληνοαμερικανικός Καζαμίας* [Greek American almanac] (New York: Atlantis, 1922, 1928).

38. *Ατλαντίς* [Atlantis], 7 December 1919, p. 4; *Ατλαντίς* [Atlantis], 22 March 1928, p. 4; "National Bank of Greece," *Ατλαντίς* [Atlantis], 9 November 1929, p. 2.

39. On the postal banking system, see Paul Henry Nystrom, *Economic Principles of Consumption* (New York: Ronald Press Co., 1929).

40. Cohen, *Making a New Deal*, p. 76.

41. Ibid., p. 83.

42. "Bank of Athens," *Ατλαντίς* [Atlantis], 2 November 1929, p. 2.

43. "Cognac Barbaresso," *Ατλαντίς* [Atlantis], 3 March 1912, p. 4; "Moscahlades Brothers: Apollo Olive Oil," *Ατλαντίς* [Atlantis], 6 January 1916, p. 9.

44. *Ατλαντίς* [Atlantis], 7 January 1928, p. 4. Other advertisements urged the public to buy books and Greek American magazines, and send them as presents to families and friends in Greece; see *Ατλαντίς* [Atlantis], 20 November 1935, p. 4.

45. Judith Butler, *Gender Trouble: Feminism and the Subversion of Identity* (New York: Routledge, 1990), p. 146.

Chapter Five

1. Gayatri Chakravorty Spivak, "The Political Economy of Women as Seen by a Literary Critic," in *Coming to Terms: Feminism, Theory, Politics*, ed. Elizabeth Weed (New York: Routledge, 1989), p. 227.

2. Scholars of autobiography have argued that the commitment to introduce critical perspectives of analysis in the study of subjectivity has led to a shift in the generic definitions

and a broadening of the range of materials included in the study of life stories. See Caren Kaplan, "Resisting Autobiography: Out-Law Genres and Transnational Feminist Subjects," in *De/colonizing the Subject: The Politics of Gender in Women's Autobiography,* ed. Sidonie Smith and Julia Watson (Minneapolis: University of Minnesota Press, 1992), pp. 115–38.

3. Spivak, "The Political Economy of Women as Seen by a Literary Critic," p. 227.

4. The historiographical, sociological, and anthropological literature on the Greek American community is very rich and diverse. The "natural" character of cultural assimilation is an assumption that can be traced, although in different degrees, across the wide range of approaches, and especially in books written in the 1960s and 1970s. See Harry Psomiades and Alice Scourby, eds., *The Greek-American Community in Transition* (New York: Pella Publishing, 1982); Evan Vlachos, *The Assimilation of Greeks in the United States, with Special Reference to the Greek Commnunity of Anderson Indiana* (Athens: E.K.K.E., 1968); Heike Fenton and Melvin Hecker, *The Greeks in America, 1528–1977: A Chronology and Fact Book* (New York: Oceana Publications, 1978); Michael Contopoulos, *The Greek Community of New York City: Early Years to 1910* (New Rochelle, N.Y.: Aristides D. Cavatzas, 1992); Edwin Clarence Buxbaum, *The Greek-American Group of Tarpon Springs, Florida: A Study of Ethnic Identification and Acculturation* (New York: Arno Press, 1980); Alice Scourby, *The Greek Americans* (Boston: Twayne Publishers, 1984); Charles C. Moskos, *Greek Americans: Struggle and Success* (Englewood Cliffs, N.J.: Prentice-Hall, 1980); Robert James Theodoratus, *A Greek Community in America* (Sacramento, Calif.: Sacramento Anthropological Society, Sacramento State College, 1971); Theodore Saloutos, *The Greeks in the United States* (Cambridge, Mass.: Harvard University Press, 1964).

5. A similar "gap," combined with a tendency to present assimilation as a natural and inevitable event, is encountered also in immigrant autobiographies and memoirs.

6. Thanos Veremis, *Μελετήματα γύρω από τον Βενιζέλο και την Εποχή του* [Studies on Venizelos and his era] (Athens: Philippotis, 1980); Ch. Chatziosif, ed., *Ιστορία της Ελλάδας του 20ου αιώνα* [History of Greece in the Twentieth Century] vols. A1, A2 (Athens: Vivliorama, 1999).

7. See Ατλαντίς [Atlantis], 1909–11, and especially the reports on anti-Greek nativist attacks like the riots that took place in Omaha, Nebraska, in February 1909 and the prohibition of fishing for nonnaturalized migrants in Providence, Rhode Island in January 1909.

8. Vlastos to J. Harrison Power, 17 October 1917, *Atlantís:* National Daily Greek Newspaper, Records, 1894–1973, Series III: Records of Legal Actions, 1889–1932, Box 17, F2, "Atlantis Legal Acts. Post Office Permit, Correspondence," Balch Institute for Ethnic Studies, Philadelphia (hereafter cited as *Atlantís* Records).

9. Thomas Pattern, Postmaster, to Atlantis Publisher, 16 October 1917, *Atlantís* Records.

10. Vasilios I. Chebithes, *AHEPA and the Progress of Hellenism in America* (New York, 1935).

11. "Η Ελληνική Αναγέννησις εν Αμερική" [The Greek renaissance in America], Μηνιαίος Εικονογραφημένος Εθνικός Κήρυξ [National Herald Monthly Illustrated], January 1928, p. 32.

12. See also *Νεοελληνικός Πολιτισμός Δυνατοί Νεοελληνικοί Χαρακτήρες. Οι κατά τους τελευταίους τρεις αιώνας αγωνισθέντες δια την αναγέννησιν του ελληνικού έθνους. Ήρωες και Μάρτυρες. Οι ηγέτες του φωτισμού των Ελλήνων. Συγγραφείς και Διδάσκαλοι του Γένους. Εθνικοί Ευεργέται. Οι ανά τον Κόσμον Διαπρέψαντες Μετανάσται* [Modern Greek culture: Powerful modern Greek characters: Individuals who participated in the struggle for the rebirth of the Greek nation during the last three centuries: The nation's authors and teachers: The immigrants who succeded in all different places on the globe] (New York: National Herald, 1927).

13. On Callimachos, see Sephes Kollias, *Δημ. Καλλίμαχος. Μια Άρτια Αγωνιστική Συνείδηση* [Dem. Callimachos: A perfect fighting consciousness] (Athens, 1963); Pol. Papachristodoulou, "Μια Γιγαντιαία Μορφή της Θράκης εις την Νέαν Υόρκην" [A great Thracian in New York], *Αρχείον του Θρακικού Λαογραφικού και Γλωσσικού Θησαυρού* [Bulletin of the Thracian folklore and linguistic treasure] 23 (1958): 403–5; Petros Charis, "Ο Διασημότερος Έλλην της Αμερικής" [The most famous Greek in America], *Νέα Εστία* [Nea Estia], Christmas Issue, 1955.

14. Callimachos considered that his work to bridge Hellenism with Anglo-Saxonism and to educate the Greek American community to become the avatar of this hybrid culture was parallel to similar modernizing efforts that were taking place in Greece at the same period and were politically represented by Eleutherios Venizelos and the Liberal Party. Callimachos dedicated one of his books to Venizelos, whom he considered had tried to "introduce the moral ideals of the Anglo-Saxons into modern Greek life." See Demetrios Callimachos, *Πώς Προοδεύουν οι Αμερικανοί. Το Πνεύμα, αι Αρχαί και ο Κώδιξ των Σύγχρονων Αμερικανικών Επιχειρήσεων* [How Americans progress: The spirit, principles, and code of modern American companies] (New York: Ethnikós Kýrix, 1934), p. 6. On Eleutherios Venizelos and modernization politics in Greece, see G. Maurogordatos and Ch. Chatziosif, eds., Βενιζελισμός και Αστικός Εκσυγχρονισμός [Venizelism and civic modernization] (Heraklion: Crete University Press, 1988).

15. *Μηνιαίος Εικονογραφημένος Εθνικός Κήρυξ* [National Herald Monthly Illustrated], September 1930, p. 1.

16. Demetrios Callimachos, *Το Ευαγγέλιον υπό Σύγχρονον Πνεύμα. Ψυχολογικαί Έρευναι—Φιλοσοφήματα επί της Ζωής—Κοινωνικά Προβλήματα—Χαρακτήρες* [The New Testament in the modern spirit: Psychological researches: Philosophizing about life: Social problems: Characters] (New York: Ethnikós Kýrix, 1925).

17. Callimachos, *Νεοελληνικός Πολιτισμός* [Modern Greek culture], pp. 186–87.

18. Ibid., pp. 282, 304, 306, 315.

19. Ibid., p. 168.

20. Ibid., p. 220.

21. Ibid., pp. 223, 257.

22. Ibid., p. 6.

23. Callimachos often condemned in his book specific modes of behavior that he considered to be very common among Greek women in the United States. He argued that female arrogance, pretentiousness, provinciality, and lack of education jeopardized Greek family life and values in the United States and could be dangerous for the preservation of Greek culture and consciousness. See ibid., pp. 156, 198–99.

24. Ibid., pp. 176, 180, 191. In these interruptions he often referred to what were commonly considered to be the most important problems of the Greek American community in that period, such as gambling, laziness, pretentiousness, and lack of education. See ibid., pp. 52–53, 104, 199.

25. Ibid., p. 331.

26. Ibid., p. 332.

27. Callimachos insisted that Anagnostopoulos's Americanism was not similar to the ill-conceived version of Americanism supported by the "100 percent" movement and whose purpose was to destroy all the psychological and intellectual treasures represented by the diversity of racial groups in the United States. Callimachos's Americanism had the ability to include cultural diversity and to transform ethnic heritage into national cultural wealth. See ibid., p. 384.

28. Callimachos defined the content of Americanism in his book *Πώς Προοδεύουν οι Αμερικανοί* [How Americans progress]. There he defined culture through references to the psychology of the people who are this culture's carriers. The Anglo-Saxon is thus described as happy, innocent, free of unnecessary passions, productive, systematic, sober, healthy, and tending to professional success. The non–Anglo-Saxon and more specifically the South European is described as neurotic, often miserable, full of overwhelming passions, physically disadvantaged, prone to failure. In this book Callimachos provided advice on how to develop the charisma of Anglo-Saxon culture by transforming one's practice of everyday life.

29. Demetra Vaka-Brown, "For a Heart for Any Fate: The Early Years of Demetra Vaka (Mrs. Kenneth Brown)," *Athene* 8, no. 3 (Autumn 1947): 87.

30. Kenneth Brown, "Demetra Vaka," *Athene* 9, no. 1 (Spring 1948). The autobiography was concluded in vol. 13, no. 4 (Winter 1953).

31. Yiorgos Kalogeras, "A Child of the Orient as American Storyteller: Demetra Vaka-Brown." Working Papers of the English Department, Aristotle University, 1989, pp. 187–93.

32. On the life of Demetra Vaka, see John William Leonard, *Woman's Who's Who of America: A Biographical Dictionary of Contemporary Women in the United States and Canada, 1914–1915* (New York: American Commonwealth Co., 1914); and Doris Robinson, *Women Novelists, 1891–1920: An Index to Biographical and Autobiographical Sources* (New York: Garland Reference Library, 1984), p. 491.

33. Her publications include *The First Secretary* (with Kenneth Brown) (New York: B. W. Dodge Co., 1907); *A Duke's Price* (Boston: Houghton Mifflin, 1910); *In the Shadow of Islam* (Boston: Houghton Mifflin, 1911); *The Grasp of the Sultan* (Boston: Houghton Mifflin, 1916); *In Pawn to a Throne* (with Kenneth Brown) (London: John Lane Co., 1919); *A Child of the Orient* (Boston: Houghton Mifflin, 1914); *Haremlik: Some Pages from the Life of Turkish Women* (Boston: Houghton Mifflin, 1909); *In the Heart of the German Intrigue* (Boston: Houghton Mifflin, 1918); *The Unveiled Ladies of Stamboul* (Boston: Houghton Mifflin, 1923); *Bribed to Be Born* (New York: Exposition Press, 1951).

34. Aristides Phoultrides and Demetra Vaka, trans., *Modern Greek Stories* (New York: Arno Press, 1920).

35. Brown, "Demetra Vaka," p. 13.

36. Ibid., pp. 14–16.

37. Demetra Vaka, *The Heart of the Balkans* (Boston: Houghton Mifflin, 1917).

38. Ibid., p. 4.

39. Vaka, *The Unveiled Ladies of Stamboul*. Before Vaka wrote this book, she visited Turkey after twenty years of absence. The book was dedicated to Prince Sabaheddine on account of his ideals about the preservation of the Ottoman empire. See also Vaka's *In the Shadow of Islam*, where she narrates the story of a feminist young woman who, as an American college graduate, comes to Turkey on a vacation hoping to work for the enlightenment of Turkey.

40. Demetra Vaka, "Demetra Vaka's Autobiography," *Athene* 9, no. 2 (Summer 1950): 36.

41. Demetra Vaka, "Demetra Vaka's Autobiography," *Athene* 11, no. 4 (Winter 1951): 51.

42. Vaka, *A Child of the Orient*, pp. 263–4 (my emphasis).

43. Demetra Vaka, "Demetra Vaka's Autobiography," *Athene* 12, no. 2 (Summer 1951): 25.

44. Vaka, *A Child of the Orient*, pp. 296–97.

45. She had just explained to him that in the United States people cremated their dead instead of burying them in cemeteries.

46. The present had been a little Greek flag, which the author herself considered a precious present, while her friend Kiamelé could not understand why it had any value at all.

47. Vaka, *A Child of the Orient*, pp. 297–8.

48. For a critical discussion of this view, see Jane Flax, *Disputed Subjects: Essays on Psychoanalysis, Politics, and Philosophy* (New York: Routledge, 1993), p. 101.

49. Analysts whose critique is located on the borderlines of philosophy, psychoanalysis, and politics have pointed out the manifestations of this type of interaction within the space of psychoanalytical practice. See Flax, *Disputed Subjects,* especially chap. 5. "Multiples: On the Contemporary Politics of Subjectivity," pp. 92–110, where Flax suggests a phenomenology of different ways of organizing subjectivities and argues that in the cases of many of her patients the inability to experience simultaneously, mutually, and distinctively different aspects of subjectivity has led to either *schizoid* (psychic experiences divorced from somatic ones) or *borderline* (affective experience fluctuating from one absolute state to another and profound sense of disequilibrium) forms of subjectivity.

50. See Shoshana Felman, *What Does a Woman Want? Reading and Sexual Difference* (Baltimore: Johns Hopkins University Press, 1993), pp. 18–19 (quote, p. 19).

51. As the author herself testifies in her autobiography, cultural literacy was also the reason that many members of the American intelligentsia at the time took interest in Vaka and her literary work.

52. In her autobiography the chapter on her visit to Turkey was quite brief. On the contrary, the same chapter in *A Child of the Orient* was quite detailed and expanded.

53. Vaka, *A Child of the Orient*, pp. 291–92 (my emphasis).

54. The description of this incident was followed by a commentary on English idiosyncrasy—more particularly, the way in which English people are extrovert when they are abroad and introvert when they remain in Britain—and by a political commentary on how fortunate it would be if Turkey were under British control.

55. Vaka, *A Child of the Orient*, pp. 276–77.

56. Ibid., pp. 254–55.

57. Ibid., p. 276–77.

58. Ibid., p. 251.

Chapter Six

1. A large number of unpublished memoirs and family chronicles are dispersed in various personal or community archives. In this chapter, I mostly use published autobiographies, because I am interested in the public diffusion of such migration life stories.

2. Georges Gusdorf, "Conditions and Limits of Autobiography," in *Autobiography: Essays Theoretical and Critical*, ed. James Olney (Princeton: Princeton University Press, 1980), pp. 28–48.

3. Doris Sommer, " 'Not Just A Personal Story': Women's *Testimonios* and the Plural Self," in *Life/Lines: Theorizing Women's Autobiography*, ed. Bella Brodski (Ithaca, N.Y.: Cornell University Press, 1988), p. 111.

4. Karolos Manos, *H Ζωή Ενός Μετανάστη* [The life of a migrant] (Athens, 1964).

5. Manos's autobiography included a second foreword, written by Theofanis Karvelas, an "intellectual migrant." Although this second commentator also pointed out the didactic character of the autobiographical writing, he drew the reader's attention more to his own views and reflections, rather than to the book's value as a supposed container of unprocessed experience.

6. Nina Ladoyianni, *Ένας Έλληνας στην Αμερική* [A Greek in America] (Volos, 1954).

7. Ibid., p. 5.

8. Manos, *H Ζωή Ενός Μετανάστη* [The life of a migrant], p. 123.

9. Emmanuil Polenis, *Εγκόλπιον Μετανάστου. Συμβουλαί, Ανέκδοτα, Ιστορικά Γεγονότα* [The migrant's handbook: Advice, anecdotes, and historical events] (Athens, 1945).

10. Ibid. p. 43.

11. Ibid. p. 46.

12. Polenis also asserted that the reason for his early migration was actually his Greek grandmother's ignorance of the "civilized ways" of bringing up a child. Ibid., p. 17.

13. Ibid., p. 18.

14. Polenis, *Εγκόλπιον Μετανάστου. Συμβουλαί, Ανέκδοτα, Ιστορικά Γεγονότα* [The migrant's handbook: Advice, anecdotes, and historical events], p. 17.

15. Ibid., pp. 77–78.

16. Ibid., p. 56.

17. Ibid., p. 68.

18. Some of the best known such guides were those of Socrates A. Xanthaky, *Ο Σύντροφος του Έλληνος εν Αμερική* [The companion of Greeks in America] (New York, 1903); and Seraphim Canoutas, *Ελληνο-αμερικανικός Οδηγός* [Greek-American Guide] (New York, 1907).

19. Canoutas, *Ελληνο-αμερικανικός Οδηγός* [Greek-American Guide], p. 11.

20. See Thomas Burgess, *Greeks in America* (Boston,1913); and J. P. Xenides, *The Greeks in America* (New York, 1922). Burgess was an Episcopalian clergyman and a member of an American branch of the Anglican and Eastern Orthodox Churches Union that sought to effect a closer union between these two churches. Xenides's book appeared under the auspices of the Inter-Church World Movement. Both authors drew their information from personal contacts with members of the Greek immigrant community.

21. As we saw in chapter 2, systematic studies of Greek immigration were also conducted in Greece in the early twentieth century.

22. Henry Pratt Fairchild, *Greek Immigration to the United States* (New Haven: Yale University Press, 1911). The thesis was supervised by anthropologist A. G. Keller. In the same category belong a number of books written by native-born American social scientists that dealt with the case of Greek migration to the United States. See Thomas J. Lacey, *A Study of Social Heredity as Illustrated in the Greek People* (New York, 1916). In the same period many articles on Greek migration were published in various American journals and magazines such as *Commonweal, Literary Digest, The Nation, Outlook, The Saturday Evening Post, Common Ground,* and *American Journal of Sociology.*

23. Fairchild, *Greek Immigration to the United States,* p. xvi.

24. Ibid., p. 237.

25. See Grace Abbott, "A Study of the Greeks in Chicago," *American Journal of Sociology* 15 (November 1909): 379–93.

26. As discussed in chapter 2, other accounts were also written in Greece by Greek intellectuals, who traveled in the United States, visited Greek communities there, and published their impressions. These accounts often dealt with contemporary debates concerning the advantages and disadvantages of Greek migration to the United States.

27. See Seraphim Canoutas, *Ο Ελληνισμός εν Αμερική* [Hellenism in America] (New York: Cosmos, 1918); Spyridon Kotakis, *Οι Έλληνες εν Αμερική* [The Greeks in America] (Chicago: S. P. Kotakis Press, 1908).

28. Canoutas, *Ο Ελληνισμός εν Αμερική* [Hellenism in America], pp. 316, 319.

29. Ibid., pp. 319–20.

30. Ibid., p.19.

31. Ibid., pp.19–20.

32. Canoutas, *Ελληνο-αμερικανικός Οδηγός* [Greek-American Guide], pp. 16–17.

33. See Robert Young, *White Mythologies: Writing History and the West* (London: Routledge, 1990).

34. The legal and political aspects of the dispute were officially recorded by the U.S. Department of State. See Decimal File 1910–1929, Box 3682 (311.674 H 84/1–311.681 SO 8/9) and Box 3683 (311.681 SO 8/10–311.682 SP 2/5), U.S. Department of State, Record Group 59, National Archives, Washington, D.C.

35. "Public Law No. 207, 65th Congress, S. 4527. An Act to authorize the payment of indemnities to the Government of Greece," Decimal File 1910–1929, Box 3683, U.S. Department of State, National Archives, Washington, D.C.

36. *Atlantís* 2088, 22 February 1909; quoted from Box 10, F. 6, *Atlantís,* National Daily Greek Newspaper Records, 1894–1973, Balch Institute for Ethnic Studies, Philadelphia.

37. "Social Ethnics. Greeks. J. H. Norris July 11, 1939. Omaha, District #2," Box A 749, "Nebraska, Greeks, Essays," Federal Writers Project, Manuscript Division, Library of Congress, Washington, D.C. The crossed-out line is thus in the original.

38. This type of articulation was discussed in chapter 5, concerning regulative biographical narratives.

39. Helen Papanikolas, "Toil and Rage in a New Land: The Greek Immigrants in Utah," *Utah Historical Quarterly* 38 (1970): 97–206.

40. Helen Papanikolas, *Αμιλία-Γεώργιος* [Emily-George] (Salt Lake City: University of Utah Press, 1987). Her latest book is *An Amulet of Greek Earth: Generations of Immigrant Folk Culture* (Athens: Swallow Press; Ohio University Press, 2002).

41. Ibid., p. 321.

42. Ibid., p. 54.

43. Ibid., pp. 38–40.

44. Ibid., p. 23.

45. Helen Papanikolas, "Magerou, the Greek Midwife," *Utah Historical Quarterly* 38 (1970): 50–60.

46. Saloutos had written several books before he turned his attention to Greek American history. See Theodore Saloutos and John D. Hicks, *Twentieth-Century Populism: Agricultural Discontent in the Middle West, 1900–1939* (Lincoln: University of Nebraska Press, 1952); *The American Farmer and the New Deal* (Ames: Iowa State University Press, 1982).

47. Saloutos referred to this career plan, in his rich correspondence with migration historians. See Section I (Correspondence), Theodore Saloutos Collection, Immigration History Research Center, University of Minnesota, Minneapolis (hereafter cited as Saloutos Collection).

48. Theodore Saloutos, *They Remember America: The Story of the Repatriated Greek-Americans* (Berkeley: University of California Press, 1956); *The Greeks in the United States* (Cambridge, Mass.: Harvard University Press, 1964).

49. The correspondence files included in Saloutos's personal archive indicate his relation with historians such as Oscar Handlin, Carl Wittke, Theodore C. Blegen, Carlton C. Qualey, and later Rudolf Vecoli and others. See Section I (Correspondence), Saloutos Collection.

50. Box 65, FF 647, Saloutos Collection.

51. "Saloutos to Handlin," 11 September 1951, Box 1 FF 6, Section I (Correspondence), Saloutos Collection.

52. Saloutos, *They Remember America* , pp. 130–31.

53. Ibid., p. 117.

54. Ibid., p. 124.

55. See "Diary, September 24–October 11, 1952," 3 October entry, p. 5, Box 15, FF 87, Saloutos Collection.

56. Ibid., 4 October entry, pp. 6–7.

57. It seems that the issue of new Greek migration to the United States was of great importance for second-generation Greek American intellectuals and historians. On July 1, 1976, Saloutos interviewed Helen Papanikolas in Salt Lake City. The seven pages of notes of this interview that he kept in his archive indicate that most of their discussion concerned the ways in which the old Greek American community reacted to the arrival of new Greek migrants and the transformations that contemporary migration was expected to effect. The historians' urge to record the early history of Greek migration was related to the changing demography of the Greek American communities in the post–World War II era. See "Salt Lake City. July 1, 1976. Lunch with Helen and Nick Papanikolas," Box 84 FF 838, Saloutos Collection.

58. Saloutos, *The Greeks in the United States*, p. 20.

Afterword

1. On the relation between theoretical engagement, cultural analysis, and the contemporary "culture in crisis," see also Nancy Armstrong, "Who Is Afraid of the Cultural Turn?" *Differences* 12, no. 1 (Spring 2001): 17–49.

2. For a compelling exploration of the relation between migration and conceptualizations of nationhood, see Prasenjit Duara, "Nationalists among Transnationals: Overseas Chinese and the Idea of China, 1900–1911," in *Ungrounded Empires: The Cultural Politics of Modern Chinese Transnationalism*, ed. Aihwa Ong and Donald Nomini (New York: Routledge, 1997), pp. 39–60. The comparison between the Chinese diaspora and Greek diaspora in the early twentieth century may offer some valuable insights into the ways in which transnational forms of identification offered the means for cultural conciliation among modernity, nationhood, and classical tradition.

3. Lisa Lowe has explored in an inspiring way the implication of migration history for the reconceptualization of Chinese identity in the present. See Lisa Lowe, *Immigrant Acts: On Asian American Cultural Politics* (Durham: Duke University Press, 1996).

4. Smadar Lavie and Ted Swedenburg, *Displacement, Diaspora and Geographies of Identity* (Durham: Duke University Press, 1996), p. 2.

5. Sotiris Dimitriou, *Ν' Ακούω Καλά το Όνομά σου* [May I always hear good things about you] (Athens: Kedros, 1993), pp. 103–4.

6. Gianni Amelio, *Lamerica* (Florence: Cecchi Gori, 1994).

Archives

Greece

Athens. Γενικά Αρχεία Κράτους [National Archives].
  Ioannis Metaxas Archive. Correspondence with Immigrants. Files 28, 31, 43, 44, 45.
Athens. Ελληνικό Ιστορικό και Λογοτεχνικό Αρχείο [Hellenic Historical and Literary Archive].
  George Perros Archive (1907–51)
  Tsimbis Archive (1902–31)
  Chronis Archive
  Paneris Archive
  Greek American Families. Pictures and Scrapbooks (1940–60)
  Costopoulos Archive (1899–1945)
Athens. Ιστορικό Αρχείο Υπουργείου Εξωτερικών [Historical Archive of the Ministry of Foreign Affairs]. Files on: Immigration, Repatriation, Missing Persons, Fugitives, Immigrant Communities, Immigrant Education, Consular Reports, Church in the United States, Press, Propaganda, Registration of Immigrants. 1900–1940.
Athens. Αρχείο Θεάτρου [Theater Archive].
  Χειρόγραφα Επιθεωρήσεων [Revue Manuscripts]. "Παναθήναια 1908" [Panathinea 1908].
  Χειρόγραφα Επιθεωρήσεων [Revue Manuscripts]. "Παναθήναια 1910" [Panathinea 1910].

United States

Minneapolis. Immigration History Research Center, University of Minnesota.
  Theodore Saloutos Collection
  Kostis Tamias Argoe Papers (1930–69)
  Greek American Collection (including miscellaneous monographs and scrapbooks)
New York. New York Historical Society.
  Diary of Alexander Evangelides (1864–1969)
New York. New York Public Library. Manuscripts and Archives Section.
  Dean Alfange Papers (1927–88)
New York. Tamiment Archive of Labor History.
  Poulos Archive
  Εμπρός. Εφημερίς Ελλήνων Εργατών της Αμερικής [Forward: Newspaper of the Greek workers in America] (Chicago), 1923–25.
  Εμπρός. Εφημερίς Ελλήνων Εργατών της Αμερικής [Forward: Newspaper of the Greek workers in America] (New York), 1935–39.
  Η Φωνή του Εργάτου. Όργανον της Ελληνικής Σοσιαλιστικής Ένωσης της Αμερικής [The Worker's voice: Organ of the Greek Socialist Association in America] (New York), 1918–20.
  Ελληνοαμερικανικόν Βήμα [The Greek American tribune] (New York), 1941–46.
Philadelphia. Balch Institute for Ethnic Studies.
  Atlantis, national daily Greek newspaper. Records, 1894–1973. Photographs.
  Gregory G. Lagakos Archive (1912–82).
  Nicholas Vagioni Archive (1902–73).
  Miscellaneous. Articles of Incorporation of Greek Associations in the United States.

Washington, D.C. Library of Congress, Manuscript Division. The U.S. Works Project Administration. Federal Writers Project. Socio-Ethnic Field Studies. Life Histories.

Washington, D.C. National Archives and Records Administration.

Consular Dispatches. T-362, Dispatches from U.S. Consuls in Athens, 1837–1906. T-648, Dispatches from U.S. Consuls in Patras, 1874–1906.

U.S. Department of State, Decimal File: 711.68. M-475, Records of the Department of State Relating to Political Relations between the United States and Greece, 1910–29.

U.S. Department of State (RG 59), Decimal File: 1910–29. "Omaha Riots. Indemnities to Foreign Nationals." Box 3682 (311.674 H 84/1–311.681 SO 8/9). Box 3683 (311.681 SO 8/10–311.682 SP 2/5).

Government Documents
Greece
Πρακτικά της Βουλής [Parliamentary proceedings]. Athens, Greece, 1901–20.

Statistique du commerce spécial de la Grèce avec les pays étrangers. Greek Ministry of the National Economy, Statistical Division. Vol. 1905–20.

United States
Annual Reports of the Commissioner General of Immigration, 1899–1930.

U.S. Department of State. *Papers Relating to the Foreign Relations of the United States, with the Annual Message of the President.* New York: Kraus Reprint, 1968. Vols. 1890–1920.

U.S. Immigration Commission. *Reports of Immigration Commission.* Washington, D.C.: U.S. Government Printing Office, 1911. Vols. 1–42.

Books and Articles
Abbot, Grace. "A Study of the Greeks in Chicago." *American Journal of Sociology* 15, no. 3 (November 1909): 379–93.

Alex, Angel. Καρδιές που Ραΐζουν [Hearts that break]. New York: Divry, 1926.

———. Το Φουστάνι της Γυναίκας μου [My wife's skirt]. N.p., n.d.

Alexopoulos, Ioakim. Μελέτη περί Εκκλησιαστικής Διοργανώσεως του εν Αμερική Ελληνισμού [Study of the ecclesiastic organization of Hellenism in America]. New York, 1919.

———. Οι Κίνδυνοι του εν Αμερική Ελληνισμού και τα μέσα Διασώσεως Αυτού [The dangers threatening Hellenism in America and the means for its salvation]. Boston, 1926.

Ålund, Aleksandra, and Raoul Granqvist, eds. *Negotiating Identities: Essays on Immigration and Culture in Present-Day Europe.* Amsterdam: Rodopi, 1995.

Aman Amerika Orchestra. *Cafe Aman Amerika: Greek-American Songs Revised and Revisited.* [Music recording.] Music World Productions, 1995.

Amantos, Konstantinos. "Το Αιγαίον και η Γεωγραφική Διάσπασις του Ελληνισμού" [The Aegean and the geographic fragmentation of Hellenism]. Ημερολόγιον της Μεγάλης Ελλάδος [Almanac of Great Greece] (1923): 345–46.

Amelio, Gianni. *Lamerica.* [Film.] Florence: Cecchi Gori Editoria Electronica, 1994.

———. *Lamerica: Film e storia del film: Sceneggiatura desunta dal Montaggio.* Turin: Einaudi, 1994.

Anderson, Benedict. "Exodus." *Critical Inquiry* 20 (Winter 1994): 314–27.

———. *Imagined Communities: Reflections on the Origin and Spread of Nationalism.* London: Verso 1983.

Andreadis, Andreas. Η Ελληνική Μετανάστευσις [The Greek migration]. Athens, 1917.

————. "Les émigrants grecs aux Etats-Unis." *Bulletin d'Orient* 212, 213, 220, 222, 226 (1908).

Angelopoulos, Yiorgos, et al. *Ταυτότητες στη Μακεδονία* [Identities in Macedonia]. Athens: Papazisis, 1997.

Anthias, Floya, and Yuval-David, Nira. *Racialized Boundaries: Race, Nation, Gender, Colour, Class and Anti-racist Struggle.* London: Routledge, 1992.

Appadurai, Arjun. *Modernity at Large: Cultural Dimensions of Globalization.* Minneapolis: University of Minnesota Press, 1996.

————. *The Social Life of Things: Commodities in Cultural Perspective.* Cambridge: Cambridge University Press, 1986.

Arendt, Hannah. *On Revolution.* London: Penguin Books, 1990.

Armstrong, Nancy. "Who Is Afraid of the Cultural Turn?" *Differences* 12, no.1 (Spring 2001): 17–49.

Asimakopoulos, I. D. "Μετανάστευσις εις Αμερικήν" [Migration to America]. *Η Σφαίρα* [The Globe], 12 May 1882, pp. 2–3.

Balanos, S. *Έκθεσις του Αποσταλλέντος εις Ιταλίαν Τμηματάρχου της Μεταναστεύσεως προς τον Υπουργόν Εσωτερικών* [Report on the Italian migration submitted by the head of the Migration Office to the minister of Domestic Affairs]. Athens, 1911.

Balibar, Etienne, and Immanuel Wallerstein. *Race, Nation, Class: Ambiguous Identities.* London: Verso, 1991.

Bammer, Angelika, ed. *Displacements: Cultural Identities in Question.* Bloomington: Indiana University Press, 1994.

Barkan, Elazar. *The Retreat of Scientific Racism: Changing Concepts of Race in Britain and the United States between the World Wars.* Cambridge: Cambridge University Press, 1992.

Basch, Linda, Nina Glick Schiller, and Christina Szanton Blanc. *Nations Unbound: Transnational Projects, Postcolonial Predicaments and Deterritorialized Nation-States.* Philadelphia: Gordon and Breach, 1994.

Behar, M. F. *Our National Gates: Shut, Ajar or Open?* New York, 1916.

Bender, Thomas, ed. *Rethinking American History in a Global Age.* Berkeley: University of California Press, 2002.

Benjamin, Jessica. *Like Objects, Love Objects: Essays on Recognition and Sexual Difference.* New Haven: Yale University Press, 1995.

Bennet, David, ed. *Multicultural States: Rethinking Difference and Identity.* London: Routledge, 1998.

Berghahn, Volker R. *America and the Intellectual Cold Wars in Europe: Shepard Stone between Philanthropy, Academy, and Diplomacy.* Princeton: Princeton University Press, 2001.

Bernard, William S., ed. *American Immigration Policy: A Reappraisal.* New York: Harper, 1950.

Bhabha, Homi. *The Location of Culture.* London: Routledge, 1994.

————. *Nation and Narration.* London: Routledge, 1990.

Bitzes, John G. "The Anti-Greek riot of 1909—South Omaha." *Nebraska History* 51, no. 2 (Summer 1970): 199–224.

Boas, Franz. *Changes in the Bodily Form of Descendants of Immigrants.* Washington, D.C.: U.S. Government Printing Office, 1911.

Boelhower, William. *Autobiographical Transactions in Modernist America: The Immigrant, the Architect, the Artist, the Citizen.* Udine: Del Bianco, 1992.

Bogartus, Emory S. *Essentials of Americanization.* Los Angeles: University of Southern California Press, 1920).

Booras, John. Αι Ελληνικαί Θερμοπύλαι [The Greek Thermopylae]. New York, 1910.

Booras Bros. *Ημερολόγιον Θερμοπυλών* [Thermopylae almanac]. New York, 1904.

Bosworth, R. J. B. *Italy and the Wider World, 1860–1960*. London: Routledge, 1996.

Bourne, Randolph. "Trans-national America." *Atlantic Monthly* 118 (July 1916): 86–97.

Brah, Avtar. *Cartographies of Diaspora: Contesting Identities*. London: Routledge, 1996.

Braidotti, Rosi. *Nomadic Subjects: Embodiment and Sexual Difference in Contemporary Feminist Theory*. New York: Columbia University Press, 1994.

Brennan, Teresa, and Martin Jay, eds. *Vision in Context: Historical and Contemporary Perspectives on Sight*. New York: Routledge, 1996.

Brewer, John, and Ann Berminham, eds. *The Consumption of Culture, 1600–1800: Image, Object, Text*. London: Routledge, 1995.

Brodski, Bella, ed. *Life/Lines: Theorizing Women's Autobiography*. Ithaca: Cornell University Press, 1988.

Brown, Kenneth. "Demetra Vaka." *Athene* 9, no. 1 (Spring 1948).

Burgess, Thomas. *Greeks in America*. Boston, 1913.

Butler, Judith. *Gender Trouble: Feminism and the Subversion of Identity*. New York: Routledge, 1990.

Buxbaum, Edwin Clarence. *The Greek-American Group of Tarpon Springs, Florida: A Study of Ethnic Identification and Acculturation*. New York: Arno Press, 1980.

Cadava, Eduardo, Peter Connor, and Jean-Luc Nancy, eds. *Who Comes after the Subject?* New York: Routledge, 1991.

Callimachos, Demetrios. *Νεοελληνικός Πολιτισμός. Δυνατοί Χαρακτήρες. Οι κατά τους Τελευταίους Τρεις Αιώνας Αγωνισθέντες δια την Αναγέννησιν του Ελληνικού Έθνους. Ήρωες και Μάρτυρες. Οι Ηγέτες του Φωτισμού των Ελλήνων. Συγγραφείς και Διδάσκαλοι του Γένους, Εθνικοί Ευεργέται. Οι ανά τον Κόσμον Διαπρέψαντες Μετανάσται* [Modern Greek culture: Powerful modern Greek characters. Individuals who participated in the struggle for the rebirth of the Greek nation during the last three centuries. The nation's authors and teachers. The immigrants who succeeded in all different places on the globe]. New York: Ethnikos Kirix, 1927.

————. *Πώς Προοδεύουν οι Αμερικανοί. Το Πνεύμα, αι Αρχαί και ο Κώδιξ των Σύγχρονων Αμερικανικών Επιχειρήσεων* [How Americans progress: The spirit, principles and code of modern American companies]. New York: Ethnikós Kýrix, 1934.

————. *Το Ευαγγέλιον υπό Σύγχρονον Πνεύμα. Ψυχολογικαί Έρευναι—Φιλοσοφήματα επί της Ζωής—Κοινωνικά Προβλήματα—Χαρακτήρες* [The New Testament in the modern spirit: Psychological researches: Philosophizing about life: Social problems: Characters]. New York: Ethnikós Kýrix, 1925.

Callinikos, Constance. *American Aphrodite: Becoming Female in Greek America*. New York: Pella Publishing, 1990.

Canoutas, Seraphim. *Ελληνο-αμερικανικός Οδηγός* [Greek-American guide]. New York, 1907.

————. *Ο Ελληνισμός εν Αμερική* [Hellenism in America]. New York: Cosmos, 1918.

Catsainos, George. *Η Σύφιλις και οι Συγκακούργοι της. Κοινωνία, Πολιτεία και Ιατρός* [Syphilis and its collaborators: The society, the state, and the doctor]. New York: Cosmos, 1922.

Charis, Petros. "Ο Διασημότερος Έλλην της Αμερικής" [The most famous Greek in America]. *Νέα Εστία* [Nea Estia], Christmas Issue, 1955.

Chasiotis, I. K. *Επισκόπηση της Ιστορίας της Νεοελληνικής Διασποράς* [A review of the history of modern Greek diaspora]. Thessaloniki: Vanias, 1993.

Chatziosif, Ch., ed. *Ιστορία της Ελλάδας του 20ου αιώνα* [History of Greece in the twentieth century], vols. A1–A2, B1–B2. Athens: Vivliorama, 1999–2003.

Chatzipantazis, Thodoros, and Lila Maraka. *Η Αθηναϊκή Επιθεώρηση* [The Athenian revue]. Athens: Estia, 1977.

Chebithes, Vasilios I. *AHEPA and the Progress of Hellenism in America.* New York, 1935.

Cheah, Pheng, and Bruce Robbins, eds. *Cosmopolitics: Thinking and Feeling beyond the Nation.* Minneapolis: University of Minnesota Press, 1998.

Chow, Rey. *The Protestant Ethnic and the Spirit of Capitalism.* New York: Columbia University Press, 2002.

———. *Writing Diaspora: Tactics of Intervention in Contemporary Cultural Studies.* Bloomington: Indiana University Press, 1993.

Christophis, Chr. *Ύλη προς Σύνταξιν Νομοσχεδίου περί Μεταναστεύσεως* [Material for a migration bill]. Piraeus, 1905.

Cinel, Dino. *The National Integration of Italian Return Migration, 1870–1929.* Cambridge: Cambridge University Press, 1991.

Clarke, John, Ch. Critcher, and Richard Johnson. *Working-Class Culture: Studies in History and Theory.* New York: St. Martin's Press, 1980.

Clifford, James. "Travelling Cultures." In *Cultural Studies,* ed. Lawrence Grossberg et al. New York: Routledge, 1992.

Cohen, Liz. *Making a New Deal: Industrial Workers in Chicago, 1919–1939.* Cambridge: Cambridge University Press, 1990.

Contopoulos, Michael. *The Greek Community of New York City: Early Years to 1910.* New Rochelle, N.Y.: Aristides D. Cavatzas, 1992.

Crook, Paul. *Darwinism, War and History.* Cambridge: Cambridge University Press, 1994.

Dafnis, Grigorios. *Η Ελλάς Μεταξύ Δύο Πολέμων, 1923–1940* [Greece between two wars, 1923–1940]. Athens: Ikaros, 1955.

Daughters of Penelope. *The 50th Anniversary of the Daughters of Penelope, 1929–1979.* Washington, D.C.: AHEPA, 1979[?].

Deleuze, Gilles, and Félix Guattari. *A Thousand Plateaus: Capitalism and Schizophrenia.* Minneapolis: University of Minnesota Press, 1987 [1980].

———. "What Is a Minor Literature?" In *Out There: Marginalization and Contemporary Cultures,* ed. Russell Ferguson, Martha Gever, Trinh T. Minh-ha, and Cornel West. Cambridge, Mass.: MIT Press, 1990.

Dendias, M. *Αι Ελληνικαί Παροικίαι ανά τον Κόσμον* [The Greek colonies around the world]. Athens, 1919.

Dimitriou, Sotiris. *Ν' Ακούω Καλά τ' Όνομά Σου* [May I always hear good things about you]. Athens: Kedros, 1993.

Drachsler, Julius. *Democracy and Assimilation: The Blending of Immigrants Heritages in America.* New York: Macmillan, 1920.

Dragoumis, Ion. *Ελληνικός Πολιτισμός* [Greek culture]. Athens, 1927 [1914].

———. *Ο Ελληνισμός μου και οι Έλληνες* [My Hellenism and the Greeks]. Athens, 1927 [1903–9].

Economidou-Sarantidou, Maria. *Οι Έλληνες της Αμερικής, Όπως τους Είδα* [The Greeks of America as I saw them]. New York: Divry, 1916.

Emke-Poulopoulou, Ira. *Προβλήματα Μεταστεύσης-Παλιννόστησης* [Problems of migration and repatriation]. Athens: Institute for the Study of Greek Economy, Greek Association of Demographic Studies, 1986.

"Empowering the Minor." Special issue of *Journal of Modern Greek Studies* 8, no. 2 (1990).

Epitropi tis Voulis. *Η εξ Ελλάδος Μετανάστευσις. Η Έκθεσις της Επιτροπής της Βουλής και Σχετική Πρότασις Νόμου* [Migration from Greece. The report prepared by the Parliamentary Committee, accompanied by relevant bill]. Athens, 1906.

Fairchild, Henry Pratt. *Greek Immigration to the United States.* New Haven: Yale University Press, 1911.

Falanga, Marika M. "Οι Φθισικές" [The consumptives]. *Ελληνίς* [Greek Woman] 12 (1932): 255.

Featherstone, Mike, ed. *Cultural Theory and Cultural Change.* London: Sage Publications, 1992.

Felman, Shoshana. *What Does a Woman Want? Reading and Sexual Difference.* Baltimore: Johns Hopkins University Press, 1993.

Fenton, Heike, and Melvin Hecker. *The Greeks in America, 1528–1977: A Chronology and Fact Book.* New York: Oceana Publications, 1978.

Flax, Jane. *Disputed Subjects: Essays on Psychoanalysis, Politics, and Philosophy.* New York: Routledge, 1993.

———. *Thinking Fragments: Psychoanalysis, Feminism, and Postmodernism in the Contemporary West.* Berkeley: University of California Press, 1990.

Folkmar, Daniel, and Elnora Folkmar. *Dictionary of Races or Peoples.* Washington, D.C.: U.S. Government Printing Office, 1911.

Foucault, Michel. *The Archaeology of Knowledge.* London: Tavistock, 1974 [1969].

———. "Nietzsche, Genealogy, History." In *Language, Counter-Memory, Practice,* ed. Donald Bouchard. Ithaca: Cornell University Press, 1977 [1971].

Freud, Sigmund. *The Interpretation of Dreams.* Trans. James Strachey. New York: Basic Books, 1955.

Galton, Francis. *Hereditary Genius: An Inquiry into Its Laws and Consequences.* London: Macmillan, 1869.

———. *Inquiries into Human Faculty and Its Development.* London: Macmillan, 1883.

Georgakas, Dan. *Greek America at Work.* New York: Smyrna Press, 1992.

Georgakas, Dan, and Charles C. Moskos, eds. *New Directions in Greek American Studies.* New York: Pella Publishing, 1991.

Gilroy, Paul. *The Black Atlantic: Modernity and Double Consciousness.* Cambridge, Mass.: Harvard University Press, 1993.

———. "Cultural Studies and Ethnic Absolutism." In *Cultural Studies,* ed. Lawrence Grossberg, Cary Nelson, and Paula A. Treichler. New York: Routledge, 1992.

Goldberg, David Theo, ed. *Anatomy of Racism.* Minneapolis: University of Minnesota Press, 1990.

Gossett, Thomas. *Race: The History of an Idea in America.* Dallas: Southern Methodist University, 1963.

Grant, Madison, and Chas. Stewart Davison, eds. *The Alien in Our Midst* (New York: Galton Publishing Co., 1923.

Greek Archives. *The Rebetiko Song in America 1920–1940.* Vol.1. [Music recording.] FM Records SA, 1993.

Hall, Stuart. "Cultural Identity and Diaspora." In *Identity: Community, Culture, Difference,* ed. Jonathan Rutherford. London: Lawrence & Wishart, 1990.

Hall, Stuart, et al. *Policing the Crisis: Mugging, the State, and Law and Order.* London: Macmillan, 1978.

Handlin, Oscar. *Race and Nationality in the United States.* Boston: Little, Brown, 1957.

Hardt, Michael, and Antonio Negri. *Empire*. Cambridge, Mass.: Harvard University Press, 2000.

Hauser, Philip Morris. *Local Community Fact Book: Chicago Metropolitan Area*. Chicago, 1938.

Hebdige, Dick. *Subculture: The Meaning of Style*. London: Methuen, 1979.

Higham, John. *Strangers in the Land: Patterns of American Nativism, 1860–1925*. New Brunswick, N.J.: Rutgers University Press, 1988.

Hoerder, Dirk. *Labor Migration in the Atlantic Economies: The European and North American Working Classes during the Period of Industrialization*. Westport, Conn.: Greenwood Publishing Group, 1985.

Hoerder, Dirk, and Leslie Page Moch, eds. *European Migrants: Global and Local Perspectives*. Boston: Northeastern University Press, 1996.

Hunt, Milton B. "The Housing of Non-family Groups of Men in Chicago." *American Journal of Sociology* 16 (1910): 145–71.

Iggers, Georg. *The German Conception of History: The National Tradition of Historical Thought from Herder to the Present*. Middletown: Wesleyan University Press, 1968.

———. *Historiography in the Twentieth Century: From Scientific Objectivity to the Postmodern Challenge*. Hanover, N.H.: Wesleyan University Press, 1997 [1993].

Ignatiev, Noel. *How the Irish Became White*. New York: Routledge, 1995.

International Labor Office. *Emigration and Migration: Legislation and Treaties*. Geneva, 1922.

Jacobson, Matthew Frye. *Barbarian Virtues: The United States Encounters Foreign Peoples at Home and Abroad, 1876–1917*. New York: Hill and Wang, 2000.

———. *Special Sorrows: The Diasporic Imagination of Irish, Polish and Jewish Immigrants in the United States*. Cambridge, Mass.: Harvard University Press, 1995.

———. *Whiteness of a Different Color: European Immigrants and the Alchemy of Race*. Cambridge, Mass.: Harvard University Press, 1998.

Janetis, Elias. *Η Αυτού Μεγαλειότης, ο Μετανάστης* [His majesty the migrant]. New York: NYL Anatolia Press, 1946.

Jannopoulo, Helen Phiambolis. *And across Big Seas*. Caldwell, Idaho: Caxton, 1949.

Jenks, Jeremiah, et al. *The Immigration Problem: A Study of American Immigration Conditions and Needs*. New York: Funk & Wagnalls, 1912.

Johnson, Richard. "Frameworks of Culture and Power: Complexity and Politics in Cultural Studies." *Critical Studies* 3, no. 1 (1991).

———. "Towards a Cultural Theory of the Nation: A British-Dutch Dialogue." In *Images of the Nation: Different Meanings of Dutchness 1870–1940*, ed. Annemieke Galema et al. Amsterdam: Rodopi, 1993.

Kallen, Horace. *Culture and Democracy in the United States*. New York: Boni and Liveright, 1924.

Kalogeras, Yiorgos. "A Child of the Orient as American Storyteller: Demetra Vaka-Brown." Working Papers of the English Department, Aristotle University, 1989, pp. 187–93.

———. " 'The Other Space' of Greek America." *American Literary History* 10, no. 4 (1998): 702–24.

———. "Suspended Souls, Ensnaring Discourses: Theano Papazoglou-Margaris' Immigration Stories." *Journal of Modern Greek Studies* 8, no. 1 (May 1990): 85–96.

Kaplan, Caren. *Questions of Travel: Postmodern Discourses of Displacement*. Durham: Duke University Press, 1996.

Katsiardi-Hering, Olga. *Η Ελληνική Παροικία Τεργέστης, 1751–1830* [The Greek community in Trieste, 1751–1830]. Athens, 1984.

Kaufman, Rhoda. "The Yiddish Theater in New York and the Immigrant Jewish Community: Theater as Secular Ritual." Ph.D. diss., University of California Berkeley, 1986.

Kitroeff, Alexander. *The Greeks in Egypt, 1919–1937: Ethnicity and Class.* London: Ithaca Press, 1989.

———. "The Transformation of Homeland-Diaspora Relations: The Greek Case in the Nineteenth and Twentieth Centuries." In *Proceedings of the First International Congress on the Hellenic Diaspora: From Antiquity to Modern Times,* ed. John M. Fossey. Vol. 2, *From 1453 to Modern Times.* Amsterdam: J.C. Gieben, 1991.

Kollias, Sephes. *Δημ. Καλλίμαχος. Μια Άρτια Αγωνιστική Συνείδηση* [Dem. Callimachos: A perfect fighting consciousness]. Athens, 1963.

Koshy, Susan. "American Nationhood as Eugenic Romance." *Differences* 12, no. 1 (Spring 2001): 50–78.

Kotakis, Sryridon. *Οι Έλληνες εν Αμερική* [The Greeks in America]. Chicago: S. P. Kotakis, 1908.

Lacan, Jacques. *The Four Fundamental Concepts of Psychoanalysis.* New York: W. W. Norton, 1981 [1973].

Lacey, Thomas J. *A Study of Social Heredity as Illustrated in the Greek People.* New York, 1916.

Ladoyianni, Nina. *Ένας Έλληνας στην Αμερική* [A Greek in America]. Volos, 1954.

Lambropoulos, Nikos. *Ιερείς και Παπάδες* [Priests and fathers]. San Francisco: California Greek Newspaper, 1935.

———. *Οι Φωστήρες* [Leading lights]. San Francisco, 1925.

———. *Ο Κακός Δρόμος* [Going astray]. San Francisco: Prometheus Publishing, 1928.

Lane, A. T. *Solidarity or Survival? American Labor and European Immigrants, 1830–1924.* New York: Greenwood Press, 1987.

Lauck, Jett. "Industrial Communities." *Survey,* 7 January 1911, pp. 585–86.

Lavie, Smadar, and Ted Swedenburg. *Displacement, Diaspora and Geographies of Identity* (Durham: Duke University Press, 1996.

Leontis, Artemis. *Topographies of Hellenism: Mapping the Homeland.* Ithaca: Cornell University Press, 1995.

———. "Women's Fabric Arts in Greek America." *Laografia: A Journal of the International Greek Folklore Society* 12, no. 3 (May–June 1995): 5–11.

Liakos, Antonis. *Εργασία και Πολιτική στην Ελλάδα του Μεσοπολέμου. Το Διεθνές Γραφείο Εργασίας και η Ανάδυση των Κοινωνικών Θεσμών* [Labor and politics in interwar Greece: The International Labor Office and the emergence of social institutions]. Athens: Idryma Ereunas kai Paideias Emporikis Trapezas Elladas, 1993.

———. *Η Ιταλική Ενοποίηση και η Μεγάλη Ιδέα* [The Italian unification and the great idea]. Athens: Themelio, 1985.

Likoudis, Emmanuil. *Οι Μετανάσται* [The migrants]. Athens: Proskopos Press, 1919.

Lowe, Lisa. *Immigrant Acts: On Asian American Cultural Politics.* Durham: Duke University Press, 1996.

Ludmerer, Kenneth M. "American Genetics and Eugenics Movement: 1905–1935." *Journal of the History of Biology* 2, no. 2 (Fall 1969): 337–62.

Lumas (Theophilakes), Eustratios. *Οι Περιπλανώμενοι* [The Vagrant people]. New York: Stamatakis CH. M., 1918.

Makridis, Nikos. *Αι Υπηρεσίαι Υγιεινής εν Ελλάδι* [Health services in Greece]. Athens, 1933.

Manos, Karolos. *Η Ζωή Ενός Μετανάστη* [The life of a migrant]. Athens, 1964.

Maurogordatos, G., and Ch. Chatziosif. *Βενιζελισμός και Αστικός Εκσυγχρονισμός* [Venizelism and civic modernization]. Heraklion: Crete University Press, 1988.

McRobbie, Angela. *Feminism and Youth Culture.* London: Macmillan, 1991.

Μηνιαία Εικονογραφημένη Ατλαντίδα [Atlantis monthly illustrated]. Vol. 1, no. 1 (January 1910) through vol. 22, no. 12 (December 1932).

Μηνιαίος Εικονογραφημένος Εθνικός Κήρυξ [Ethnikós Kýrix monthly illustrated]. Vol. 1, no. 7 (July 1915) through vol. 25, no. 9 (September 1939).

Michaels, Walter. *Our America: Nativism, Modernism, and Pluralism.* Durham: Duke University Press, 1995.

Michalaros, Dimitris. "The Chronicle of Halsted Street." *Athene* 24, no. 1 (Spring 1963): 44.

Moskos, Charles C. *Greek Americans, Struggle and Success.* Englewood Cliffs, N.J.: Prentice-Hall, 1980.

Mumford, Lewis. *The Story of Utopias.* New York: Boni and Liveright, 1922.

Ngai, Mae. "The Architecture of Race in American Immigration Law: A Re-examination of the Immigration Act of 1924." *Journal of American History* 86 (1999): 59–86.

Nystrom, Paul Henry. *Economic Principles of Consumption.* New York: Ronald Press Co., 1929.

Olney, James, ed. *Autobiography: Essays Theoretical and Critical.* Princeton: Princeton University Press, 1980.

Ong, Aiwa. *Flexible Citizenship: The Cultural Logics of Transnationality.* Durham: Duke University Press, 1999.

Ong, Aiwa, and Donald Nomini, eds. *Ungrounded Empires: The Cultural Politics of Modern Chinese Transnationalism.* New York: Routledge, 1997.

Papacosma, Victor. "The Greek Press in America." *Journal of the Hellenic Diaspora* 5, no. 4 (Winter 1979): 45–61.

Papachristodoulou, Pol. "Μια Γιγαντιαία Μορφή της Θράκης εις την Νέαν Υόρκην" [A great Thracian in New York]. *Αρχείον του Θρακικού Λαογραφικού και Γλωσσικού Θησαυρού* [Bulletin of the Thracian folklore and linguistic treasure] 23 (1958): 403–5.

Papanikolas, Helen. *Αιμιλία-Γεώργιος* [Emily-George]. Salt Lake City: University of Utah Press, 1987.

———. *An Amulet of Greek Earth: Generations of Immigrant Folk Culture.* Athens: Swallow Press; Ohio University Press, 2002.

———. "The Greeks of Carbon County." *Utah Historical Quarterly* 22, no. 2 (April 1954): 143–64.

———. "Magerou, the Greek Midwife." *Utah Historical Quarterly* 38 (1970): 50–60.

———. "Toil and Rage in a New Land: The Greek Immigrants in Utah." *Utah Historical Quarterly* 38 (1970): 97–206.

Papazoglou-Margaris, Theano. *Χρονικό του Χώλστεντ Στρητ: Ελληνοαμερικανικά Διηγήματα* [Chronicle of Halsted Street: Greek-American short stories]. Athens, 1962.

Park, Robert. *The Immigrant Press and Its Control.* New York: Harper & Brothers, 1922.

Passerini, Luisa. "Becoming a Subject in the Time of the Death of the Subject." Paper given at the Fourth European Feminist Research Conference, Bologna, September 2000. Available online: <www.women.it/cyberarchive>

———. *Identità culturale Europea: Idee, sentimenti, relazioni.* Florence: La Nuova Italia, 1998.

———, ed. *Across the Atlantic: Cultural Exchanges between Europe and the United States.* Brussels: P.I.E.–Peter Lang, 2000.

Patterson, James. "The Unassimilated Greeks of Denver." *Anthropological Quarterly* 43 (October 1970): 245–49.

Pavalko, Ronald M. "Racism and the New Immigration: A Reinterpretation of the Assimilation of White Ethnics in American Society." *Sociology and Social Research* 65, no. 1 (1980): 56–77.

Pentzopoulos, Dimitri. *The Balkan Exchange of Minorities and Its Impact upon Greece.* Paris: Mouton, 1962.

Peyser, Thomas. *Utopia and Cosmopolis: Globalization in the Era of American Literary Realism.* Durham: Duke University Press, 1998.

Phoultrides, Aristides, and Demetra Vaka, trans. *Modern Greek Stories.* New York: Arno Press, 1920.

Polenis, Emmanuil. *Εγκόλπιον Μετανάστου. Συμβουλαί, Ανέκδοτα, Ιστορικά Γεγονότα* [The migrant's handbook: Advice, anecdotes, and historical events]. Athens, 1945.

Poster, Mark. *The Information Subject.* New York: Routledge, 2001.

"Πώς θα σωθώμεν από της ερημώσεως" [How are we going to be saved from desolation?]. *Η Σφαίρα* [The Globe], 17 March 1907, p. 1.

Pozzetta, George E., ed. *Nativism, Discrimination, and Images of Immigrants.* New York: Garland Publishing, 1991.

Protonotarios, Athanasios. *Το Προσφυγικόν Πρόβλημα από Ιστορικής, Νομικής και Κρατικής Απόψεως* [The refugee problem from historical, legal and state perspectives]. Athens: Pyrsos, 1929.

Psomiades, Harry J., and Alice Scourby, eds. *The Greek-American Community in Transition.* New York: Pella Publishing, 1982.

Repoulis, Emmanuel. *Μελέτη περί Μεταναστεύσεως μετά Σχεδίου Νόμου* [Study and bill on migration]. Athens, 1912.

Richards, Barry, ed. *Crises of the Self.* London: Free Association Press, 1989.

Roberts, Kenneth. *Why Europe Leaves Home.* Indianapolis: Bobbs & Merrill, 1922.

Rodgers, Daniel. *Atlantic Crossings: Social Politics in a Progressive Age.* Cambridge, Mass.: Belknap Press of Harvard University Press, 1998.

Roediger, David, ed. *Towards the Abolition of Whiteness: Essays on Race, Politics and Working Class History.* London: Verso, 1994.

Rogers, James Allen. "Darwinism and Social Darwinism." *Journal of the History of Ideas* 33, no. 2 (1986): 265–80.

Rosen, Bernard C. "Race, Ethnicity, and the Achievement Syndrome." *American Sociological Review* 24, no. 1 (February 1959): 47–60.

Roussopoulou, Agni. *Οδηγός Ιδρυμάτων Κοινωνικής Πρόνοιας* [A guide to social welfare institutions]. Athens, 1936.

Rozakos, Nikos. *Το Νεοελληνικό Θέατρο στην Αμερική, 1903–1950* [Popular modern Greek theater in America, 1903–1950]. San Francisco: Falcon Associates, 1985.

Saloutos, Theodore. *The Greeks in the United States.* Cambridge, Mass.: Harvard University Press, 1964.

———. *They Remember America: The Story of the Repatriated Greek-Americans.* Berkeley: University of California Press, 1956.

Saneth, Edward. *American Historians and European Immigrants 1875–1925.* New York: Russell and Russell, 1965 [1948].

Sassen, Saskia. *Guests and Aliens.* New York: New Press, 1999.

Saunier, Michel. *Το Δημοτικό Τραγούδι της Ξενιτιάς* [Folksongs about migrancy]. Athens: Hermes, 1990.

Schneirov, Matthew. *The Dream of a New Social Order: Popular Magazines in America 1893–1914.* New York: Columbia University Press, 1994.

Scourby, Alice. *The Greek Americans.* Boston: Twayne Publishers, 1984.

Sedgwick, Eve Kosofsky. *Between Men: English Literature and Male Homosocial Desire.* New York: Columbia University Press, 1985.

Showalter, Elaine, ed. *Speaking of Gender.* New York: Routledge, 1989.

Singh, A., J. Skerrett, and R. Hogan, eds. *Memory, Narrative, and Identity: New Essays in Ethnic American Literatures.* Boston: Northeastern University Press, 1994.

Skliros, Yeoryios. *Τα Σύγχρονα Προβλήματα του Ελληνισμού* [The contemporary problems of Hellenism]. Alexandria: Grammata, 1919.

Smith, Sidonie. *Subjectivity, Identity and the Body: Women's Autobiographical Practices in the Twentieth Century.* Bloomington: Indiana University Press, 1993.

Smith, Sidonie, and Julia Watson, eds. *De/colonizing the Subject: The Politics of Gender in Women's Autobiographies.* Minneapolis: University of Minnesota Press, 1992.

Sollors, Werner. *Beyond Ethnicity: Consent and Descent in American Culture.* Oxford: Oxford University Press, 1986.

—————. *Neither Black nor White and Yet Both: Thematic Explorations of Interracial Literature.* New York: Oxford University Press, 1997.

Sotiropoulou, Chrisanthi. *Η Μετανάστευση στον Ελληνικό Κινηματογράφο* [Migration in Greek cinema]. Athens, 1994.

Spivak, Gayatri. "Foundations and Cultural Studies." In *Questioning Foundations: Truth/Subjectivity/Culture,* ed. Hugh J. Silverman. New York: Routledge, 1993.

—————. "The Political Economy of Women as Seen by a Literary Critic." in *Coming to Terms: Feminism. Theory, Politics,* ed. Elizabeth Weed. New York: Routledge, 1989.

Steiner, Edward. *On the Trail of the Immigrant.* New York: Fleming H. Revell Company, 1906.

Stepan, Nancy. *The Idea of Race in Science: Great Britain 1800–1960.* London: Macmillan, 1982.

Stoianovich, Traian. "The Conquering, Balkan, Orthodox Merchant." *Journal of Economic History* 20 (1960): 234–313.

Talbot, Winthrop. *Americanization, Principles of Americanism, Essentials of Americanization, Technic of Race-Assimilation: Annotated Bibliography.* New York: H. W. Wilson Co., 1917.

Taylor, Carol M. "W. E. B. Dubois's Challenge to Scientific Racism." *Journal of Black Studies* 11, no. 4 (1981): 449–60.

Theodoratus, Robert James. *A Greek Community in America.* Tacoma, Wash., Sacramento, Calif.: Sacramento Anthropological Society, Sacramento State College, 1971.

Theotokas, Yiorgos. *Δοκίμιο για την Αμερική* [An essay on America]. Athens: Ikaros, 1954.

Todorova, Maria. *Imagining the Balkans.* New York: Oxford University Press, 1997.

Tournakis, Ioannis. *Διεθνής Μεταναστευτική Κίνησις* [International migration movement]. Athens, 1930.

—————. *Μετανάστευσις και Μεταναστευτική Πολιτική* [Migration and migration policy]. Athens, 1923.

Triantafyllidis, Manolis. *Έλληνες της Αμερικής. Μια Ομιλία* [Greeks of America: A speech]. Athens, 1952.

Vaka-Brown, Demetra. *Bribed to Be Born.* New York: Exposition Press, 1951.

—————. *A Child of the Orient.* Boston: Houghton Mifflin, 1914.

—————. *A Duke's Price.* Boston: Houghton Mifflin, 1910.

—————. *The First Secretary.* With Kenneth Brown. New York: B. W. Dodge Company, 1907.

—————. "For a Heart for Any Fate." *Athene* 8, no. 3 (autumn 1947) through 13, no. 4 (Winter 1953).

—————. *The Grasp of the Sultan.* Boston: Houghton Mifflin, 1916.

—————. *Haremlik: Some Pages from the Life of Turkish Women.* Boston: Houghton Mifflin, 1909.

—————. *The Heart of the Balkans.* Boston: Houghton Mifflin, 1917.

————. *In the Heart of the German Intrigue*. Boston: Houghton Mifflin, 1918.

————. *In Pawn to a Throne*. With Kenneth Brown. London: John Lane Company, 1919.

————. *In the Shadow of Islam*. Boston: Houghton Mifflin, 1911.

————. *The Unveiled Ladies of Stamboul*. Boston: Houghton Mifflin; Cambridge: Riverside Press, 1923.

Valaoras, Vasileios. "Κληρονομικότητα και Περιβάλλον" [Heredity and Environment]. *Επιστημονική Ηχώ* [Scientific echo] (April 1936): 50–54.

————. *Ο Ελληνισμός των Ηνωμένων Πολιτειών* [The Hellenism of the United States]. Athens, 1937.

Vardoulakis, Mary. *Gold in the Streets*. New York: Dodd, Mead, 1945.

Verdicchio, Pasquale. *Bound by Distance: Rethinking Nationalism through the Italian Diaspora*. London: Associated University Presses, 1997.

Veremis, Thanos. *Μελετήματα για τον Βενιζέλο και την Εποχή του* [Studies on Venizelos and his era]. Athens: Philippotis, 1980.

Vlachos, Evan. *The Assimilation of Greeks in the United States, with Special Reference to the Greek Commnunity of Anderson, Indiana*. Athens: E.K.K.E., 1968.

Vlavianos, S. "Ψυχολογία του Σύγχρονου Ελληνικού Λαού" [Psychology of modern Greek people]. *Ψυχιατρική και Νευρολογική Επιθεώρησις* [Psychiatric and Neurological Review] (1903): 219.

Wald, Priscilla. *Constituting Americans: Cultural Anxiety and Narrative Form*. Durham: Duke University Press, 1995.

Weatherford, Doris. *Foreign and Female: Immigrant Women in America, 1840–1930*. New York: Schocken Books, 1986.

Xanthaky, Socrates A. *Ο Σύντροφος του Έλληνος εν Αμερική* [The companion of Greeks in America]. New York, 1903.

Xenides, J. P. *The Greeks in America*. New York, 1922.

Yans-McLaughlin, Virginia, ed. *Immigration Reconsidered: History, Sociology and Politics*. New York: Oxford University Press, 1990.

Yiannopoulos, Periclis. *Έκκλησις προς το Πανελλήνιον Κοινόν* [Call to the Panhellenic public]. Athens, 1907.

————. *Νέον Πνεύμα* [New spirit]. Athens, 1906.

Young, Robert. *Colonial Desire: Hybridity in Theory, Culture and Race*. London: Routledge, 1995.

————. *White Mythologies: Writing History and the West*. London: Routledge, 1990.

Žižek, Slavoj. *For They Know Not What They Do: Enjoyment as a Political Factor*. London: Verso, 1991.

Zolotas, Xenophon. *Μετανάστευσις Οικονομική Ανάπτυξις* [Migration and economic development]. Athens, 1966.

genetics, social engineering and, 23. *See also* eugenics

Geneva Convention, 8

Gennadeios, Ioannis, 82

Gennadeios Library, 82

ghettos, 39–40

globalization: American culture as global, 15; exaggeration of, 5; historicizing, 5; nationalism undermined by, 4. *See also* transnationalism

Going Astray (Lambropoulos), 132, 223n19

Gold in the Streets (Vardoulakis), 1–2

"Great Idea," 54–55, 72

Greece: American philanthropic institutions in, 82, 222n61; Andreadis's research on migration, 56, 212n18; autobiographies of migrants as viewed in, 173; commerce between U.S. and, 135; cultural adaptability of Greeks, 65, 67–68; cultural backwardness of, 68–69, 77, 84, 175; desire to migrate in self-representation in, 65, 67; emigration as little studied, 203n7; feminist movement in, 114; government interest in Greek communities in U.S., 69–73, 89; "Great Idea" in, 54–55, 72; individualism as characteristic of, 195; International Service for the Protection of Migrants in, 61; labor migration as massive phenomenon in, 53; migrants arriving in, 8, 199; migrants defined by, 62–63; migrants visiting as tourists, 82–83, 139, 222n61; migration agents in, 61; Migration and Expatriation Law, 62; migration bill of 1912, 59–60; migration bill of 1913, 62; migration in national debates in, 51, 53–56; migration seen as contagious in, 64; migration seen as multifaceted phenomenon in, 56–63; multiplicity of terms for migration, 66; national character and migration, 58, 64–69; national consciousness and migration, 58, 68; nation and diaspora in, 53–55; as nation of migrants, 56, 86, 198; natural resources as scarce in, 57; Ottoman rule in, 53; Piraeus, 76, 140, 141; population exchanges with Asia Minor, 55, 57, 65, 75, 103; post–World

War II migration from, 173; racism debate in, 199; residential tax on Greeks residing in U.S., 71–72; royalists and antiroyalists, 150–51; seafaring identity of, 65–66; as Southern, Balkan, and European, 14; the state and emigration, 59–63; War of Independence of 1821, 53, 124, 154–55, 156, 176; women's emigration controlled in, 60–61; in World War I, 125. *See also* Athens; Greek diaspora; repatriation of Greek migrants

Greek-American Bank, 139

Greek American Progressive Association (GAPA), 139, 152

Greek Colonies around the World, The (Dendias), 66

Greek consulates, 70

Greek diaspora: as colonies, 66–67; Greek representation of, 16; merchants in, 136; and nation in Greece, 53–55; political developments devastating, 97. *See also* Greek migrants in U.S.

Greek language, 127–29

Greek migrants in U.S.: amateur theater of, 131–35; American Hellenic Educational Progressive Association, 82–83, 139, 152, 220n32; Americanization separating public and private spheres, 107, 120, 205n20; American social scientists on, 179, 229n22; antimigrant violence, 185–86; autobiographies of, 171–96; bohemianism among, 175; *café aman*, 129, 130; chronicles of, 178–86; communities referred to as colonies, 66; community guides and directories, 178–79, 229n18; consolidation of Greek American identity, 150; as contributing to progress of Greece, 68; cultural exhibitionism in, 126; as distinct category of diasporic Greeks, 63; Fairchild on, 179–81, 184, 229n22; folksongs on experience of, 87–89; fraternal associations of, 152, 220n32; Greek American Progressive Association, 139, 152; Greek government attempts to cultivate relations with, 61–62; Greek government reports and legislation on, 59–63; Greek government transnational

popular culture: Greek migrants consuming, 136–37, 142; post–World
War II Americanization of, 173. *See also*
entertainment
private and public spheres. *See* public and
private spheres
progress, 68, 69, 77, 82, 164
prostitution: controlling women migrants
to combat, 61; Greek migrants compared
with prostitutes, 77; Immigration
Commission gathering data on, 26
Protestantism, 43
Protoporos (journal), 97–98, 105–6, 115,
219n20
psychoanalysis, 42, 126, 210n75, 228n49
psychobiography, 147–70; Callimachos's
sketches as, 154; migrant subjectivity
and, 149–58; of Vaka, 158–70
"Psychology of Modern Greek People, The"
(Vlavianos), 67
public and private spheres: Americanization
separating, 107, 120, 205n20; ethnic
culture as private, 120, 222n58; in short
stories of migration, 106–7, 114–15,
122; time divided according to, 120,
222n58
publishing companies of Greek migrants,
93, 94, 132, 138

race: in American nationalism, 22; Boas
on, 210n69; classification for new
immigrants, 29–33; migrant subjectivity
affected by, 15; miscegenation, 36, 37;
racialization, 15, 168; social problem
emerging from, 23, 24. *See also* eugenics;
racism; whiteness
racism: antimigrant violence and discrimination, 185–86; experience of migration
and, 199; psychoanalysis in analysis
of, 210n75; scientific versus cultural,
43, 45
radio, 133, 136
recording companies, 129
Red Scare, 31
reformed subjects, Greek migrants in U.S.
as, 80–90
religious celebrations, 107–8, 220n34
remittances, 52, 53, 139, 140, 172, 173

repatriation of Greek migrants, 73–80; in
amateur theater, 132; autobiographies
of repatriated migrants, 172; folksongs
about, 87–88; to former socialist countries, 200; percentage who returned, 53,
74; Saloutos's research on, 191, 192–95;
short stories of migration on, 109–10,
118; sick migrant returning home to
die, 109–10; women wanting to marry
returning migrants, 111
Repoulis, Emmanuel, 62
residential tax on Greeks residing in U.S.,
71–72
Rethinking American History (Bender),
204n9
"Return, The" (Evrotas), 220n27
revues, 77–78
Roberts, Kenneth, 38–42, 209n65, 210n69
Robertson, Roland, 28
Roosevelt, Theodore, 25
roots, and essentialist notions of origins, 5
royalists, 150–51

Saloutos, Theodore, 187, 191–95, 231n57
San Francisco Greektown, 74
sanitation, data collected on immigrant, 30
Sassen, Saskia, 8, 50
Saturday Evening Post, 38
Saunier, Michel, 87
Schaulust, 126
science fiction, 23
scientific racism, 43, 45
self: essentialist notions of, 11; in memories
of the homeland, 118; technologies
of, 21–49. *See also* identity; self-
representation; subjectivity
self-improvement, 175
self-representation: commodities in
migrant, 129, 130–31; desire to migrate
in Greek, 65, 67; diffracted images in, 2;
parody in migrant, 134–35, 143
short stories of migration, 93–122; as
collective, 98–99; deviation stories, 102;
forgetfulness in, 105; in Greek migrant
publications, 95; homeland and America
stories, 100–103, 219n22; interruptive
events in, 105; labor as subject of,
108–10; location as preoccupation of,

100; memories of the homeland in, 116–20; as minor literature, 95–96; as most appropriate genre for experiences of migration, 98–99; private and public as distinct in, 106–7, 114–15, 122; readership addressed by, 96; reality related to fiction in, 99–100; recurrent themes in, 99, 100, 101; religious celebrations in, 107–8; sanitarium and asylum as locations for, 109; time as represented in, 103–8; women migrants as represented in, 101, 102, 110–16

Skliros, Yeoryios, 65

smoking, 130–31

social Darwinism, 30

social engineering, 23–24; Americanization as, 24, 47; Chicago school of sociology and, 49; and emergence of migrants as recognizable subject, 24, 197; and eugenics, 35; immigration problem as problem of, 15–16, 24

socialist stories, 105–6, 110

social politics, 22–24

social problem: emerging in early twentieth century, 22; migration perceived as part of, 25, 33, 197; social difference causing, 23, 24

social reform: migrants as subjects of, 33; nativism and cultural pluralism inspiring, 24; and social engineering, 23. *See also* social engineering

songs, Greek, 129–30

Sons of America, 206n17

Southern/Eastern European migrants: conceptualizations of subjectivity and culture affected by, 13–14; eugenics and, 35–37; national debates on migration, 50–56; as "new immigration," 25–33; popular images of, 37–45; U.S. government report on, 60. *See also* Greek migrants in U.S.

Spivak, Gayatri Chakravorty, 93, 149

standard of civilization, 27–28, 33

standard of living, immigrants seen as lowering, 41

steamship companies, 61–62, 75, 135, 138–39

Stepan, Nancy, 34, 36

stories, short. *See* short stories of migration

"Studies and Methods of Americanization" series, 211n93, 219n16

subcultural movements, 137

subjectivity: eugenics as project of subjectivation, 33–37; as historical process, 10, 204n14; new forms in United States, 176; social engineering and subjectivation, 23–24; in Vaka's work, 158–70. *See also* migrant subjectivity

syphilis, Greek migrants suffering from, 74, 77

ta tragoúdia tis xenitiás, 87

tax on Greeks residing in U.S., 71–72

Taylor, Carol M., 207n29

temporality. *See* time

territoriality, in discourses of Greek nationhood, 53–55. *See also* deterritorialization

theater: amateur theater of Greek migrants, 131–35; Osborn on immigrants and, 44. *See also* Greek theater

Theotokas, Yiorgos, 85–86

They Remember America: The Story of Repatriated Greek Americans (Saloutos), 191, 192–95

Third World, cultural difference associated with, 5–6

time: circular temporality, 103–4, 105, 106; dream-time, 116–17; homogenous, 104; migrants suffering time lag, 119; public and private, 120, 222n58; in relation to labor, 105–6; as represented in short stories of migration, 103–8, 116–20, 122; simultaneity of, 117, 118

tourism: autobiographies of migrants and, 176–77; Greek migrants in U.S. visiting Greece as tourists, 82–83, 139, 222n61

Tournakis, Ioannis, 56, 57–59

trade (commerce): between Greece and U.S., 135; Greek migrants' attitude toward, 136; seen as parasitic, 31

Transatlantic Greek Steamship Company, 138

transatlantic migration: Canoutas on, 178; in globalizing American history, 204n9; and historiography, 7–8, 171, 203n7;

whiteness: American citizenship defined in terms of, 22; distinction among stocks of white race, 43; new immigration and white supremacy, 29; skin whitening, 221n46; Vaka on American racial hierarchy, 168; whitening of ethnicities in America, 15. *See also* Anglo-Saxon Americans

Why Europe Leaves Home (Roberts), 38

Wilson, Woodrow, 125

women: feminism, 114, 134; Greek men marrying foreign, 113, 132; madonna/whore binary, 115; in Vaka's work, 160–66; the women left behind, 110–11. *See also* prostitution; women migrants

women migrants: absence in migration history, 195, 201; advertising of products for, 138; in Alex's *My Wife's Skirt*, 133–34; Anglo-American women contrasted with, 114; Callimachos on, 155–56, 226n23; Canoutas ignoring, 184; and circuits of subjectivation, 12; commodity consumption and, 130–31; embroidery by, 224n31; folk representation of, 88–89; fraternal associations for, 220n32; Greek government attempt to control, 60–61; Immigration Commission gathering data on, 26; picture-brides, 88, 101, 102, 220n33; in short stories of migration, 101, 102, 110–16

Xanthaky, Socrates A., 229n18

Yiouroukopoulos, Thanos, 220n25

YMCA, Greek branch of, 82, 222n61

Žižek, Slavoj, 42